HMS Life

A Journey of transformation from wayward lives

First Edition 2007

John Bullock & David Crabb

HMS Life
A journey of transformation from wayward lives
First Edition 2007
by John Bullock & David Crabb

Printed in the United States of America

ISBN 978-1-60477-205-0

•

Original Front cover designed by Clare Nicholas – www.contactme.net/ Clarenicholas

www.xulonpress.com

Foreward

When Dave & John first talked about writing this book, it was with some trepidation that we, as their wives, turned the pages to read of our husbands 'past lives.' What would it be like to read? How would we feel finding out about their previous life styles - life styles that took them to hell and back in many different ways. Now, as we stand on the other side, as it were, having read the book, we realise how amazing God is! - the different journeys that the four of us made, in particular Debbie as a pastor's daughter, who would ever have imagined we would end up in fantastic marriages all knowing the grace of God in our lives. Dave, John, Sheila, Debbie born in 1955, 1958, 1957, 1969 respectively - God doesn't make mistakes and when these four were born, He knew they would end up together in ministry with a wealth of experience and wisdom for life not only for themselves but for the many people who will listen and read their story. This story is about the miracle of transformed lives and we all hope that as you read the following pages, you will find the One who is still in the transforming business today.

Sheila & Debbie

Dedications and Acknowledgements

ᢀᵖ

We wish to dedicate this book to our beloved wives, Debbie and Sheila, without whom the telling of this journey could not have happened. The stabilising effect their respective lives have had upon ours must be acknowledged. During times when both authors have felt cast adrift on memories of the seas of degradation and self humiliation, we have been fortunate to have those who have steadfastly believed in us. We spent some time considering who we could ask to write a forward for this book and both of us have concluded that they are, above all, best qualified to do so.

We both acknowledge that our respective times in the British Royal Navy have helped to fashion us into the unique characters we have become. Our parallel journeys are uniquely connected through similar, in fact almost identical events, which have revealed what we believe to be fountains of revelation knowledge that have found their origin beyond human senses.

We submit our account to you, the reader, in the hope that you will find yourself somewhere in these pages. You are also a unique individual just waiting to be discovered, you are much more than you think you are and like us, you too can come to the place where your thinking gradually coalesces with the God of absolute, unconditional love. Our prayer is that you too will find Him among these pages – life being the supreme canvas upon which the great artist creates the masterpieces that are, in His time, revealed. We carry within us His purpose if we would but seek it. We hope you will not be deceived into thinking this is just another 'book about God.' We believe there are powerful and effective principles within that have been thoroughly tested in lives that are becoming examples of His good will extended toward all peoples.

About the Authors

John and David believe that you have in your hand a unique story. They both joined the Royal Navy at about the same time in the early 1970's, at very young ages [16 & 15 respectively], leaving at a similar time, the late 1970's. They served on the same class of ships – County Class Guided Missile Destroyers. Both experienced alcohol abuse and self abuses of various forms, until, independently they came to faith in Christ during the same year, 1984. Both attended the same Bible College, becoming ministers within one year of each other. Both lead churches and have travelled and lived in East Africa, still sharing a working interest in that part of the world to this day.

Due to their earlier experiences, they had to take the longest yet also the shortest route to gain and walk in their true identities. Longest in the sense that even before they were grown men they had been 'programmed' so extensively that it was a long route to change their mindset. They took the shortest route, in the sense that their decision to give their lives to Christ changed the course of both their lives overnight. It is true to say, the journey has been very dark at times, but in recent years their paths have been illuminated to a degree that they would not have thought possible. Today they are free men who are fulfilling their potential in every sense of the word; living proof that the gospel of Jesus Christ really works.

In connecting with one another they have discovered together incredible insight through a shared experience. The belief that you are alone can foster feelings of separation, even abandonment to simply exist in a world where you fail to relate with anyone at any significant depth. Their accounts hold no bitterness towards any persons and certainly not towards the Royal Navy. In fact, they are both grateful for the opportunity to have served in Her Majesty's Navy. Rather, their intention is to share the effects of imposing an identity upon the canvas of two lives that had already lost any sense of their uniqueness. They were both already carrying baggage in their young lives and when influenced by the new imposed identities, or when coming under pressure, they simply could not cope. Therefore it is stressed that the intent is not that anyone or any organisation should be perceived to be either the architect, or in any way responsible for the experiences described in this book.

It has to be said that many of the experiences described hitherto are quite graphic. Both John and Dave feel the need for this is justified. Both authors have had extensive experiences that lead them to believe that the church generally still struggles to understand and accept those whose backgrounds are rooted either in abuse or immorality which causes debilitation in the life of a believer. Therefore their intention is not to glorify in anyway whatsoever the experiences in themselves, in fact, they are confident that you too will quickly conclude the tragedy contained herein. Neither of the authors considers themselves 'trophies,' nor presupposes any sense of self aggrandisement. Moreover, most of what has been revealed has been difficult and at times painful to admit to and subsequently write, but the conviction to do so has far exceeded any misgivings on their part. Of course they both believe that they are 'new creations' in Christ Jesus and they have been given all they need for life and Godliness. The working of this into their souls is a journey on which, like all other believers, they have experienced the hindrances and attacks of this world, their flesh and the devil. They believe that the natures of these attacks are designed to wear down believers if at all possible. Some may wish to debate that assertion, whilst good men and women continue to fall or fail in some way, and the church continues to be apparently impotent to help, except to "tut! tut!" or judge, and even distance themselves in incredulity. Both authors have been in that place of thinking, "there must be help somewhere?" This then is their story, and their discoveries that come from their cumulative years of lives out of balance to lives that are being brought back into balance - within the wonderful love and grace of Christ the Saviour.

Both John and David are now married. John is married to Debbie and has two children. David is married to Sheila with two children and six grandchildren. John leads a church in Porth, South Wales and David leads a church in Rugby, England –they remain very close friends and still write and travel together.

Contents

Title page i

Dedications and Acknowledgements v

The Taxi – About the authors – Introduction

Chapter One	Every effect has a cause	23
Chapter Two	New Entry	35
Chapter Three	Fixing the masks	49
Chapter Four	Fixing the masks (2)	65
Chapter Five	Returning to life	83
Chapter Six	The first meeting of like minds	115
Chapter Seven	Early days in ministry	133
Chapter Eight	There is always a victory	149
Chapter Nine	Magnifying moments	159
Chapter Ten	Living in the reality of our new Identity	165
Chapter Eleven	You Decide	175
Chapter Twelve	The dwelling place of God	189
Chapter Thirteen	You can because you are	201
Chapter Fourteen	More than a conqueror	207
Chapter Fifteen	You are perfect	217
Chapter Sixteen	How big is your God?	227

Chapter Seventeen   Moving the Core 241
Chapter Eighteen   Eating from the wrong tree 247
Epilogue 255

The Taxi

The taxi pulled up and a figure stumbled out of its back door holding a half eaten portion of fish and chips. He had been heavily drinking since 4:30pm and it was now late in the evening. He was disheveled; dry vomit covered the front of his shirt. In the previous few hours he had been beaten up, had a sexual experience of some sort, lost or had his money stolen and been paralytic drunk since two hours into his night out. What are we describing? We are describing a regular occurrence at the foot of the gang-plank of one of Her Majesties warships in the 1970's. We know because we have been that man and have seen countless others acting out that scene. It was normal. We were boys at risk in a world that wanted to take captive our souls. We were promised love, drawn toward it grasping, longing, and pursuing a phantom - our adopted parents (The Navy) giving us the freedom to find it if we could. What we found, instead, was an imposter - the imposter wanted all of us, enticing our young, inexperienced flesh until we had given ourselves over to its slavery. The imposter dressed as a woman even though he was a man and as a man even though he was a woman. We were caressed - at times our heads hung limply, tingling flesh deluded in a loving embrace, our nemesis camouflaged as a lover. We were intoxicated until we cried, 'I want you, I need you, take me, I'll do anything, be anything just as long as you offer me love. You have no gender and it matters not because you have taken me beyond the line, my senses heightened and your pursed lips whispering freedom as I give myself over to a deeper level of slavery. I gasp for the pleasure of each breath you release drawing you into my inner being. I am captured, owned now, given over completely - free at last.' That is what our inner world told us: boys at risk as the outer world observed the stages of our humiliation. The taxi drivers knew our story well!

Introduction

L ife's experiences all have their own degree of influence in shaping our individual characters and personalities; therefore these chapters are not the ravings of dispirited or disillusioned souls, but rather this book contains the honest reflections of two men who have rediscovered that life holds purpose and direction, within the context of eternity.

Neither of them was particularly very good with numbers. However, here were two distinct numbers they would never forget. Over thirty years later they are imprinted upon their souls, for David D/121275N and John D/143004T. These numbers began as sequential prefixes ordained to impress themselves upon anonymous bearers. However, now they were fast becoming identities that were to leave their own unique impressions upon the landscapes of existing, marred and abused lives.

These numbers were known as their official numbers and would follow them throughout their careers in the Royal Navy. They were the main identifying prefixes on their identity cards, along with their photographs. They were on all documentation that concerned them, even finding their way onto most of their clothing. David was to become Junior Radio Operator [2] D W Crabb D/121275N and John became Junior Seaman [2] J Bullock D/143004T.

At such young ages any unique aspects to their characters were already under threat. The early years of life were likened to being a template that was to be erased, in order that a new image could emerge that was acceptable to Her Majesty's Navy. With so many erasures already, their lives were fast becoming likened to a confused pastiche, impossible to discern between that which was a shadow perhaps of something else, or original and to be left alone. In truth they now realise that many characteristics of their very young lives were to be overwritten, some simply enhanced, others discarded completely with accompanying, sarcastic disdain. Much of what occurred during their sojourn into service life was precipitated by events that had already taken place and in effect, had left their own significant markers that waited silently, almost magnetic in their nature, attracting other similar encounters that seemed to grow in magnitude and consequence.

Although they both served on various other ships, much of what they share pertaining to their naval experience is centered around the times they both served on Guided Missile Destroyers. Below is a very brief insight into what that life was like.

The DLG Experience (Destroyer, Light, Guided)

⚓

W hat an unforgettable experience it was to live and work on a GMD - a Guided Missile Destroyer. The ships were referred to as "County Class" because they each took their name from a British County. Thus, we had the Kent, the Fife, Norfolk, Glamorgan, Hampshire, Devonshire, Antrim and London. The ships were further referred to as DLG's or Destroyer Light Guided.

We both had our best days in the navy whilst serving on this class of ship – John on the Kent and Dave on the Fife. The atmosphere was inimitable. Both of us lived in 3D mess which was home to us at the front or "forrard" end, three decks down in the ship. The scene in 3D mess in full swing was a sight to behold. In our era The Navy had just phased out the traditional daily ration of rum, only to replace it with three cans of beer a day for everyone of age (18 years). This meant that those who didn't want their daily rations could hand them on. Quite literally some guys had a crate of beer to themselves every day. At certain times of day one could hear a constant sound of cans being opened.

The Navy had a game called "Huckers" which is similar yet more complicated than the game of Ludo. The mess square (communal area) would see games being played in a crowded, smoke filled atmosphere with sailors in varying degrees of undress lounging about the place, some dangling off the top bunks which were three high. What a place it was - loud, no space, unhealthy, obscenities and banter passing back and forth, yet creating a sense of camaraderie that is rarely equaled. The forty five or so ratings (navy personnel) grouped together in a way that almost replaced a man's family.

Visitors would be "lashed up", the term used to describe naval hospitality, in this instance through beer. In some ports it was not uncommon for celebrities to pay a visit. The custom was to place a can of beer at the guest's feet. This ritual could be carried out deftly and without words, the visitor ending up with endless cans surrounding his feet. Often people would arrive in a dignified manner and have to be carried off the ship in an undignified manner, drunk - or to use naval slang, *'crappers,' 'minging' or 'shytus.'*

Girls were referred to as *'parties'* therefore any matelot (slang taken from the French word for sailor), who was acting in a girly fashion would be referred to as, "You big party". It wasn't long before a sailor got indoctrinated into navy slang which was referred to as "pusser" or "Jack speak" and was almost a language in its own right. A few examples: a *sprog* was a young recruit, a drink was a *wet*, toilets were *heads*, a night out was a *run*, a wall was a *bulkhead*, a homosexual was a *brown-hatter, mincer* or *raving nosh*. A Wren (Women's Royal Navy) was a *split*, a Submarine was *a boat*, the sea was *the oggin*, a wave was a *goffer*, Hot Chocolate was *kai*. A Chinaman was a *choky*; a good looking girl was *essence*. To get a girl was to *trap*, to work was to *turn to*, to avoid work was *to loaf*, to mess around was to *skylark*, an afternoon off was a *make-and-mend*, a beard was a *full-set*, food was *scran*, to catch a venereal disease was to *get a dose*,

The Navy was the *Andrew* and so it went on. Suffice to say, life on board ship was another world with its own language.

The DLG's were armed to the teeth with Sea Slug long range surface to air missiles; 2 times quadruple sea cat short range surface to air missiles, twin four point five gun turrets that fired shells rapidly, twin Bofars and large machine guns. In addition the ships carried an arsenal of small arms. Each ship carried a Helicopter with anti-submarine capability and also a Land Rover. There were Chinese laundrymen on board, a tailor's shop, a Naafi (the Armed Forces grocery shop) and even a cobbler. The ships were like villages, the canteen could be turned into a church, a cinema and it even had its own TV studios. On board were Surgeons, Padres and Physical Training Instructors. The ships were war machines, yet our homes. In foreign ports we would be ambassadorial, housing cocktail parties for local dignitaries. We had soccer teams, rugby teams, hockey teams and many others representing us in each port.

Life on a ship could move from great delight to extreme despair, all because someone of a higher rank made a decision, and this could sometimes be due to nothing more than a change of mood. Officers were called "*Pigs*" and though obeyed were in the main tolerated rather than respected by the lower deck ratings. Working clothes were *number eights*, overalls were *number nines* (hence punishment being referred to as number nines); n*umber tens* were tropical whites. *Number twos were* second class dress uniforms and *number ones* were your best uniform. We wore berets on our heads and steaming bats (special navy boots) on our feet. Payment came through ritual every fortnight whereby we queued, marched to the table, removed our hats, (known as doffing your lid), recited our official numbers, placed the caps in front of us and the money was placed on the hats. This was where the ships regulators (policemen) checked our haircuts to see if we were at regulation standards. The week without pay was known as *blank week*. To do almost anything we had to put in a request form, this applied for an afternoon off, to go on leave or even to grow or remove a beard. This procedure of request forms was referred to as *slapping in*.

Generally the food on board was both good and plenteous, but this could depend on who was on duty in the *galley,* (the kitchen). The Navy provided breakfast, lunch, four o'clockers and supper, which was in fact a full dinner. In addition it was possible to buy chocolate and sweets (known as *nutty*) from the Naafi. Each morning we awoke to *"Call-the-hands"* piping over the tannoy system. A twenty four hour day was split into the following watches: forenoon watch - 8:00am until 12:00pm; afternoon watch - 12:00pm until 4:00pm; first dog - 4:00pm until 6:pm; last dog - 6:00pm until 8:00pm; first watch - 8:00pm until midnight, middle watch - midnight until 4:00am and morning watch - 4:00am until 8:00am.

Life at sea was busy and we worked every fourth watch as well as our normal working day, the only exception being the afternoon off if one had done the middle watch. There were further exceptions if the ship was in defence mode, action stations, or in a different watch system. The whole ship worked off a system of starboard and port watch. Warships are constantly being cleaned and painted - it is a tedious necessity. In the 1970's the Cold War was in full force and we were often doing mock battles against the *Ruskies,* as the Russians were referred to. The propaganda was hot and we considered ourselves elite. At that time we truly believed that no other navy in the world could 'live' with us. A friend was not just a mate but a *hoppo* or *winga*. When you were ashore it was every *hoppo's* unwritten duty to look after one another. It would be considered the lowest form of life to desert or let down a friend in need; if he was drunk or in a fight, you would be expected to stand with him and ensure his safety. This is just a glimpse of life on board a DLG in the mid 1970's; we hope this will provide a suitable context as we now share more details of each of our unique stories.

Chapter One – Every effect has a cause

The ship lays at anchor in the harbour, too large to tie up alongside the jetty. The Captain has mustered the ship's company on the helicopter flight deck for his customary chat before anyone is allowed onto the liberty boat for shore leave. The usual speech is given, concerning the importance of realising we are ambassadors for our country. Information is imparted as to the wonderful places of interest, the historical significance, the educational opportunities and experience of being in another part of the world. Then the warnings are given - the lists of places no naval rating must be found in. Out come the note pads and pens as we hurriedly write down the forbidden zones, knowing that as far as we are concerned these are actually the places of interest for many real sailors.

Like creatures of instinct, moths to the light, no amount of threats or the certain retribution that would fall in the form of naval discipline would stop us, no sir!

We were "Typical Jack," the identifying prefix for most sailors, an identity that was almost impossible to deny. A few hours later you would see him, slumped over a half full glass, muttering something that seemed to him pure wisdom.

There was another, falling over the woman old enough to be his mother, winking and signalling his intentions to his compatriots. He would be found days later outside the sick bay, waiting for his session with the ship's surgeon, as he desperately tried to convince the surgeon that the stinging, as he urinated, had nothing to do with his sexual indiscretion those nights before. Another is found doubled up in the corner of the bar, the contents of his stomach testimony to his evening's end. Yet another is found outside talking animatedly to a young girl, seeking to convince her that he is different, his wedding ring having been left in his locker on the ship.

In truth, "Typical Jack" was just another lost and empty soul who had taken on an identity that would leave its own particular and significant marker on the scarred and pitted landscape of a life that had completely gone astray. What a miracle to no longer be typical, to discover the uniqueness everyone deserves to find....

Some events that we share over the next few chapters may make difficult reading, we share these things in order to set the scene if you like, to illustrate how the canvas of a life can be formed and subsequently overwritten by successive changes in our identities for all kinds of reasons. Therefore, it may seem at times that we are overly gratuitous in sharing specific details concerning our respective stories, it should be understood that the only reason for this is to further illustrate the awesome workings of God, in being both willing and able to lead such individuals into their uniqueness.

John's beginnings

I realise now that I had grown up in the shadow of my older brother Kevin. At one stage he was the "cock of the school," that is, the one with the reputation as the best fighter. He gained us notoriety in our village, causing a great deal of trouble as we entered our teenage years. Still, as we progressed through our early years Kevin and I, later joined by brothers David, Ian and our adopted brother Nigel, had what would be considered a fairly normal upbringing. We were a working class family brought up in a Yorkshire village and my dad had to work long hours just to keep us. Our parents worked hard to do their best for us but being a large family we were relatively poor. I look back with pleasure at my earliest years, we had a very large, extended family and our lives were immersed in family life.

My parents had fifteen brothers and sisters between them, so there were lots of cousins who we would gather with at my Grandmother's house for tea each Sunday. These were happy times when we would get up to all kinds of mischief and I have memories of preparing Granddad Farrington's cigarettes in a rolling machine and trying them out. We also helped ourselves to his homebrew beer and wine. Grandma Farrington would hold us spellbound with monologues about her life, speaking about characters as if we knew them - her whole life seemingly revolving around 8 Creswell Lane, Staincliffe in Dewsbury, Yorkshire.

On Sundays a big spread of cold meats and salads would be laid out, followed by fruit and Carnation cream. It was a feast. I was particularly friendly with my cousin Steven as we were only a few months apart in age. As the years went by, Steven and I went on holidays together, we had a period where we wore the skinhead gear of Doc Martin boots, Levi Jeans with braces and Ben Sherman shirts. How could I know then that before my fortieth birthday I would conduct his funeral? He was killed in a car crash whilst living and working in Germany. It was a sad time as our family gathered to prematurely pay our respects to Steven.

The event helped me to focus on the different ways our paths had taken. How innocuous those pints of beer seemed to Steve and I during the holiday of our early youth. Later we would both progress toward fighting a drink problem, and for Steve that would be until he ended up slumped in his crashed car, having left the road he was travelling on.

He was in Germany to start a new life having gone through divorce and heartache. Steve and I had created an image during our holidays together of trying to look and talk like hard men. Neither of us was. In fact, during that period, I had to live in the aftermath of my brother's reputation. Kevin's was such, that we were known as 'The Bullocks', and being a Bullock caused me to run for my life on more than one occasion, as kids from other gangs would attack us simply because of the name we carried, therefore our identities were already somewhat tainted. This was as a result of my brother's antics.

By the age of 14 I was already 5 feet 10 inches tall and was different in my thinking to most of our gang. I was able to get into pubs and clubs from the age of 13 and spent my time playing sport and chasing girls. I had virtually dropped out of school altogether, regularly playing truant ('slamming' as we called it). My friends and I were all sexually active at a very young age, our lives seemingly revolving around discussing who was the toughest and who could drink the most Tetley's Bitter (Beer).

Village life gave me a myopic view on life in general; as a result I developed very narrow views and had no real idea of what my life was to become. My brothers and I were often a disappointment to our parents, regularly bringing trouble with us into the home. We were without doubt a real source of worry to them, constantly at loggerheads. I was, in effect, trying to live a double life, attempting to be a man, which in reality my parents knew of course I was not – I was a boy. I would lie in an effort to find my way out of situations; with my parents constantly having to bring me back into line. This became a repetitive characteristic of my young life, posing or trying to be something I knew deep down I was not.

When I was 14 my prowess as a soccer player gave me the experience of a lifetime. None of the crowd I associated with was academic and 90% of us wanted to be professional footballers. I had played for a team since I was seven and represented my schools throughout. On Saturdays I played morning and afternoon. On one particular day a scout from Bradford City Football Club was watching us. I scored eight goals in the morning and five in the afternoon. After the game I was approached and asked to go down to Bradford City. Subsequently, I trained with them on Monday and Thursday evenings and in the school holidays we had the privilege of training with the first team. I had supported them from the terraces and now I was training on the pitch at Valley Parade.

In those days I had skinny legs and the coaching staff nicknamed me "Stickman," after a senior player called Warren Raynor. It was quite something for me during those school holidays to train with some of my idols like Cess Podd, Joe Cooke and Ronnie Brown. Occasionally during the night training I would have a lift with the late Yorkshire and England wicket keeper David "Buster" Bairstow, who some years later tragically took his own life. David was a part time player at the club at that time. Several of my friends were attached to football clubs - David Nichols, who had been capped by England at under 15, signed apprentice for Huddersfield Town, as did David Jackson for Manchester United, and John Hall and Tibby Zsabo for Bradford. Two others, David Wood and Colin Racher were at Bradford City with me but none of us signed professionally.

It seemed, however, that I was destined to go down a different path, although later I was told that Brian Edwards (manager) and Bobby Kennedy (youth manager) had been interested in signing me as an apprentice. However, my fixation with The Navy began to dominate my life. The fixation grew strong during a holiday with my cousin Steve to the Isle of White.

We were there during Cowes week and the Warship HMS Ajax, along with the Royal Yacht "Brittania", was taking part. Steve and I mixed a lot with the sailors who were on a "rig run" (navy slang for wearing uniform) and joining the RN became an obsession for me. I suppose I saw it as an escape from the mundane. I had completely wasted my education and was dominated by the thoughts of travel and the apparent glamour that went with the naval identity. At that point I wanted to join the navy more than anything; little did I know then that within a few weeks I would have done so.

Dave's beginnings

A recurring experience began in my very early years. As a little boy of about five years old a regular pattern of sexual abuse began to take place, lasting until I was about eleven or twelve. I knew that what was happening was injurious but I did not know why? It was too difficult for me to argue against, or stop what was happening, for I had no real frame of reference, or context within which to put these experiences. I was just a frightened little boy who only wanted to please.

At the same time this was happening, I was also being badly bullied. I was very late developing and very small for my age, therefore I became a natural target for bullies. At a young age I was already suffering from a victim mindset. I was learning not to fight back - either because of fear or because of emotional abuse from the one who was abusing me sexually. I was becoming a liar to make up stories that depicted me in a much better light. It soon became a habit to put on a mask over a scared boy, who was so ashamed of his apparent weakness and inability to cope with these events.

Another thing I had learnt to do was to minimise what was happening to me. I fooled myself into thinking that this sort of thing was normal. Of course, I could not, at that time, even begin to see how wrong I was to think that way. I would not have dared to talk to others about what was happening. Privately I had already accepted responsibility for it; this was a secret which I must never tell anyone about.

On one occasion, one of the boys who would bully me quite regularly goaded me to such an emotional state, that I became completely uncontrollable. I threw a house brick at him that broke the nail off his big toe; I then hit him in the eye with a large wooden fence stake and left him with a badly cut eyebrow. This would be the condition I would need to be in before I would dare fight back. I now understand that that is why I would often drink whilst in the navy to the extent that I was no longer in control, for then I found the "front" to do the things that deep down I guess I truly wanted to be able to do.

I developed an amazing fantasy life. I would often imagine myself as some kind of "super hero," more than able to conquer the fiercest of enemies. I remember my brother and me creating our own masks, badges, utility belts and capes, making our debut appearance as "Cat man and Cat boy." We were shocked that no one took us seriously as the feared crusaders against crime we were convinced we were.

I tried hard as a youngster to create an image that I thought was acceptable to my Dad, who I loved so much. He was my hero, but I always felt that I had failed him. My dad came from a generation where you would be expected to be able to stick up for yourself. I had tried to do this, but my failure was something I always saw as a divisive factor in our relationship. I would often do drastic things in order to gain my parents' (particularly my Dad's) attention, such as self harm, lying and running away from home. Sometimes I made up stories that painted me in what I thought was a good light, yet, inside myself, I knew they were just lies. I wanted to be like my dad who always knew what to do, in my eyes he was tough, never afraid - he knew how to sort people out, and I had seen him do it.

One memory I have is going out with dad one day as a four or five year old. In those days Dad had a small wooden seat on the cross bar of his bicycle which I would often ride on. We were going along nicely and I was tapping the spokes with my foot wondering what would happen if I pushed my foot, just that few inches further. I soon found out. Over the handlebars went dad; out came his false teeth clattering into the gutter, ending in pieces. I ended up with a badly grazed thigh and an extremely sore foot. Still, at least he knew I was there!

The time came when I decided to impress my parents with my ability to woo and win the opposite sex. The trouble was I had no idea beyond kissing what to do with a girl. On one occasion I started dating a girl who was way ahead of me emotionally and sexually, I was still only about eleven years old and would often go to her flat to "listen to records." Her mother suffered from rheumatoid arthritis and was confined to a wheel chair; her father had died some years before. One afternoon she was lying on her bed and I recall her saying to me, *"Come on Dave, be a Bear with me."* I had no idea, fortunately, that this was an invitation for a sexual encounter and ended up parading around her room roaring and growling in a very "bear like" fashion.

As I was now in the mood for further impressing her, I decided to show her how I could make myself faint through a process of hyperventilation and holding my breath. Oh how I impressed her - I fainted so well that I ended up breaking my nose on my way down to her bedroom carpet. When I got home with my nose badly swollen I simply told my dad I had been in a fight and this seemed to impress him greatly. My girlfriend dumped me! The truth soon came out and I was totally devastated at the giggles and smirks of those around me.

How I hated myself, words like, useless, weak and liar became part of my identity as far as I was concerned. It seemed impossible for me to initiate any kind of change in my life, I was, it would seem, resigned to these recurring issues. There were however a few occasions when circumstances seemed to have a more favorable outcome.

I would have been about fourteen and my brother Nigel was nine. We were given some money and off we went to the circus. I was wearing a very old anorak that was slightly ripped on the zipper. As we were queuing up a group of lads came over to us and it was immediately clear they were looking for trouble. One of them, a mean looking individual who I was convinced was probably the toughest lad in Rugby, started pulling my zipper until it completely came away. He blew smoke in my face and started pushing both me and my brother around. I was scared but afraid to allow myself to get angry. However, something just seemed to break within me.

Perhaps it was because my brother was there - the way Nigel was looking at me with eyes that seemed to say, *"Do something Dave."* Eventually I put my hand up and pushed this lad's hand away from my anorak. That simple act ignited such anger in him that he declared, *"Right, so you want a fight do you?"* In truth it was the last thing that I wanted but I knew that it was going to happen.

We left the queue and went around the back of the Big Top. By this time a huge crowd had gathered into a large circle and already my opponent was dancing around as though he had won. He had a flat nose, and he was obviously an experienced fighter; I was imagining myself lying on the ground with blood all over my face. I could already see the jeering faces, my brother's disappointed face and most of all the disappointment in my Dad's eyes. I just knew I was going to get the hiding of my life.

He came at me straight away, fists swinging wildly. I was amazed at how simple it was for me to grab him around the neck in what was my favorite wrestling move, the side headlock. Oh how I squeezed! With all my might I squeezed until I could hear him gagging. To make it look even better I thumped him a couple of times in the face until at last I could hear him begin to squeal. I asked him if he had had enough and he immediately indicated to me he had. However, I did not want to let him go. It seemed to me at this moment that he had asked for this anyway and surely he was to blame for all the pain I had endured over the years. Wasn't I justified to hold on that little bit longer? Maybe I should hit him until he bled to really impress everyone?

Thoughts like these went through my mind in a matter of seconds. Eventually though, as he was turning purple, I let him go. I have never had the heart to really want to hurt someone. Nigel was cheering as were some others. The exhilaration I felt was incredible and I almost wanted it to happen again.

After the crowd dispersed the other lad and I began to chat with one another. He gave me a cigarette that I dutifully smoked, trying hard to suppress the dizziness and nausea I felt. It seemed to me at this time in my life that the "secret" was well and truly covered over now. Nigel did a great job of relating the tale to my Dad, in fact he embellished it to such an extent I almost believed his version myself.

I got to know my opponent very well over the next few months. He introduced me to new experiences that were to have more negative effects in my life. Apart from the abuse I had suffered in my younger years my experience of girls was almost non-existent. This was soon to change. His bedroom was directly opposite the bedroom of a neighbour. As we hid in the darkness of his room a woman who must have been in her thirties stood, and we watched, as she seductively removed all of her clothes. He informed me that this had become a regular occurrence in his life and he was proud to share it with me. My body began to respond in ways that up to then I had little experience in.

Before long I had developed an amazing masturbation habit, I say amazing because I was at it almost constantly. Over the weeks I would meet with my friend and watch fascinated by the exhibitionism of this neighbour. Eventually my friend's mother caught us, the clandestine meetings ended and suddenly I was no longer welcome in the home. The guilt I felt at being caught during our shameful, voyeuristic assignations was profound to say the least. Yet the habit only seemed to get worse as I drew so much comfort from it.

Over the next few months I began experimenting more and more with girls. Just before I joined the navy I met a girl with whom I had a fairly heavy encounter. I threw my heart at her, I was in love - she was very experienced, and I was convinced I was to spend the rest of my life with her. This was my very first sexual encounter and I assumed we would eventually just get married, but other things were happening in me that were to change the whole course of my life for almost nine years, love would have to wait!

These were just a few of the recurring things I would take with me when I joined the Royal Navy as a fifteen year old: fear, emotional and sexual abuse, a fantasy life that was completely out of control, self-esteem issues, and a hidden sexual identity crisis. On top of these would be stamped - D/121275N.

Two young boys, at risk, would now enter a man's world. We could not have known the effects that this would have upon our already damaged lives. John had clearly taken on an identity through his associations with brothers and friends that was wholly performance related. I (David) had also built up a huge mask in a desperate attempt at acceptance. Both of our identities were wholly false and we would now also experience further contributions, which would require us to enhance, change or dispose of vital parts of our core characters.

The story we will tell is not about blame. The next chapter will look at early experiences in the Royal Navy and we would both want to make it clear that these reflections are not an attempt at reassigning responsibility, or justifying aberrant behaviour. Rather, we are endorsing the fact that both of us were already wallowing in a sea of uncertainty and compromise. Being a service man would require another identity change and discipline would be enforced. In fact, it would be fair to say that some characteristics imbibed whilst serving in the navy have been useful upon entering into ministry in the church. Peer pressure of a new, distinct kind would also have its effects. The following chapter will also reveal how these early character defects can simply continue and, unless they are challenged, bring further damage and confusion into your life.

Chapter Two – New Entry

John

I was 16 and Dave was 15 when we found ourselves pulling in to Plymouth station to begin our six weeks basic training at HMS Raleigh near Torpoint, Cornwall. In this chapter we will both share different aspects of the training regime we encountered.

Our purpose is to further impress upon you the danger of imposing one identity upon another and what can happen when you begin to live from a 'perceived identity,' rather than who you truly are in your core character.

D143004T is the number that I (John) became on September 14th 1974; it was late afternoon as the train pulled in to Plymouth station. The new recruits were met by someone in uniform who bundled us off in a navy wagon to HMS Raleigh. Raleigh was and still is the Royal Navy's basic training establishment in Cornwall.

For some years I had been using mascara to blacken the fluff above my top lip so that I could get into pubs. I would need it no longer because moustaches were not allowed in the Royal Navy. The long hair I had got used to was also outlawed. Thinking it would be helpful, I had already had a short hair cut but within 24 hours it would be shorter still.

The navy barber kindly asked me what style I would like. Thinking he was being generous, I obliged him with my preference. Of course he was mocking me; there was in reality just two styles – a tuft on top, or all off. Most of the recruits in my class had just left school; we were, in the main: thin, gaunt and now bald. Between 20 and 30 of us were placed in one long wooden room. From now on it would be referred to as "The Mess." The irony, as I would learn to appreciate over the next five years, was that it would never be allowed to resemble anything like a mess. Cleanliness was a naval obsession. Over the next few weeks of basic training I was taught that both personal cleanliness and tidiness of one's living quarters was not an option and failure in either area brought severe punishment. To be deemed to be a "crab" (one who didn't look after his personal hygiene), was akin to being called a "brown hatter," (homosexual). You dare not be labelled as either or you would pay dearly.

My strongest memories of those first couple of days in the "New Entry" block was getting kitted out with uniform and smoking "blue liners/guerrillas," the navy's own brand of cigarette. Blue Liners cost 50 pence for three hundred so no one bothered too much about "crashing the ash" (sharing cigarettes). We would sit around the "spit kits" (metallic bowls that resembled giant ashtrays), telling jokes and stories from our past. Within a day we had new nicknames. There were the obvious ones like "Taff" for the Welshmen, "Jock" for the Scotsmen or "Paddy" for the Irish recruits, but other nicknames were given due to character traits or infirmities. One poor lad's voice was breaking (and it took the whole of our training to do so). One night he interrupted the flow of conversation from his bunk with a pathetically squeaky voice and was immediately labeled "Squeak". I became "Bulky" due to my surname and not my physique!

Having gone through the process of New Entry we were moved to another part of the camp and placed in our divisions. The divisions were named after Admirals and I was placed in Hanson. Each division had a long row of barrack rooms - six in all - housing recruits who were on week one to six respectively of 'Part One Naval Training.' This is where we were introduced to discipline, navy style. It was tradition that the "Top Mess," the recruits, who were in week six, would keep those behind them in order. The top mess formed their own kangaroo court with a number of judges and one top judge.

The rumours of what went on had drifted over to new entry and so it was with some trepidation we faced our first night in Part One training. In the early hours of the morning we got our first encounter with the "Top Mess." The door burst open and a number of recruits wearing gas masks, with white towels for wigs, sauntered into our Mess. It was impossible to know who they were – it was a very menacing scene. We were in beds neatly arrayed down each side of the long room. "Where's Thomas?" shouted one of our tormentors, "we're looking for Thomas". With that they proceeded to tip us out of our beds and ransack them. The Thomas in question was an imaginary mouse - he had a lot to answer for. Sometimes this would be repeated two or three times a night. Tradition declared that we had no option but to take it. To fall foul of the top mess meant appearing before the judges in the kangaroo court. This would usually take place in the early hours of the morning and it was a terrifying experience. Punishment could mean anything from being paraded naked through the entire division covered in plimsol whitener, being pulled along by string that was attached to your private parts; to being kept in a cold shower long enough to make you cry with the pain. Yet another was to be ordered to run the gauntlet. This bordered on unbelievable cruelty and meant running through one barrack room length, whilst being beaten all the way along by the entire top mess who had pillowcases filled with marching boots. Both Dave and I endured this indignity. Teeth were sometimes lost and bones could be broken. There was no opt-out and definitely no complaints procedure – it was naval tradition and the superiors turned a blind eye to it. This was accompanied by great fear and psychological torment.

Another feature of Part One training was the lack of sleep. We were shocked out of our sleep at 6:30 am (the non swimmers earlier, for this would be when they would *learn* to swim). A duty Petty Officer would arrive with his entourage, the lights would be switched on and he would bellow something designed to interrupt a deep sleep. One of the Petty Officers became known to us as the "Fat PO" he had a cruel streak and would hammer a stick on the metal lockers next to our heads. "OUT!" he would scream, occasionally beating the bed so that your legs had to move swiftly to avoid the stick. The Petty Officers would systematically go through the barracks and then return to make sure that no one had dared to stay in bed. Punishment from the fat PO for such a breech would be to hang by the arms from the rafters until he completed his rounds. This would reduce even the hardest among us to tears. Why this was allowed I'll never know, but we were bullied and brutalised by a system that had adopted us at puberty.

Today we live in a different era and the account I have described would never be allowed. I can remember after my announcement that I was joining the RN being given the following comments: "You'll be bullied you know", or "you'll never survive the discipline". My inner response was to decide that rather than be bullied I would fight. This course of action caused me a few beatings early on but eventually stood me in good stead. I became mentally tough and soon realised that wearing the same uniform, having similar haircuts and living in a confined space had the affect of dismantling people's images. This was because there was no hiding place; we shared practically every moment together so it wasn't possible to hide one's weaknesses. I used this to my advantage and almost conned my way through my navy career by creating a false impression that I was tougher than I really was. I pulled this off by getting in first and calculating a few fights. Secretly, I was aware that some of my comrades-at-arms were much stronger than me. I was a fitness fanatic in those days and weighed no more than 12 stone (160 lbs), but being a runner I didn't have the upper-body strength that many had. In part I bluffed it. I refused to back down and made it known that I would take retribution in some way if I was beaten. In the early days it was about survival - that is survival in the sense of having a life that was worth living. After all there was nowhere to hide on a warship and to show weakness would result in bullying of some kind. We recruits had been pitched together from a variety of backgrounds. Every young recruit had been an infant and Dave and I recognise the role our formative years had played in our adoption of our navy identities.

Dave

I can identify with all that John has just shared. **February 15th 1971** (decimal day) I stood on the platform at Birmingham New street station to catch the 'Cornishman' down to Plymouth, to join HMS Raleigh, the training establishment. The whole joining up procedure had taken less than two Months. Dad decided this would be a good time to tell me about the facts of life, he muttered something about 'strange people' and to be careful, and that was that. To be honest, I hadn't a clue what he was going on about, it was still all so very unreal. I was excited, this was an adventure and I was basking still from the attention I had been receiving from my parents. We had a sumptuous meal, at a very expensive restaurant the evening before and now both mum and dad in tears waving me goodbye.

Sitting in the smoke filled compartment with three other hopefuls I decided to inspect the contents of the carrier bag mum had packed for me. Sandwiches, of course, some crisps, a selection of confectionary for my sweet tooth, and a carton of Kiaora orange juice, Oh, and my 'DC Superman comic.' The only other things I was required to take were some toiletries, a clothes brush, shoe cleaning kit, and a few items of clothing, this was all contained in a "good food costs less at Sainsbury's paper carrier bag."

Somehow I felt as though I did not fit in with my compatriots. They had cigarettes, beer, and a couple of editions of *playboy*. The feelings of adventure diminishing, I was now alone, responsible only to myself, and I needed friends. I was also dying to have a look at one of those magazines. I decided to go to the buffet car and bought my very first pack of cigarettes, (20 Extra), telling the counter staff they were for my dad. On my return I offered them around and was quickly accepted and found worthy of speaking to, (I still couldn't get hold of that magazine though). But success, I did get my first bottle of beer. I also got almost nine years for my 'running away' on this occasion in Her Majesty's Royal Navy.

The big wake up call came when we arrived at Plymouth station. There was a lot of shouting and swearing, and several petty officers were marching around barking out orders. We were very quickly bundled on to the back of a naval wagon, and taken to the Torpoint Ferry; from there we crossed over to Torpoint, where the training establishment was situated. The memory of standing on the ferry, listening to the chain clanking as we were pulled slowly to the other side remains with me. I had all kinds of misgivings, wondering what on earth I had got myself into. It was nothing like I had read in the glossy brochure. Everyone on that was smiling, and they were all so friendly looking. The officers in the brochure were all looking benevolently at the guys who were either playing chess, or at a snooker table. Up to now not one of these officers had spoken to me as a human being; in fact, they spoke with a kind of contempt in their voices.

I recall the incredible feelings of excitement as I saw for real my first naval warship. HMS Eagle (an old aircraft carrier) lay at anchor waiting to be broken up, having been decommissioned. There were many other vessels I noted their armament, which meant little to me at the time. However to a young 15 year old they were totally cool. Guns, missile systems, flags flapping in the breeze, the whole picture acted as a stimulus, and helped keep the feelings of cultural shock at bay. My first glimpse of real sailors, as a frigate made its way out of harbour. Ratings stood to attention in their bell-bottom trousers. Yes! I had made the right decision I was sure. The feelings of isolation however, soon began, there was a postal strike on, and therefore I could not even send a letter, and my parents were not on the telephone then. That seems strange in our world of mobile everything. However, my dad somehow managed to get a letter to me via a local careers office and their own mail delivery system. I can remember vividly the tears cascading down my face as I read that letter. My parents seemed almost an eternity away. One line remains with me even to this day, "keep your chin up son, I know it seems hard now, remember we love you."

I felt totally cut off, and I am convinced that my boyhood ended that day. For most of that time I was very unhappy. I felt robbed of some very important years, and I constantly experienced homesickness. The cruelest part of it all was that because I joined at fifteen, at any time during those three years until I reached my 18th birthday, I could have left, as those years were classed as boy's service. Of course I was either not made aware of that, or I simply did not under-stand that was the case. At any rate, I was awaiting a call from either mum or dad begging me to come home. That call never came. So, in pride, I had to maintain the façade. Each time I came home on leave in my uniform, I again had the experience of being the centre of attention. I put on a mask that basically told everyone how much I loved naval life, and the freedom of being my own man. I didn't need anyone.

On returning back to my base after a few days leave, I would be found at the back of the NAAFI building crying my eyes out. Or sitting in a lonely bar, listening to depressing records on the juke box, fooling no one, not even myself. I had decided to start smoking as I was convinced this was not only cool, but felt it made me look tough. I also started to drink a little, my favourite tipple then being 'brown ale.' I would go to the bar and with as deep a voice as possible, order a bottle of Newcastle brown or the like. Most times I was served out of sheer pity I'm sure.

However, my real singularity became most apparent to me on my first morning, February 1971, in the mess deck at HMS Raleigh, Benbow division. I was the youngest amongst all of the new entries, in fact I was the youngest on the whole establishment. Most of my compatriots were between their early to late twenties, I was still only fifteen. Apart from the brutal hair cut the second most important facet of naval ablutions was to ensure you were clean-shaven at all times. This was not a problem, as the only hairs on my face were the wisps of fair hair that most boys have, that once removed, seemed to take years to make their appearance in the form of more manly stubble.

Our class Petty Officer was a decent chap. I will never forget my absolute pride when on that morning he told me to have a shave. I could not wait to get to the bathroom and wield the new razor my dad had given me before leaving. On my first visit to the bathroom I was to discover what normal practice was on all ships on which I served. The men tended to stand at the sinks naked, shaving and then showering afterwards. It was clear to me that this was going to cause a problem. I arrived with my towel firmly knotted around my tiny waist. At 5ft 2" and only just seven stone in weight (98lbs), 29 inch chest, blonde hair and bright eyes, I was tiny in every way compared to the fully developed men around me. I had no underarm hair at all, a mere tiny wisp of pubic hair only just beginning to sprout. I was just a boy and I was at risk.

What horror then when the towel was suddenly and deliberately snatched away with the cry, *"What you got under there then, Skin?"* This was to become my next identity, *"Skin,"* a derogatory naval nickname for anyone not yet developed and considered virginal. The utter humiliation I felt as several men mocked me in my now vulnerable state. *"Not going to do much damage with that are you Skin?"* *"Only good for stirring coffee with, hasn't even taken the silver paper off it yet!"* I didn't know what to do; I didn't want to run, as I knew that would attract even more attention. At the same time I was feeling totally humiliated, as I was now the centre of everyone's attention? Someone else grabbed me and simulated sex, as he pushed against me I realised to my horror that he was fully erect. This act didn't seem to bother anyone except me, I was utterly devastated. Here then came my next identity, for I was not only *'Skin'* but attached to that was also the word *'Essence'*. This was the naval way to indicate that in somebody's opinion you were considered to have sexual potential.

If this had been the very first time anything like this had happened to me, perhaps it would not have had the debilitating effect that it did. It is hard to describe the effect this incident had upon such a young life. I can recall many nights weeping many tears and struggling with inner conflicts over my sexual identity. However, to realise that there were some men who would find me sexually attractive was not only shocking to me, it also raised incredible questions in my mind because of those things that had happened in my past. Was there something about me that attracted this sort of attention? Did this mean my sexuality was questionable?

So '*Skin and Essence*' was to become my identifying title from now on. How relieved I was then that Mum and Dad were not able to come to my passing out parade. How utterly humiliated I would have felt had they known my nickname. Somehow I had to find a way of ensuring that that name did not follow me to my next establishment. Some people ask, even today, "Why did you not report these things to your superiors". It is hard to answer that question when you cannot perceive the pressure we lived with daily to conform to a particular identity. To admit to having been abused in some way was tantamount to admitting to homosexuality, which unlike today, was perceived as something totally unacceptable.

To further convince me of my need to rid myself of this new name, an incident that occurred at my next training establishment reinforced the conviction that was forming in my mind. I was stripped naked, put into a kit bag and hung outside a three storey building for about three hours. My friends thought this was really funny but I was terrified and afraid to move around too much in case the rope broke leaving me to drop at least twenty feet to the ground. When I was eventually discovered I was simply in trouble for missing one of my classes. It was amazing that nothing was done about this kind of bullying. I was in a bad way, dehydrated through sweating profusely, scared and totally humiliated. You were simply expected to deal with it - no wonder the need for a new identity.

I realised that I could not continue as I was, without further, perhaps more serious abuses taking place. I also experienced more serious sexual abuse during my training, which utterly devastated me and left me so damaged that I realise now this was the time a plan began to form in my subconscious mind.

Fortunately, during this time in my training an older man befriended me. He was an Australian who had moved to Britain and had joined the navy and become a Field Gunner. He took pity on me and became my best friend during this part of my training. On more than one occasion someone was beaten up for giving me a bad time. He was a true friend whose care I will never forget. However, it became very clear to me that if I did not discover a way to protect myself and start fighting back, I would very soon face more serious issues. It is incredible as I look back and compare society now with what was allowed, even expected just 36 years ago. The regime was really quite brutal, and little was done to either discourage bullying or even put a stop to it altogether. Young boys like me, fresh out of school with no work experience whatsoever, (my only job having been a paper round) were definitely at risk and should have been better protected.

Of course I was not the only one; there were others who suffered far worse than me. There were also some experiences that everyone went through. The parade ground abuse was sickening, the tirades that these instructors thought up were devastatingly offensive and in many cases extremely provocative. It often turned to physical abuse, one instructor's favourite past time was straightening lad's caps by hitting them on the head with a piece of wood. Hearing him walking behind you, never knowing if it was going to be your head was more than disconcerting.

On one occasion a fellow class mate was forced to run around the perimeter of the parade ground, with an SLR (Self–Loading–Rifle) above his head 21 times, just because it was his birthday. Unfortunately for him he had dared to smile during drill. This experience resulted in him collapsing and breaking his nose. He was then required to clean the blood from the parade ground with a toothbrush and bucket of water. If a recruit dared to faint, during drill, on the 'hallowed turf' of the parade ground, he would be dragged off in a fashion that scraped the toes off his 'bulled' boots, thus, causing him hours of work in restoring his marching boots to parade ground standard. No sympathy would be offered whatsoever!

Some of the nicknames that were given were harmless; eventually mine became "Buster" after the naval diver Buster Crabb. But to be labeled "Skin and Essence" was humiliating and during that time of my training I sank into a very deep depression. As I said, I was 5ft 2" when I joined up and barely weighed 7 stone. Whilst in my Part One training I went down to just over 6 stones (84lbs) and on one occasion I was sent for another full medical. How I remained sane during those six weeks I still do not know, for some reason there was a stubbornness within me that caused a determination to finish the course, which I did. Part of that stubbornness I now realize was connected to wanting validation from my father and if that meant enduring what I was going through, then so be it.

I still remember a few days before completing my Part Two training at HMS Mercury deciding that my identity would have to change. I thought back to my younger days and my fascination with super heroes. I would change; I would do things to cause people to have a different view of me. I would model myself on some of the guys around me; become a real "Matelot". Somehow I would find the courage to begin to stick up for myself, I would drink, fornicate, do whatever was necessary to destroy this sensitive but vulnerable boy called David "Skin and Essence" Crabb.

In both of our cases there came a conscious decision to change. We realised that our own unique identities could not even begin to prepare us to just survive the system of which we were now a part. Already our singular personalities were gradually diminishing, lost in a sea of variances that created further confusion and inconsistency in our young lives. The identity crisis, if we but knew it, would be years later. We were still in the throes of finding ways to bolster ourselves in a way acceptable to those around us, which would also bring the protection we so desperately needed. The question to be asked was - would those new self induced identities fool everyone? Would the masks stick?

Chapter Three – Fixing the Masks

⟨ornament⟩

The purpose, through our stories in this chapter, is to reveal how we went about creating new identities that were designed to protect us. These identities, in fact, brought further debilitating experiences into our lives, because they were not a part of our core characters. Sadly, it is so easy to convince yourself that the persona you are seeking to create is actually the real you. Living in this lie for a long period of time causes great harm and will eventually contribute to a person becoming totally confused as to what their true identity is. What must it have been like for the "Man in the Iron Mask," portrayed in the movie of the same name, after years of wearing this device, being faced for the first time with his true reflection.

John

During my time in the "Mob" (another name for the navy) my sporting prowess gained me a lot of respect and this was another certain way to avoid being 'put on' or bullied. In 1975/76 I was the runner up in the 200 metres Navy Juniors Championship. This meant that I went on to represent the

Navy in the Junior Combined Services at Aldershot. I was down to run in the 200 metres and came in fifth, which was a great disappointment to me. In truth, it was very difficult for us to compete with the Army and Air Force as we were often at sea and thus had limited opportunities or facilities to train. We had to train running around the upper deck which was possible on County Class Destroyers. The shock of doing so poorly in the 200 metres led me to fill the space in the 1500 metres race. I was ill-prepared and came last; it was one of the most embarrassing moments of my life as I finished a straight behind the other runners. Why had I been so foolish as to enter a race that I was so badly prepared for? I can smile now looking back, but it was a long return journey on the coach. I was, however, a serious athlete at the time, having realised that it gained one such a good standing and I had added incentive in the fact that I loved sport. I trained practically every day and on joining HMS Kent made it into the first eleven football team.

On my debut I was the youngest player in the team and to be included was immensely prestigious. During my time on the ship I played many times for her. One of the highlights was beating the Moroccan navy in one of their premier stadiums in Casablanca. I also played in Germany, France, Turkey, Malta and Gibraltar and many parts of Britain. After leaving the navy I would go on two football tours to Malta during which we beat the Malta youth team at the then national stadium in Gzira, and lose to Valletta who were Maltese champions at the time, again at the national stadium – the Malta trips were one of the highlights of my life up to that time.

For a period of time, HMS Kent was guard ship in Gibraltar. One of the few bright spots of being there was to play football in front of relatively big crowds for the Kent. We had a very good team and played under floodlights on the hard surface. Wherever we went we would play – this included our trips around Britain and meant a lot of extra time off. Whilst in Gibraltar I also took part in the grueling Rock race on three occasions. I enjoyed the identity of being an athlete and it certainly paid high dividends.

It wasn't long before I leaned toward the Physical Training Branch (PTI). I was drawn to the image of the Physical Training Instructor (known as Club-Swingers). The respect, the demeanor, the lifestyle and even the kit were a draw. Several people within the branch convinced me that I should indeed become a PTI. It wasn't possible to join the navy as a PTI; one had to gain some time in one's own branch before transferring to the Physical Training Branch. I considered it an ideal job. I loved sport and the role carried with it much prestige. Having gained enough seniority I put in my request form but by the time my apti- tude test came I was serving in London where we didn't have a PTI.

Due to my lifestyle in London and poor preparation it was with some trepidation that I set off for HMS Temeraire, the navy's school of Physical Education in Portsmouth. For three days the staff at the school put us through the most grueling physical and mental stress that I had ever known. The discipline was incredible. From morning to night we were on the go from gym tests to trapeze work over the pool. We were required to give lectures on impossible subjects, and on one occasion I was asked to tell my story in front of the whole school. I was humiliated by a Chief PTI verbally destroying me... The Gym was sacred ground where to walk was a major crime – we had to 'double' (a kind of running on the spot with forward movement) at all times. When we sat we had to slap our knees, when we got up we had to slap the floor. When spoken to by staff we had to respond at the top of our voices with "Staff!" Each evening we would go back to our barrack room and just collapse waiting to rise early for another grueling day.

Another feature was kit inspections whereby we would be given short notice to appear in either gym kit or number one uniforms. We were thrown in the pool in our number one's only to have to reappear in them, in a given amount of time, up to parade ground standards. I was ill-prepared and although I completed my aptitude test, I failed and was told to re-apply later. It was a real blow to me and I felt like crying, a dream died and it was not long after that I decided I wasn't going to stay in the navy. My failure to join the PTI staff was merely the death of one identity – I had several others to fall back on. Some of these had been fashioned back in basic training and would be added to through my diverse experiences during my time in the RN. For example, on completion of my naval training, I was sent along with a large team to work on an exercise taking place in Malta. It was my first trip overseas. In the three weeks that I was there I did the usual things, got infatuated with a Maltese girl, got regularly drunk and greatly enjoyed my time. Little did I know that within days of arriving back in Britain, I would be sent back out to Malta!

The flight was from RAF Brize-Norton in Swindon, there were several of us heading out to RAF Luqa in Malta. About four were going to join HMS Kent. The Kent was to be my home for the next two years or so. I arrived on the dock side at St. Angelo where the Kent was birthed under going a SMP (self maintenance period). I remember climbing up the gangplank of the imposing ship and being led down to the forward mess deck 3D, the next few hours would be something I will never forget.

The Mess was three decks down relatively near the front of the ship. Some 45 people lived in 3D mess and on this particular day there was a "clean ship" so everything was upside down and appeared calamitous. There were lockers emptied out into the centre of the Mess square and lots of people busying themselves doing this and that. I was shown to my bunk and locker space, my first thought was how I am going to store all my kit in there – the lockers seemed so tiny.

The bunks were arranged three high on either side of the passage way and continued down the full side of "the Bulkhead" (the wall). It took some getting used to as you were so close to others. As I began to unpack my things, a burly sailor wearing a full beard came round to me, he rubbed his hand on my chin, presumably weighing up the stubble before declaring for all to hear, and "I'm giving you one tonight." "Oh no the rumours about homosexuality are true," was my first thought.

What was happening? I was convinced that I was going to be raped and I was looking for the signals to suggest that he was kidding me on - the signs were not forthcoming. What should I do? Perhaps this was normal initiation? I was petrified - here I was a sixteen year old boy who was about to be raped. Should I tell somebody? It is hard to imagine what it was like to join a warship in those days, the first few days or even weeks' one had to establish oneself or you would face misery. The battle for credibility was enormous and it was established by proving that you were, "one of the boys". One major slip-up or show of weakness could destroy your life. Subconsciously, I knew this and decided to do nothing except put up a fight and hope for the best. I went ashore and got drunk in anticipation of a bad night ahead. In the event, nothing happened but the power in what I am saying is: I didn't know that nothing would happen.

Initiation into the real navy (on board ship) was an incredible experience. There was a 500 man crew on board Kent which made it into a small village. Life on board for the average lower deck sailor was to live in a cesspit of degradation. The air was blue and one was never far from stories of sexual conquest and innuendo. Although I never experienced any homosexual abuse or activity, you will know as you have read Dave's account that he did experience abuse. The innuendo of homosexuality was ripe but as I said previously it was completely unacceptable to indulge in any homosexual activity or to divulge that one was in fact "gay". To do so would mean immediate dishonorable discharge. How times have changed! Nowadays, one can be openly gay. Dave and I find this hard to reconcile knowing what life is like on a warship at sea.

Looking back I greatly enjoyed this period of my life on the Kent as I moved between adventure and boredom; adventure in the various ports of call and boredom at sea. I hated what was for me the tedium of being at sea. I now had no real desire to be a sailor or for my role as a Radar Plotter, but my desire was for the accompanying lifestyle that being a sailor offered. However, the identity of "sailor" meant one thing in one place and an entirely different thing in another. In the naval port of Portsmouth we carried the title of "Skates" and were considered the lowest of the low, whilst in non naval ports we were treated like celebrities. It was hard to adjust but one thing we were consistent at was taking enjoyment to the limits. It was considered to be a good thing if you could be classed as an "animal". One who had no values or moral code! It wasn't long before I was selling my soul.

The Gut

It was a balmy spring night as I (John) took my first step onto the infamous "Gut" or Straight Street in Valletta, Malta. The year was 1975 and I was still 16 years of age. It was to be a night to remember. The Gut was like a very long alleyway consisting of bars, brothels and little else save a tattoo artist where I had my first tattoo. Once seen never forgotten - it was a hub of decadent life - a scene of wild unadulterated lust and debauchery. As we proceeded down the Gut that particular night I looked to the right to see a girl sat at a bar

raising her top to reveal a perfectly formed pair of breasts -
she beckoned us with an inviting smile. Wow, I was going to
enjoy the Gut. Up and to my right a homosexual was being
dangled by his legs out of a bedroom window. Later, I would
learn that his name was Frankie and that he was a permanent
fixture down the Gut in those days.

I moved on not yet knowing that this night was to be the
night when I would have full sexual intercourse for the first
time. Previous to this I'd had lots of sexual experiences but
not full penetration. After a few bottles of the local brew
"Hop Leaf" a friend of mine from Southern Ireland suggested
we find ourselves a prostitute.

It wasn't difficult but not all of them were beauties.
We decided on "two's up," we would only go for one who
would take two of us on. I can't remember if this decision
was based on lust or security but we promptly began to find
the one. She wasn't much...short, plump and in her mid to
late thirties. Needless to say she wasn't going to turn down
some easy money from two inexperienced boys and she led
us up the dimly lit stairway into a cheap, badly painted room
with a double bed, stool, sink and little else. She gave us
both a "Johnny" (condom) and my mate was first, I sat on the
stool and watched the spectacle as his youthful innocence
diminished further, I never asked him if it was his first time
as well. A few groans later it was over and it was my turn.
We changed places and another few groans later it was all
over for me as well.

As we rearranged our clothes she began to mother us and
told us that she had a husband and five children and that she
did what she did because she was so poor. I doubt that she
enjoyed the experience and it didn't exactly light up my life
but I was no longer a *Cherry Boy* the naval term for virgin. It
mattered little to me at the time that I had lost the glory of my
virginity so cheaply. I can recall looking down on the ample
flesh of the woman - old enough to be my mother – who had

just absorbed my virginity and I felt sorry for her. We began a strange conversation for two who had just engaged in a sexual act as her mothering instincts took over. Sometime later I found myself in a brothel in Izmir, Turkey. It was a debt prison where women were reluctantly forced into prostitution. The place was unbelievable, one literally shopped for women in shop windows. I'll never forget my thoughts, even as one who would abuse the system, for the not so pretty ones who were dressed very provocatively offering themselves at half-price. The thought still brings a tear to my eyes. In other places we sailors would find ourselves in situations where animals were having sex with women. What have we done to our world?

That night down the Gut my mate Willie and I grinned as we left the premises and proceeded to get very drunk. I had no idea at the time how much sexual experiences can scar a person's life. That night would cost me much more than the money that I had handed over. It always does but you can't see it until you understand your true identity. Apart from my name, official number and navy directive I didn't have a clue where I was heading in life or even where I wanted to go.

As previously stated I had experienced a lot of sex before this night but never full penetration. Some years later I sat under the late Dr. Ed Cole's teaching on the "Glory of Sex". As I listened to his great discourse on God's intent I wept at the realisation of what I had been with regard to my sexuality. I had no idea that the answer to this and all matters pertaining to life were wrapped up in identity. I had begun to masturbate aged seven, this was long before I could ejaculate but I remember talking to some masturbating peers about "getting the feeling." It is true to say that from the age of seven until my conversion to Christ at 25, I had some kind of sexual experience practically every day. This would involve numerous women over the years and a daily habit of masturbation. I saw this as being normal for a healthy, young man-of-the-world. It may well be usual but it is not normal. It is certainly not God's intent. In those days I was dominated by the thought of sex and before long I visited other brothels and generally slept around when ever possible. I now know that you will always read life through the identity that you have assumed. The answer really is to take off your invisible glasses, whatever label they have, and look through God's perspective.

When my time on H.M.S Kent came to an end I was a different person from the young lad from the Yorkshire village in Bradford. I was now one who had travelled widely and experienced much. I was surprised to find that I had been drafted to London. I was to take up a position of "Buffer's party" at Firs House which was on Queens Gate Terrace in Kensington. Firs House was the home of the Wrens who worked at the Communication's Centre under Whitehall. The male staff were outnumbered by at least ten to one and my life was about to take a dive. It was remarked that Firs House was a paradise draft for a young, single 18 year old man and that is certainly how it appeared. In my experience there was role reversal there. For example, the women chatted up the men and it was normal for the girls to ask the boys to dance and more.

Every Tuesday and Thursday we had our own disco in the resident bar and I soon descended into deeper levels of decadence. On arrival in London, I had a girlfriend in Blackpool and at first I tried to remain faithful to her but I didn't hold out for long. I lived with four other sailors in the upstairs of a big house on Birkbeck road in Acton in West London. It was normal to wake up and stroll over bodies that one was meeting for the first time.

During a night out with my housemates down the West End we picked up a sixteen year old girl who had run away from her home to the bright lights of London. She accompanied us back to our house and before morning she had slept with all of us. It was the first time that I had been unfaithful to my girlfriend and the next day I felt remorseful even turning down the chance to sleep with the girl again. The remorse that I felt that day would not last as my waywardness got easier. However that one night stand resulted in me contracting venereal disease. This was a heavy price to pay.

It was at Birkbeck road that I smoked my first joint and true to say my stay in London was like one big party. I had lost all sense of control and began to drink at lunch times as well as in the evenings (it was during this period that I did my PTI aptitude test). I arrived in London as an athlete with a steady girlfriend, I left one year later as a wreck but my next draft would be as different again. H.M.S Vigilant based on Carlingford Loch in Northern Ireland was my next place of work. I went from London to Whale Island as it was known – the infamous H.M.S Victory naval gunnery school. It was here that I was turned into somewhat of a soldier for my new role. Through arduous training I became an expert in the small arms of the day – the SLR rifle, The small machine gun (SMG) and the Browning 9mm pistol. So, in 1977 I found myself on a ferry at Liverpool heading for Belfast. In order to look inconspicuous I had been allowed to grow my hair long and for the one and only time had a full beard, this was so that we would not stand out as servicemen.

On the Ferry I met other crew members of the Vigilant. I had several pints of Guinness and got my head down in a bunk on the overnight crossing. The next morning, a little hung over, we were transferred to the back of a military vehicle. As we headed down to the infamous Warren Point, which was the scene of the IRA's bloody murder of members of the Parachute regiment, I remember wondering whether I would survive.

As pleasant as London had been I was about to experience the antithesis. The Vigilant was a converted tug that had been specially adapted to patrol the Loch in an attempt to stop the gun-running of the terrorists. I was to be part of a twenty-six man team consisting of sailors and marines. Our job was to search ships coming in to Warren Point and traverse the narrow water ways of the border, searching people, small craft, farm houses and the like. Similar to my initial experience on HMS Kent, arriving on the Vigilant was a shock to the system, as there were not enough bunks; we operated a system of one in and one out. We were often wet, cold and miserable and to cap it all there was a very real danger that we would kill or be killed. Along with our sister vessel "H.M.S Alert" we were the only naval personnel on active service anywhere in the world at that time – the Falklands war would, of course, change all that.

I soon had the sense of going from being a playboy in London to a frightened little rabbit in the midst of the Northern Ireland of the seventies. For six long months we did patrol after patrol, boarding ships at all hours of the day, holding people at gunpoint – I was a trained searcher and entered people's worlds uninvited. It was the most difficult patch of my then short life, I hated it and it was during this time that my decision not to stay in the navy was enforced. I was beginning to see that having some control of one's destiny was very appealing. I didn't want to do what I was doing but had no choice, I was under command.

Though we would not dare show fear during our time on the Vigilant we were scared and I certainly prayed for protection to a God I didn't know. Not only did we need protection from the terrorists but also for the times that we were out on the open sea. From time to time we had to cross the Irish Sea to go to Scotland. On more than one occasion we stood on the bridge of the ship with life jackets on waiting for the order to abandon ship. Not that we would have lasted long in the kind of seas we faced. During these times at sea I suffered terribly from sea sickness and felt so ill that I think I would have welcomed the IRA shooting me.

After leaving the Vigilant I went home to Blackpool for a long leave and realised now, looking back that I was suffering from Post Traumatic Stress Syndrome. I had never heard that term at the time but that is what it was. For long periods I didn't want to get out of bed and when I did I got excessively drunk. First the Kent, then Firs House followed by the Vigilant in Northern Ireland and I was not yet 20 years of age.

My next ship was H.M.S Londonderry which was under-going refit at the naval base in Rosyth in East Scotland. It was from here that I would leave the navy some 18 months later. As the ship was in refit we were seconded into unre-lated and various roles, I ended up working full-time in the gym which was a delight. However, I had put my required 18 months notice in and though I had some second thoughts I decided that on the due date I would leave my life as a sailor. Though I would indeed leave the navy, I would find that it would not be so easy for the navy to leave me. By this time, identity on top of identity was having its effect and I had lost all contact with anything real in my young life. I was directionless and without any real vision for my future. The navy had forged an identity that I wouldn't easily shake off even after I left to re-enter civilian life.

Finding myself back in "Civvie Street," was a strange experience. My naval identity was stamped right through me. Nevertheless, as had been the course of my life hitherto, I wandered between identities feeling that time was on my side. With the little money I had received on exiting the RN I purchased a Side-Stall in the Winter Garden's amusement arcade in Blackpool. My Dad had one opposite. His was "Hoola Hoop" and mine was one where the "punter" had to get several balls in the same slot. It looked easy but in reality was very difficult. The idea was that in inclement weather the unsuspecting holiday-makers would seek shelter in our amusement arcade. The job was then to lure them onto one's stall by persuading them that they had a very good chance of winning a giant teddy bear. The trick was to keep them playing until they had spent way beyond the worth of the teddy. In reality they bought the teddy several times over. In order to succeed the stall holder had to be hard of heart and have the gift of the gab. I had neither and this coupled with the fact that hardly anyone came into the arcade meant that my new career was short lived.

I dreamed of being different and longed to find some kind of Bohemian lifestyle that would keep me free of the mundane. After the Blackpool Illuminations of 1979 I went off to Spain for a holiday and to ponder my future. We were in Magaluf and I had my usual drunken binge. I was with a girlfriend and some friends and felt like I needed a rest when I got home. Ever the adventurer I remained unsettled as a civilian and longed for the out-of-the-ordinary lifestyle that I had lived in the previous five years.

Much to my surprise it wasn't long before I was back in a navy environment as my next job was working for the navy as a civilian Store-Keeper. HMS Inskip was a shore base near Preston in Lancashire. It was an easy job but with little prospects. I did, however, enjoy working again in a naval atmosphere. I made a lot of friends but knew that I wouldn't be staying for long. I didn't, and in the spring of 1981 I set off along with a friend to travel around Europe in a converted ambulance. Now, I was a Bohemian and was looking to live in freedom. We travelled through France, Andorra, Spain, Monte Carlo, Italy, Germany, Switzerland, Luxembourg and Belgium. In a nutshell the idea was to travel, eat, drink and have sex. It was a memorable time but didn't serve to release me from the enemy of longing within.

As my friend Simon and I headed south from our homes in Blackpool we were looking for blessing although we would not have used that word. We foolishly believed that if we could get "blessed" in some way then we would be fulfilled in life. How wrong! I had this image of sunshine, fun, sex and frequently moving on to the next batch of people. We experienced the above list and more but didn't bargain for the poverty, persistent dysentery, scabies and breakdown in relationships! I returned at the end of that summer penniless, 14 lbs lighter having had the trip of a lifetime but still unfulfilled. I had spent my 23rd birthday in Monte Carlo getting drunk and swimming the famous harbour in the early hours of the morning. I was a good raconteur and could, after several drinks, keep an audience enthralled with the incredible life I had had since leaving school but who was I? Truth is: I was several people rolled into one. The thinker, the adventurer, the athlete, the animal, the polite young man, the man who could fall in love, the man who could move from one partner to another, the perennial underachiever. The seeker, who had found many dead ends and who didn't know who he was and what potential lay within him. At that time I had no qualifications (quite unbelievably I would go on to get my first O level in the Welsh language, studying in Welsh) so educationally I couldn't articulate some of the deeper moments in my thought process. I have since learned the following: "if you perceive education to be expensive try a life time of ignorance." Like Dave, I was walking around with an IQ of 134 but without an education. Again, if I had not found my identity, I would have continued in that state and would have probably remained so until I obtained an early death through some misadventure or other.

Whilst being a great adventurer I was also the definitive misadventurer. At times I was full of life and mischief yet, at other times, I was full of regret, melancholy and doubt. One confused cookie. Before the time of my conversion to Christ I was living in Blackpool and working in the Post Office. My nickname at the time was "Beer God". By now I had worked as a waiter, a builder's labourer, and greengrocer and sold seafood on Blackpool beach. I had been a hardened drinker since my navy days and lived in the dichotomy of trying to stay fit for sport whilst being a heavy drinker. A few years on and my drinking habits were out of control. Although I tried to stay sober from Monday to Thursday, I would usually begin my weekend on Thursday night with a few pints of beer. After finishing work on Friday lunchtime I would drink until closing time and occasionally through the night. Saturdays would see me drinking from teatime through to about 4:00 am then Sunday lunch I'd have a few more. Exhausting stuff!

Merely to write about it is draining now but that was my routine for about five years. I did some crazy things in those years and as I have alluded to I was wearing several masks, each mask portraying a different identity. I would not have wanted to be any one thing at the expense of the others, simply because being; for example, just "The Beer God" would have been too one-dimensional and horrifying in prospect. The truth is I had never found me!

Chapter Four – Fixing the Masks (2)

✑

Dave's account

It was almost my first "run ashore" in a foreign port, Tangiers in Morocco and I had promised myself prior to joining my first ship to do something about my identity. I wanted people to perceive me in a different light. Here was my big chance to prove myself a man. There must have been a dozen of us, loud, brave and looking good in our uniforms. I had plenty of money, having had nothing to spend it on during the weeks we had spent at sea on exercise. We had previously visited Gibraltar for a few days; I had only one chance to go ashore there due to my duty requirements. That had been a pretty miserable affair as I was alone and didn't really know where to go. I had a tourist's visit really. I went to the top of the "rock" on the cable car, saw the Barbary Apes, then I visited the other side of the "rock" to the lovely "Catlan" bay. Arriving back on board ship the first thing I was asked was, "did you get a bit?" This was almost always the first enquiry a sailor made on someone returning from shore leave. It was expected that graphic details would follow.

Well, here in Tangiers, just across the water from Gib' our first stop was a dirty; grimy bar that I failed to realise was, in fact, a brothel. Almost as soon as we entered, several near naked women who got us all beers greeted us. One woman came over to me, sitting next to me on a bar stool. I recall that her English was very limited; she was able to get me to buy her a drink (known as *sticky greens*), that I noticed cost over twice the normal price. Once she had her drink she began kissing and masturbating me, she also gave me several huge "love bites" on my neck that appeared like massive bruises. She whispered her intentions into my ear making it abundantly clear what she wanted to do with me. I was, without doubt, enjoying the experience with this near naked woman, I felt as though I was being treated as a man.

Here I was sixteen years old and already in my first brothel. It didn't occur to me what danger I was in, or that indeed I would be required to go the full distance. I was quite content whilst in the kiosk to buy her drinks and partake in some heavy petting. However, she was clearly not going to allow me to get away with just that. I noted that my compatriots were passing a cap around among themselves, collecting enough money for, in their words, *"Dave to break his cherry,"* meaning to have my first encounter with a prostitute. I wasn't so innocent that I didn't know what that meant. There was no way I was going to go with this woman. Not only was she old enough to be my mother, she had a mouth full of gold teeth, she smelt awful, and in my mind was archetypical of the films we were shown in training concerning women of this kind and the terrible diseases you could catch were you to go with them. However, I was also strangely fascinated with this woman who was allowing me to do things, that prior to this, I had merely fantasised about. It was as though these women had a certain agenda they would abide by. Everything was about getting the client to go one step further, to spend that little extra cash, for me this was not about cash. I had not at that point descended far enough in my moral sensibilities nor in desperation to even want to go any further with this woman.

Suddenly, the new identity I was seeking to create as "one of the boys" was being challenged. I ran! It must have been well past midnight when the others arrived back on board ship. I could hear them laughing and talking, once or twice I knew I heard my name mentioned, I was dreading the morning, I knew I was in for some stick. Sure enough, the impending humiliation came. I was informed that the money raised was used by one of my so-called friends. However, my excuse of feeling sick coupled with the fact that because I was under 18 years old I was required to be back on the ship before midnight (known as having Cinderella leave); seemed to be accepted. Almost two weeks later however my "so called friend" joined a large percentage of the ships company at the sick bay with his dose of Gonorrhea.

In my innocence I too visited the sick bay convinced that I had caught some kind of terrible disease, due to the love bites I had on my neck and other parts of my body. The 'doc' had great fun over the next couple of weeks stringing me along with tales of horror concerning how various bits of my body may well drop off should I be infected. Nevertheless, part of me had enjoyed the experience and I would fanta- sise about it for a long time. Catching a venereal disease in the RN was a serious matter, as it was classed as a 'self inflicted' injury (just as getting sun burned was) and could even, on occasions result in disciplinary action, particularly if it resulted in a man having to be put on light duties.

The trip to Tangier only lasted about four or five days after which we went back to Gibraltar for a two-week AMP (assisted maintenance period). It was in Gibraltar that I thought I had fallen in love again with another prostitute. Her name was Leila, Moroccan in origin; she had been working in the nightclub I was frequenting quite regularly now. I didn't realise she was a prostitute. I simply thought she was some kind of hostess who got the guys to buy drinks. I eventually began to realise what her role in the club was as I bought her more drinks, it became clear that she was willing to grant "certain favours." I genuinely liked her and we chatted and petted, sometimes for hours. Provided I bought expensive drinks regularly, I could spend as much time with her as I liked. On occasions I poured out my heart to her and recall a very intimate moment with her where she too expressed real emotion over her own life situation, a rare occurrence with a prostitute. Normally, in order to exist within the degrading world they had chosen would mean cutting themselves off as much as was possible from any kind of emotional attachment, especially with a client. I think my youth attracted her to me; I was just a scared kid looking for a mother figure. She must have been in her mid to late thirties, I was still only sixteen. Looking back, it seems that for both John and I, older women, at that time in our young lives were a real attraction. We both agree that we were probably looking for mother figures, yet confusing the role of a real mother's love, with something that in effect was a perversion and no real substitute. Remembering that at this time (in our mid teens) we had both began to experience world travel, having up to that point lived very localised lives in our respective homes in Bradford and Rugby. I think Leila actually liked being with me, she was very tender toward me and probably felt safe. Once I fully understood her role in the club my feelings changed a little and though I liked her company, I knew she was not for me. I felt somewhat betrayed by her and eventually stopped frequenting the club.

My next journey to the Mediterranean was to take place a few months later and this was to last for nine months. However, we returned to the UK for a short time first before going on a four-month trip to Copenhagen, Stockholm, Oslo, and then the Norwegian Fjords, ending with a trip to Germany just in time for the beer festival. It was during the trip to Copenhagen that I managed to erect a mask that was to remain in place for some considerable time. By this time I was approaching my seventeenth birthday. I had by now had a string of encounters with women, often one night stands with only one purpose in my mind - sex! Each time I had an encounter it was as though I was reinforcing the new identity I had chosen. It was as though the sensitive, in my eyes weak, even moral David Crabb was being gradually destroyed in order for the new version to emerge.

During this period of my life, memories of the previous abuses were pushed far back in my mind, I was too busy now enjoying this new identity that seemed to offer me so much. I had not only crossed the line in terms of my morality, but now I was toughening up in all kinds of ways. Emotionally I had learnt to ignore my homesickness, even at times not going home for weekend leave, but rather taking trips with friends for an 'adventure' as we saw it. The adventure would usually result in liaisons with women, drunkenness and excesses of all kinds. I tried smoking marijuana but it never really did much for me, alcohol was my preference. I was also in the habit of picking fights, usually with people far bigger than myself. Again, this was all a front designed to make my mark. I only dared to do it once I was inebriated and usually with the belief that my mates would stop it before it went too far. This became a normal practice with me; it was a way of seeking to establish myself. I even did it on my first date with Sheila (who was to become my wife), yet on that occasion afterwards I did not get the usual buzz, rather, I felt ashamed, that I had let myself down somehow.

On the nine month trip around the Mediterranean I had the opportunity to visit places of real interest. Rome, Athens and such like places. However, for that whole nine months I descended into what can only be described as an orgy of wasting, debilitating life events that bore no resemblance to any kind of normality. On my eventual return I had accumulated over six weeks leave and had finished a full commission on my first ship, that is, two and a half years service. However, my mission was still to find a way of fixing the mask so that it truly became my identity and bring me the acceptance and protection that I wanted.

Both my parents knew that their son was very different from the young boy who had left home at 15. I had experienced life at a "fast-forward" rate and was truly determined to convince all those around me, concerning the new identity I was choosing to live from. I was clearly quite obnoxious, drinking, cursing, fighting, womanising, single or married, it made no difference to me. Strangely though, I seemed to feel the acceptance and validation from my father who had also served in the navy for 15 years. I felt as though I was one of the boys, 'Skin and Essence' was dead at last, now my orgy of self abuse really started. My father seemed so proud of me, particularly when I performed for the crowds, I could always be counted on to be the loudest and rudest in whatever scenario we found ourselves in.

My six weeks at home were an embarrassment to all those around me who loved me. I spent hundreds of pounds on drunken binges. I sought out girls, I would lie and tell them anything to get what I wanted; I wasted money trying to impress them. Old school friends couldn't believe what I had become. Some were clearly impressed; others were frankly disgusted with what they now saw. I simply didn't care anymore. My typical day would start as soon as the pubs opened. A sailor's favourite pastime was the aptly named DTS [dinner time session]. The object was to get as drunk as possible, sleep it off in the afternoon and start again early evening.

It was during the trips to Scandinavia and Germany that I really learnt to abuse drink. I had dabbled with drink before joining the navy, but now I had the chance to truly imbibe. Three things happened immediately. First of all I noted that it enabled me to at last find acceptance among those who, up to now, seemed to find me an object of scorn. Secondly, I discovered that the drinking made me feel happy, carefree and guilt free. Thirdly, drinking gave the effect of being totally uninhibited; I could do things that were normally out of character for me, or that fear stopped me doing.

During the early 70's, Copenhagen was experiencing a time of liberality that at that time seemed to us like heaven on earth. On my first run ashore I couldn't believe my eyes as most of the girls did not wear bras (very unusual at that time). At some places in Sweden we found nude beaches that we would often frequent. We would spend days on the beaches, taking beer, wine, bread, cheese, having what was known in the navy as a 'banyan.' We could hardly believe our luck, skylarking with these women in the sea and on the beach, getting them drunk in the hope of conquest.

On one occasion, we were having such a fantastic time that we were tempted not to return to the ship. I do recall that we were glad to leave when we did, some parents had approached the Captain with complaints and a minor diplomatic disaster was imminent. As the ship slipped out of the harbour that afternoon, there were the girls watching from a distance, parents with them, all with angry, accusatory faces. Once out of the harbour and certain we were not returning we all broke into ribald laughter, another conquest, we didn't care, we had got what we wanted, and those girls just became another story to tell and to boast of.

This was why it was usual practice before letting us ashore that the captain mustered us all on the flight deck with a list of places that were out of bounds to naval personnel. Again, we all had our pencils and scraps of paper taking down the details, as we knew that these were the places **to** go. We were duly warned that were we to dishonour the flag in anyway, retribution would ensue in the form of naval discipline. Yes, we laughed and boasted of the things we had done. The stories would resound around the ship's company for months until they were all out of proportion to the actual events that had taken place. 'Black catting' was a favourite pastime of sailors, this was when one man shared a story, and another would have to share something that was considered by all as the better tale. Hence, the one upmanship whilst ratings were ashore. The bigger animalistic behaviour the greater the standing amongst your peers, who truthfully all knew the stories were sometimes being grossly exaggerated. This led to a very dangerous game being lived out on runs ashore.

The sad thing as I look back to that time is that I rarely visited any places of interest. One of Copenhagen's sites is the mermaid in the harbour. The local police arrested my friend and I as we were found draped over her having deposited the contents of our stomachs all over the statue.

The first thing we did on these visits was to seek out the red light district. Every bar we went into had blue movies showing. As the drinking continued we would find our courage and go to the live sex shows. These went far beyond mere strip tease; couples would be on stage engaging in all kinds of degrading sexual acts, in all kinds of sickening scenarios. Drinks would cost three or four times the normal price and the staff were not coy in making sure you were constantly drinking. No one would be allowed to remain were they discovered not to be drinking. At the end of the shows the female and male performers would engage in what was called, "the petting session.'" Men were taken into kiosks where sexual favours were dispensed at a certain price. Women would literally be draped over our laps in a scene that could easily have been mistaken for an orgy. We degraded them and ourselves in a shameless drunken frenzy.

On other occasions we would meet with girls at disco's or in bars, buy them drinks and seek sex within moments of speaking to them. It seemed so easy. By the morning we couldn't even remember their names. Some of us would end up at the sick bay days later with venereal disease; some were just lucky and got away with it. Remember most often the type of girls that would go with sailors on one night stands were the kind who had many one night encounters. Sometimes this would even be with a friend, thus, it was very easy during a prolonged stay in a Port for disease to spread through a crew. Whether we had made anyone pregnant didn't bother us at all, we knew our ship would be leaving harbour soon enough and the chances of us ever meeting the girls again were very slim. We would lie, cheat, do whatever was necessary in order to achieve our goal.

My young mind was gradually sinking into a world of sordid images that I was to discover would not go away. I had no concept of what I was exposing my soul to; in my drunken state I was taking huge risks. It is difficult to describe what being in a bar full of drunken sailors is like to someone who has never experienced it. Unless you were part of it, it would have been a terrifying experience; literally anything could and often did, happen.

One of the most famous places for sailors to frequent was the afore mentioned 'Gut', in Valetta, Malta. As John mentioned previously, the 'Gut' was an incredible scene of decadent life. It was almost a mile long street full of bars and brothels, the idea being to go down one side and up the other drinking in every place. Impossible, but it never stopped a sailor trying. The finale of a night out would be what was called the "Zulu Warrior." Tables would be cleared and a circle formed with one table in the middle. Trouser legs were rolled up, men slapped their knees and a rhythmic chant began, in our case: *"We're from Fife, we are brave, we're from Fife, we are brave, Haul 'em down you Zulu Warrior,*

Haul 'em down you Zulu chief chief chief chief. Allelele zumba zumba zumba hey" At some point someone would spontaneously emerge from the crowd, he would be the Zulu Warrior.

Clutching his glass, his "silk" removed from his uniform and tied around his head. He mounted the table and commenced his own strip show. The quality of the Zulu Warrior would ultimately be gauged by what happened when he reached his underpants. If his courage endured and he went all the way, his reward was that all present threw the contents of their beer glasses all over him. He truly would be considered, "The Zulu Warrior." This procedure was enjoyed all the more if there was the added shock factor of a civilian audience, therefore, it could be carried out at what was deemed the venues of most risk. Needless to say it was during this trip that I attempted my very first "Zulu Warrior." At last the mask was up. I was able to begin the building of a new identity that hopefully would offer me some kind of protection. Because I now had some degree of reputation I was able to lie more convincingly. On return from almost every run ashore I would revel in my stories of how many girls I had pulled, how many fights I had been in, my whole life was getting out of control.

On a trip to Wilhelmshaven, in Germany, my reputation was further enhanced as a drinking man. I only made it as far as the dockyard canteen, full of drunken sailors from our own ship and also German ships. We sat at a long table where you were served with four litre glasses of beer and a huge glass of schnapps. You were invited to stand on the table, down all four glasses of beer and finish by downing the schnapps. At the bottom of the schnapps glass emerged a pornographic image as your reward. Of course I just had to do it, as I knew this too would enhance the reputation I was gaining in my mess deck. I couldn't understand all the fuss, the beers went down as did the schnapps and I was still standing. The cheers and slaps on the back caused me to swell with pride as I downed a few more schnapps for ultimate effect.

It was at that point that my memory began to play tricks on me. I was so far gone that I have no recollection of how obnoxious I became. I insulted one of the barmaids by grabbing her and making obscene remarks and suggestions. I became very aggressive, offering to fight anyone. When I went outside to the toilet and the fresh air hit me, I fell totally unconscious. I was covered in vomit and the remains of unfinished drinks. Fortunately for me some German sailors took me back to my ship, carrying me on their shoulders. They laid me ceremoniously at the bottom of the gangway with my arms folded over my chest as though I was dead. I have a vague recollection of the Officer of the watch calling me and informing me that if I made it up the gangway on my own all would be well. I told him in no uncertain terms to come and get me. He personally declined the invitation; rather he sent a couple of burly seamen to take me to the sick bay. It was here that I experienced my first of many stomach pumps (due to alcohol poisoning), not that I remember much about it. My next memory was opening my eyes to see the guard who had been detailed to watch me over night. His first words were, *"you are in the rattle mate, Officer of the day's table in thirty minutes."* This was naval procedure for misdemeanors.

My crime was so serious that I eventually made it to the Captains table. A Naval defaulter is best understood as a form of disciplinary procedures that culminate in appearing before the Captain. At this point you have the choice to accept the Captain's judgment, or you can opt for court marshal. A sailor rarely took up this 'kind offer.' I agreed with the Captain that my actions were deplorable and I should be willing to accept whatever punishment he meted out. Ten days number nines and a fine were my 'reward' for that escapade. Number nines, (as previously mentioned, a reference to naval overalls usually worn during menial and dirty tasks), also meant no shore leave, and reporting for extra duties regularly during the day. It was worth it in my mind, for now my reputation was indeed becoming an identity I was proud of. Other forms of punishment would hit your pocket – it seemed that the navy could, at will, impose a fine upon you even for something seemingly as innocuous as being a few minutes late for duty.

I was still just under eighteen years old, on the surface now a beer swilling Zulu Warrior, the womanising, fighting, and swearing matelot who couldn't care less. In reality I was a scared, home sick child who had no idea who he was anymore. I knew that much of my exterior world was simply a lie, yet I was totally unable, even unwilling to change it, for I believed this new persona brought me acceptance and a degree of protection. This mask was to remain in place for many damaging years, as I sank deeper and deeper into a mire of my own making.

At home I had a girl friend that I had also started a sexual relationship with. Each time I came home on leave I would look her up and buy her things. She returned my generosity with sex. It was an arrangement we were both happy with, we even went on holiday together. It was shortly after that she informed me she thought she was pregnant. I glibly said that we would get married with no real understanding of the huge ramifications this could have upon my life. This was an incident I became quite proud of, bragging to my mates how I had almost got my girl friend "up the stick!" As it was, it transpired that she wasn't pregnant but just late having her period. When my father found out he found a way of ending the relationship.

Some of the things we did were sickening and unbelievable. Other girls came and went, to my shame I cannot even remember their names or what they looked like. In our mess deck we had what was referred to as a "Gronk board." On this board was pinned photographic proof of women men had scored with. The idea was that the guy who scored with the ugliest woman and had photographic proof won the prize of a crate of ale. Everyone was buying Polaroid cameras; some of the images appearing on the board were totally pornographic. Some guys even posted pornographic pictures of their wives. We didn't care! We were all living, for different reasons, behind masks and identities that were like twisted images, belying the true identities that were now seemingly lost forever beneath a mass of filth and degradation.

Yet, I need to re-emphasise here, many of us were just boys under eighteen years of age. What I was oblivious to was how much damage I was actually doing to myself, how expert I was becoming in erecting defense mechanisms, masks that told the world a lie concerning my true identity that was now lost. I truly had no idea who I was any more, neither did I really care! I had discovered methods of getting my own way, I knew how to intimidate people, I had found ways of communicating a personality that people seemed to accept and, at times, fear. Yet beneath it all was a frightened needy boy who didn't really know what he wanted anymore.

Just before my eighteenth birthday, laying in a hotel room in Portsmouth after a run ashore that had proven boring and uneventful; I awaited the return of my mate who had stayed behind for one more drink. On his arrival back to the room he brought in two young women with him. Literally within minutes we had sex with them, oblivious to potential dangers, not bothered whether we got them pregnant, another conquest to brag about and pretend that I had really enjoyed. Laying in the bed next to a woman whose name I did not even bother to discover, I began to realise how shallow my life had become. Was this identity that seemed to offer me what I thought I needed really worth it? Disquieting thoughts like this began to plague my already troubled mind, yet there were no apparent answers and no reasons as to why I should change my course in life.

The following morning was awful. The women were not what they had appeared to be in the darkened room of the hotel and whilst still under the influence of drink. Worse still, they seemed to want to know who we were, where we were from, future meetings and the like. We lied to them, telling them false names and addresses, telephone numbers that did not exist. The girl I had been with seemed genuinely upset, in fact devastated when she realised we had simply used them. We had achieved what we wanted to achieve, now we just wanted to get back to the ship. On another occasion I remember meeting up with the wife of a Royal Marine. I wasn't concerned at all that she was married; all that concerned me was getting what I wanted. I had no concept at all as to what this was doing to my soul, how years later it would still affect me, inducing feelings of guilt and shame that are impossible to describe. I justified it because she had told me they had an open relationship. The morality of it all never, at that time, bothered me too much, for it all added credibility to the mask I was creating. This hurting, frightened boy was lost somewhere beneath it all and I was determined he would never make another appearance.

At this time in my life I, like John, experienced the indignity of a venereal disease. It is difficult to describe to people some of the scenes that had become normal to me. In Plymouth there were places like, "Diamond Lil's Showbar," where transvestite entertainers coupled with live strippers, gave the average sailor a "good night out". Outside on Union Street the naval patrols would be waiting for the drunken fights to begin. Ferrying *baby sailors* (young recruits) back to their ships where they would face up to their misdemeanors the next morning, as they joined the defaulters queue.

My time on HMS Fife came to an end. I enjoyed six weeks leave, which I spent drinking and looking up my old girlfriend, until I eventually returned to the shore base I was drafted to - HMS Warrior. This was at a NATO (North Atlantic Treaty Organisation) communications centre in Northwood, Middlesex. I would remain there for about twelve months. In the first couple of weeks there I further enhanced my reputation by sleeping with my friend's girl friend. Though I put on a bold front, I was thoroughly disgusted with myself. My friend did not complain out of fear of getting involved in a fight with me, he found another girl and we merely continued as though nothing had happened.

It was while I was at Warrior that I found myself in big trouble again. During another drinking bout (which were becoming a regular part of my life), I ended up completely inebriated to the extent that I was so confused that I urinated all over another chap's bed, thinking it was the toilet. He discovered me collapsed in his room and, whilst unconscious, gave me the hiding of my life. This action on his part was considered the lowest of the low - to take advantage of a drunken man was something a sailor never did. Fortunately for me I didn't feel a thing, in fact I didn't even know it had happened as I was so drunk. I awoke to find myself locked in the cells with a guard and a medical orderly with me. My nose had been badly broken; at one point they put me on oxygen as I could not breathe properly. I had fractured ribs and was covered in cuts and bruises. I had, I was informed, lost a lot of blood - I was a mess! I was brought before the captain, who I must say seemed genuinely concerned at my condition. I lost two weeks leave as well as getting a heavy fine and 14 days number nine's punishment. I think this was the very first time I recall a naval officer showing any kind of real concern for such a young man. He could not understand why I had allowed myself to get into such a state. I was good at my job, had my future ahead of me, why was I living such a destructive lifestyle? I took my punishment fairly well, but I was on the look out for the guy who had beaten me as I was determined to get him back. The navy became aware of this and drafted him to another establishment, I never did find him.

After my next ship – HMS Galatea, which I was on for another full commission, I was stationed at GCHQ Cheltenham, discovering here that in fact I had a brain and share with John, strangely enough an IQ of 134. It was whilst on the Galatea that we spent long months in the Icelandic 'Cod war,' involving fishery protection duties. We were often in the frightening place of placing our ship in between the Icelandic gun boats and the trawlers whose nets they were attempting to cut. Apart from the many storms we encountered in that time, we were constantly in a state of 'alert' and our own ship was rammed a number of times. One particular incident required us to return to Rosyth for major repairs. We never came under fire from the gun-boats, but it was a very scary time when being rammed in such dangerous waters. It would only require a couple of minutes before someone would perish were they to end up overboard. You can see from the photographs the terrible danger people were often in during this time. I was eventually recommended for communications specialist training, passing an Admiralty interview board, which again revealed to me that I was in fact capable of producing far more in my life than I was doing at that time. This would have required me to learn Russian, Chinese or Arabic languages and it was determined that I was more than capable of doing so, I was also recommended for officer training at this time. Had I been willing to co-operate with the educational require-ments I believe I was more than capable of accomplishing this, however I was not emotionally mature enough and turned it all down. It was whilst I was at GCHQ (Government Communications Headquarters) that I tendered my 18 month notice to quit the navy before being drafted to my final ship HMS Dido.

It is true to say both John and I had grown to enjoy the decadent slide from relative innocence into abusive lifestyles that would take years to recover from. The scene had now been set, the masks firmly in place, - we were hardened by our experience of life and the masquerade was in full swing. Later, when Christianity began to influence our lives, we began the second part of our parallel journeys. Our wounded and tarnished hearts began to discover real love. We would both go through incredible times of pain as God fashioned us into our understanding of unconditional love. We both became Christians, unbeknown to each other in 1984 and this second part to our incredible stories would be no less an adventure than the first. In many ways it goes beyond the ingenuity of the most creative, fictitious mind to make-up. The next two chapters describe how our lives changed at this point and how our masks began to be dismantled. That is, all that was false, damaged and confused.

Chapter Five – Returning to Life

John

On March 14 1984, I sat in a Blackpool church and heard these words from the preacher, *"Jesus will take you as you are."* Those words hit me like a sledge hammer and that night my life changed. In those few moments, my life took on a whole new meaning. At the time I was working as a postman in Blackpool and early the next morning I was literally walking the streets saying, *"Jesus, I love you"*. Can you imagine that, knowing what you know about my past! No doubt many a prayer had been uttered before that time but never had I said, *"Jesus, I love you"*. The fact was in the space of just a few hours I felt like I did, it seemed like He had accepted me and I was having a tremendous sense of being set free.

Sometime later I would stand before an open fire in our family home. Mum, Dad, and four brothers all present and I face the inquisition of, *"What on earth has happened to you?"* I could only reply, I can't explain, I can only say that something has changed on the inside. It had and that is how it began for me.

It was during my time on the Kent in 1975 that I first got to know a true Bible believing Christian. His name was

Andy Reid and I met him whilst undergoing punishment onboard ship. He was a steward and I had to help him whilst undergoing extra duties having been arrested for criminal damage by civilian police in Gibraltar. Andy talked to me in a way I had never heard even though I had been to church (Anglican) as a young child. This man seemed to make Jesus come alive and during a time in Gibraltar he took me along to a church. Secretly, I could see that this group of people had reality and something I had never experienced but it wasn't long before the stigma of being associated with Christians caused me to disassociate myself from them. I believed in God but definitely didn't want the Christian life. Again, it must be remembered that I was sixteen and life on board ship could be merciless. Now, in 1984, in Blackpool, the navy behind me, I was experiencing what Andy and subsequently his friends had told me about all those years before. On the night that I stood before my family in Blackpool as a brand new Christian I had no real idea of what the Bible taught. It seemed to me in that interim period, between my visit to church in Gibraltar and my conversion in Blackpool that I had exhausted life. I had done most things that it is possible to do, I now felt ready to follow Christ. My commitment was real and heartfelt.

I couldn't get enough of Christianity as my lifestyle changed rapidly. I felt like I was a recipient of incredible joy and a sense of well-being. It was infectious and my friends began to see that I had really changed. I seemed to go from one exciting encounter with God to another as I embroiled myself in church life. I hadn't understood, at that time, what being a follower of Christ really meant. I had responded to the call and "came as I was." It wasn't long before I was a regular at the Elim Pentecostal church in Blackpool.

My enthusiasm was limitless and, in my view, I had found the ultimate and it was as if I was made for this very hour. I couldn't get enough of church and Christian activity and every time I told my story, it was like the highlight of my life. I knew early on that I wanted to serve God but I had no formal qualifications and underneath my boundless enthusiasm was the issue of the "baggage" of my past life. However, from the word go, I was a keen Bible student and wanted to learn as much as possible, I became an avid reader particularly of Christian biographies such as 'Run Baby Run' and 'the Cross and the Switchblade,' books that describe the conversion of Nicky Cruz (a hoodlum) and the role that Rev. David Wilkerson (a New York pastor) had played in it. It seemed to me that I had entered a wonderful world, the extent of which I had previously not known existed.

Dave – returning to life

I first met Sheila whilst at HMS Warrior Northwood, just before joining my next ship HMS Galatea. We had began writing to one another for a little while due to a mutual friend suggesting we did so, after a while we lost contact until I decided to try again. As soon as we met for the first time I knew that I would marry her. Like John, I was carrying an incredible amount of baggage. Sheila came from a good family, although not yet a Christian herself, I knew she was morally and emotionally stable and somehow subconsciously I understood that I needed that balance as well. My life began changing to a degree from that moment. Certainly the sleeping around stopped altogether, but the other areas like drinking, going on the 'runs ashore' continued.

There is no doubt that once I had married her and began to have a young family, I also began to realise there were, at the least, terrible aspects to my identity that I was not proud of. There were many areas of my life I had never even shared with Sheila that took over ten years before I could begin to open up to her. We have now been married for over thirty years, yet there are still wounds that have taken some time to heal.

I recall a time I was asked to be a God parent to one of my brother's children, I felt quite guilty making a lot of promises in a church, when I was not certain of either where I stood before this God I was making promises to, or even how I felt about faith and religious matters in general. It was at this time that both Sheila and I made our first tentative steps towards finding faith. We visited the church where we were married and made some enquiries. Before we knew it we were enrolled into a confirmation class which was to last about seventeen weeks. We enjoyed the class and the company and some time later were confirmed at the church we were married in.

I was looking forward to our first morning in church as a newly confirmed couple. I felt proud as I put my 50 pence piece (which after all would have got me at least a pint of bitter), into the offering bag. I must admit I was slightly disappointed at the actual confirmation service. Sheila and I had gone together and knelt before the Bishop. I had done the reading after it was agreed that I was so good at it! I don't know what I was expecting: Flashing lights? A voice from heaven? Perhaps an angelic visitation? But there was nothing. The Bishop muttered a few words concluding with, "Bless this couple," that was it. I was very disappointed that God had not, as far as I could see, turned up to our confirmation. We took our children, sat down in the pew, as we awaited the start of our first Sunday meeting. Unfortunately, we had children who did not understand that they were required at this moment to be absolutely silent. There was a rather large, unfriendly looking woman sat just in front of us, who, when hearing Peter asking one of his endless questions, turned, and went, "shhhh!!" I was so angry and was very tempted to verbalise an expletive that was running through my mind at that precise moment! Instead, as I marched angrily out of the church, I opted to visit my other church "The Black Horse" and downed a few draughts of bitter.

On succeeding Sunday mornings, Sheila would ask if we were going to church. I would find all kinds of reasons as to why it was not possible and after a short time we forgot about it altogether. No one visited to find out why, after our first visit, we no longer came. I found solace at the bottom of the pint glass each Sunday where I was able to imbibe of the spirit or sing my head off if I wanted to.

With hindsight I can now see that there was pride in me and an unwillingness to let go of my identity which was now so deeply ingrained within me. I went to church because I thought by doing so I was being good, thereby fulfilling what God wanted of me. Like many, I had this idea that you, "got good to get God", rather than "in getting to God you got good."

There were deeper matters to be dealt with, for with every mask that needs to be ripped off there lies an ugly mess beneath, which can often take a great deal of time to heal. However, first it must be faced up to. Seeing yourself for the first time can be a very sobering experience as shown in the film, 'The man in the iron mask' and as previously eluded to, that is what I really needed, the sobering experience of seeing myself as I really was. I had tried all kinds of jobs, I began my civilian life as a milkman, an RAC salesman, and I then began a job as a van salesman selling paperback books, soft pornography and other general magazines. I also had a job in a pub as a barman which I really enjoyed.

Eventually, I became a manager of two shops and had achieved, in my own eyes, some status; however the truth was that we were now in tied accommodation, coupled with a terrible wage. I was as trapped in this job just as I had felt whilst in the navy and there was no easy way out. If I found another job, it had to be one that offered accommodation as well. I was also working incredible hours for almost no reward whatsoever. My drinking got worse and was aided by the fact that I'd found another pub where I would often work when the owner wanted a night off. The pay was casual and I could drink as much as I wanted, for me this was heaven on earth.

My life was spinning out of control again; I would arrive home, often totally drunk and in a state of oblivion. On one occasion I stumbled through the shop, which was the only access to our flat, knocking over stands, scattering merchandise all over the shop floor. I was so confused one night that I opened the door to our wardrobe thinking I was in the toilet; needless to say it was embarrassing the next morning. Again, the mask was firmly in place. My identity was confusing to me, let alone those around me. Was I really just a total drunk? Did I love my family? Did I care about anything? No one ever asked me, no one dared.

Then it happened. Suddenly, unexpectedly, I was confronted by an area manager and a managing director of the company I worked for. There were concerns generally, but also evidence of misconduct in that certain procedures had not been properly carried out, that were my responsibility. It was clear that the company had been looking for a way of getting rid of me for some time as I was becoming a nuisance, but they needed an excuse. The result of all of this was that I was sacked through gross misconduct. It was a shattering experience for me, one which no amount of drink was going to change. Not only did I feel totally exposed, I also had to face myself. This was something I could no longer avoid. Now I would lose my job and we would be evicted from our home. I had to face the fact that I had not just let myself down, but I had placed my young family in jeopardy as well. The self hatred I felt at that time I cannot fully describe, yet to my credit I did not allow it to turn to self-pity. I knew that I was solely responsible for this situation and had to do all I could to get my family out of it.

Thoughts of "doing myself in" soon left me as one evening my little son took my hand and with real concern in his voice said, "Daddy what's wrong?"

That day I went out with a resolve not to return until I had found another job. We received a tax rebate that helped a little and I found employment working with a Chinese firm that involved selling bean sprouts and mushrooms all over the Midlands and further North. It was very hard work, demeaning, no status, poor wages - but it was work and brought in a much needed income. I would be at the small factory for 6.00am to wash and bag the bean sprouts, and then I had to go to a village to collect a couple of hundred boxes of mushrooms, then out on the road sometimes until 11.00pm. At weekends I worked in a pub to supplement my wage. Little did I know that in all of this God was at work within me, dealing with my pride and stripping away aspects of my confused identity that would reveal some of my "Core Characteristics."

We were re-housed in a council house that needed a lot of work which I eventually completed. During this time I believe God began to strip away the mask I had worn for so long. For quite a while I felt very exposed and vulnerable. However, it was also a time when some good attributes began to show up. One thing that naval life had instilled in both John and I was a degree of self-discipline. I worked hard. I brought our house into a good state of repair, in fact a home we could be proud of. My drinking did not stop completely, but I rarely allowed myself to become inebriated any longer.

I eventually began another job working in a news warehouse on permanent nights. This required me cycling 11 miles to and from work. During this time I contracted bronchitis and then a nasty bout of pneumonia due to the fact that I would often get very wet in bad weather, having to work all night with no heating. The conditions were terrible, the small warehouse being nothing more than a converted garage. I had to continue to work or I would not be paid, therefore it took a number of months before I recovered from the pneumonia, fortunately I was still, young, strong and extremely fit.

Around this time I joined the Royal Naval Reserve, thinking that I would rediscover something that was missing from my life. It was only after I became a Christian that I realised that far from finding something good, I was, in fact, slipping back again into ways that would do me harm. The association with the navy was causing less admirable qualities to make a reappearance, later we will see the need to cut yourself off from the past in the things that will not benefit your future.

In November 1984 Sheila and I, together, became Christians. It happened when my youngest brother Tim had become a Christian, some time later both my parents also became Christians. This really spoke to Sheila and I as my Dad had been anti-religion all of his life, due to his parents having been spiritualist mediums. After our commitment, it became immediately apparent that something was happening within us. My cursing and swearing stopped immediately, without me even noticing at first. Drink became less important, until on our first Christmas we decided to stop drinking altogether. Other members of my family became Christians - my other brother and his wife, my sister and her husband, all of the children in the families. It was an incredible time.

Some of the debilitating aspects of my life seemed to be dealt with immediately, whereas other areas took more time. One thing was clear to me however: I was in this for the long haul. I realised even as a very young believer that there would be a life- long journey ahead of me. The nature of that pilgrimage was not merely learning about my new found faith in terms of having the correct theology - no, I have discovered over this past twenty one years that I can believe all the correct truth yet still miss out on the life that

Jesus taught. I have discovered that abundant life starts now, as does Heaven.

John

Recently, during the writing of this book, Dave and I sat in our hotel in the stunning Gunwharf Quays in Portsmouth. This new development is quite staggering and has trans- formed the Portsmouth that we knew. The site is built on the old H.M.S Vernon which was a training establishment and barracks in our navy days. What we see is almost a picture of the story that we have told – the old has gone and the new has come. Since we began to return to Portsmouth in recent years we have found that it still has a haunting feel to it in regard to the time when we were boys in blue suits. It is almost as if one can revisit the sights and smells, redis- cover the lifestyle and see clearly into a world from all those years ago. We feel almost tearful as we write and recount our experiences then, our redemption and subsequently our restoration and reformation. The pain has been felt, the tears have been shed but we have made it thus far. We can still see that world as it was, incredible, magnetic and seductive and what is more we can still see it through the wild eyes of uninitiated youth. We recount nostalgically the hub of life on a naval base or warship, the world on our doorstep and the world at our feet. It is a bygone day that could never be repeated and we were there, we have first hand accounts of "The Andrew" (One of the old terms for the Royal Navy).

Through the eyes that we look out from now we feel fortunate to have been involved, just to have been there even though what was left of our innocence was maligned and tarnished – damaged internal beauty redesigned as it was inadvertently prepared to abuse others. There can be no doubt that our story reflects a modern day miracle of profound substance, most miracles are worked out through process and it has certainly been a process and continues to be so.

Still, after our conversions, the journey had to continue, despite the wounds, regardless of the memories and the things that still sought to haunt us and draw us back into ways of thinking that must constantly be challenged and overcome. We have learnt and still continue to grow in doing this through learning to love and to live according to God's required level.

As you can imagine, our coming to Christ was accompanied by masses of baggage. We were bringing the scars and experiences of all that we had been and seen in our lives up to that point. Yet, and this is the mystery, God had hand-picked us to serve him in the manner that we do today. We believe that anyone who comes to Christ will make it as long as they allow him access to their hearts. Now with over 20 years of respective ministry we believe that that single fact has enabled us to come through much testing and become the influencers that we are today. However, back to our story...

One thing that Dave and I know we hold in common is that at the time of our conversions we gave God open access to our hearts. In the final analysis, it is the heart and nothing more that gives us our true identity. It is living inside out to the degree that eventually what is on the inside will be seen on the outside. Our story, captured in these pages, is one of redemption and identity. The first part of that duality was instant the second part has been and continues to be in the making. We can only say that in 1984 as we became Christians, we could never possibly have seen what he had in store.

Now that you have come to this part of our story we want to ask you outright. Do you have a personal relationship with Jesus Christ? If not why not make sure that you have right now. You can do so by praying the following prayer:

'Lord Jesus I come to you to ask for your forgiveness. Please forgive me of my sins. I am sorry for all my wrong doing; come into my life and be my Lord and Saviour. I thank you for dying for me and receive new life by faith.'

If you prayed that prayer then we would love to hear from you so please contact us at the following address:

The Gatehouse,
Pontypridd Road,
Porth.
Rhondda.
South Wales
CF39 9PF
Or email: johndeb@rhondda.fsworld.co.uk
            dave@rugbyelim.org.uk

Part two of our book is designed to help you to understand your true identity by looking at what the Bible has to say concerning you first as a human being and second as a Christian. What is true for one is true for another. If you apply the truth that will follow you are destined to make it beyond your wildest dreams.

'John as a little boy'

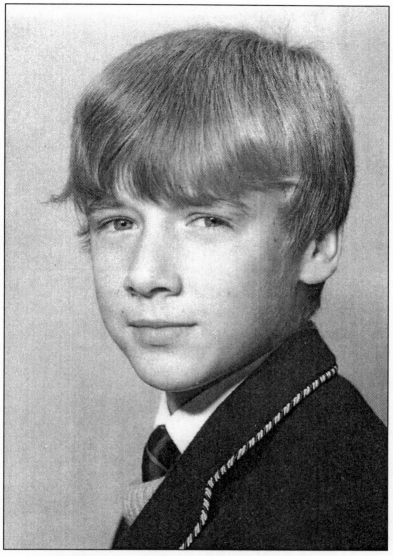

'Dave's last photo before joining the Navy'

'Benbow Division HMS Raleigh

'Dave and friend at Raleigh'

'John, new recruit, at HMS Raleigh'

'Dave on leave'

'John on first home leave with brothers'

'John with mum'

'Icelandic Gunboat Baldur ramming Dave's second ship, HMS Galatea'

'Pictures from Icelandic Cod War'

'HMS Fife – the Kent was an identical class of ship'

'Dave singing in a bar on leave'

'John with brother Ian just prior to going to serve in Northern Ireland'

'John Driving Rigid Raider Craft in Northern Ireland'

'John with brothers Kevin and David on tour in Malta'

'Sheila, Dave's wife'

'John with Deb, Chris and Beth'

'Dave in the present day'

'We still like to be beside the sea, John and Dave in
North Wales'

'Where it all began, Crest for HMS Raleigh'

PART TWO

W e all began our Christian lives somewhere and somehow. For me (John) I heard that preacher in the Blackpool church say, 'Jesus will take you as you are.' That was enough for me - I came just as I was! You know by now what Dave and I were so what has it been like to make this part of our journey with our Lord and Saviour and how has it affected how we are today? We know for sure that neither of us deserved the wives that God had prepared for us.

Had Dave and I known everything that God had in store, back in those early days, I think we would have turned around, for in reality it was a much bigger decision to follow the Lord than it was to be a boy entering Her Majesty's Navy. This time it would be exposure of hearts rather than our souls (mind, will, emotions) and our bodies – this time the pain would be much deeper, but this time it would produce great blessing…Little did we know in our days of licentious living that God had prepared fantastic life partners for the pair of us.

Now, I, John, look back at over 20 years to February 14th 1987. It was the day that Debbie and I got married. I had genuinely prayed that God would grant me the privilege of being deeply in love with the person that I walked down the aisle with (given my promiscuous background that could be classed as gross cheek!). However, He definitely answered that prayer but like so many things in my life my coming together with Deb was not normal. Debbie is ten years my junior and was the daughter of my Pastor, at that time, Jim Thompson. Whereas, I had grown up outside of the church, Deb had been in the church since she was in the womb. The age difference (Deb was just sixteen when we met) meant that our love affair would not be appreciated by all. Looking back, this period in my life began the process of my continued search for understanding about the unconditional love of God. In short, some people were cruel. We even heard that some folk were so disturbed that they were meeting together to pray that God would bring an end to our relationship. They were - to some degree - understandably confusing my old identity to the new one. God was looking at what I would be whilst some folk were judging the present by looking at what I had been. This was not the sailor and the saint - this was two saints. It has taken me twenty years to write down my feelings on this but there are great lessons to be learned. Debbie was not just my ideal girl but has proven to be my ideal partner in the ministry and without doubt my greatest confidant and friend. God knew this when he matched us together. We have two wonderful teenage children and we can honestly say, hand on heart, our love has grown and deepened over the years to the degree that we are more in love after twenty years of marriage than ever. She continues to be my dream girl and I could not possibly find the words to express the depth of my love for her. During my illness and accompanying darkness in 2000 I penned these words now recorded in my book, 'The Royal Law':

Those feelings have never ebbed. During our courtship we took every opportunity to be together. Deb would even turn up during my fifteen minutes breaks at work - every touch seemed fantastic and I couldn't quite believe God's favour on my life.

I had first seen Deb stood at the front of the church where I became a Christian. She was strumming her guitar and leading us in worship. I remember her being eye catching but the age difference and the newness of my faith meant that I didn't give it a second thought. I had a girlfriend at the time and was coming to terms with that relationship in line with my new-found faith. The relationship had grown into one of convenience but was now loveless and was destined to come to an end. Over a period of time I got to know Deb and it became obvious that we liked each other. At this stage I felt, for obvious reasons that it was forbidden love and that nothing would come of it. But it was obvious to both of us that our feelings were not diminishing but growing stronger.

We would do anything to be together, I even enrolled at some guitar lessons that Deb was teaching! (The fact that I still can't play today says something about my intent then), anything to be in her company. However, we could not show our feelings in public and our relationship remained covert. What would her mum and dad think? I decided to find out and it was during a conference at Butlins in Bognor Regis that I approached the subject. I was with Dorothy, Deb's mum and mentioned that I'd noticed that Deb had been showing feelings toward me. Dorothy, thinking that I was saying, 'your daughter is pestering me' replied, with words to the affect of, 'well she's young and impressionable and it will wear off, but if it's a problem then I'll have a word with her.' 'Oh no,' I said, 'it's not a problem, I actually like her attentions.' 'Well in that case lets see how it develops' she quickly replied. 'What, you don't mind' I said disbelievingly. 'No, Jim and I can accept that.' It was a eureka moment for me, her Mum and Dad accepted our relationship. I knew that as long as they accepted it then it didn't matter what others thought. I am eternally grateful to Deb's parents for the door they opened that day because their decision would cost them dearly in terms of the ensuing misunderstandings in the church they were leading.

After my meeting with Deb's mum at Bognor Bible week everything changed and our relationship was now out in the open. I arrived back in Blackpool the following Saturday and heading straight to meet Deb that night I kissed my new girlfriend and future bride for the first time. What that meant to me then and has subsequently meant to me over the years is enough, in itself, to thank God for the rest of my life. The great lesson here is that the past need not determine the future - in fact it ought not to under any circumstances. I had come a long way and after all that I had been and done, on our wedding day I had the privilege of walking down the aisle with a virgin.

....

Now we have shared some of our respective stories with you, we want to take you further on into another amazing aspect of our journey. We hope you have been able to say the previous prayer and mean it from your heart, as the next chapters of our stories will deal with how God has changed us, continues to change us and why we believe the journey will never end, until we reach a place of complete maturity and are transformed into the image God always meant us to reach.

This next part of our story will actually reveal to you some vital keys in understanding how God is more than able to not only undo damage in your life, He is also able to unravel the complex personality traits that remain. Please stay with us now as this is in our opinion the most amazing part of the whole story.

Chapter Six – The first meeting of like minds

Dave and I first met during a two week mission at the Elim church in Rugby. We had been students at Elim Bible College but at different times and our paths had not crossed. The year was now 1987. Dave and Sheila were assistant pastors at the church in which he is now the senior pastor. We enjoyed a great time but had no idea just how God would entwine our lives in future times.

We think it is fair to say, although it wasn't obvious, we were suffering identity crisis. How could we not? The images and needless to say some of the habits of our past lives were still with us. It is hard to imagine the struggle that ensues when people with our background begin to work out the call of God on their lives. Many times we have had cause to use the cliché, "We wish we had known then what we know now," but alas that is impossible for it is in the outworking of what we were then that lends power to our ministry today. The key to it all is "identity". You cannot be what you are until you know who you are. We were now Christians, called to the ministry, having been through Bible College but we didn't know who we now were. These ancient words have become life to us:

"Dear friends, let us love one another, for love comes from God. Everyone who loves has been born of God and knows God. Whoever does not love does not know God, because God is love. This is how God showed his love among us: He sent his one and only Son into the world that we might live through him. This is love: not that we loved God, but that he loved us and sent his Son as an atoning sacrifice for our sins."[1]

Without doubt the main message of this book is that God loves us with unconditional love and following on from this, the main requirement of us is that we will love others at the level we have received the love of God.

For the early part of our Christian lives even in the ministry we were riddled with guilt – giving out life to others but never quite believing that we could give life to ourselves, or at least fully escape our pasts. Guilt is like a dam holding back all that you have inherited in Christ. Guilt is a thought blocker. Guilt reduces constructive, positive thinking to the degree that we become blinded to it. Guilt destroys our future. Yet, guilt need not exist in the life of a believer.

We have learnt that you will always read life through the identity that you have assumed. Is your identity that of a forgiven person? If you are willing to give total forgiveness, you will receive total forgiveness. I think we were both men who would give total forgiveness but with our backgrounds it was difficult to believe God for it for ourselves. The pressures of ministry and the deluge of our past lives combined to take both of us into burnout and the possibility of breakdown. As a Christian, until you sort out the identity issue, you are more susceptible to emotional and psychological illness than the non -Christian.

---

[1] 1 John 4:7-10

How can it be any other way when one is now conscious of sin (a word incidentally that would not have been part of our vocabulary or indeed our understanding). It is right to be conscious of sin but we also need to know how to be free of guilt. The subconscious way is to live in such a way that we never fail or sin therefore we can be guilt free – that is logical. Certainly, this is a trap of Satan because he knows that if this is the standard, to live guilt free, then no Christian can keep it. He knows what makes us tick and can tempt each of us accordingly. This was never God's standard, to live guilt free. God's way is for you to love your way out of guilt. The deeper you walk in love the more you will walk free of guilt. It is so and it works.

We were put in blue uniforms at 16 years of age and given a license to sin and world travel to boot. Sin scars a person's life and we had, as our story reveals, been good at sinning. Another thing about sin (which is falling short of the mark) is that it cuts grooves in our thinking. Grooves that are not easily eradicated no matter what one goes on in life to do. We were preachers with a past. It is easy now with the understanding that we have gleaned to pass off the pain that we suffered due to this in our earlier years of ministry.

There were times when both of us felt like we were losing our minds, this as a result of the cocktail of the haunting past and the responsibilities to be pure in the present. We needed tenderness and understanding as the ministry took its toll due to our inadequate understanding of who we were. Guilt is powerful and touches the psyche in a deep and disturbing way. As we looked for tenderness we both found judgment at times, sad to say, from fellow leaders, who had determined to "rid us of our weaknesses".

There is simply no hiding place when you fill a pulpit once or twice a week. The preacher lives out his life in the arena of the public eye. The tension is unbearable when you are still struggling to be what the Bible says you already are.

We didn't know who we were and subsequently we were "living in the new out of the old." The only remedy is to allow the word of God to re-program your subconscious mind. It will take repetition!

Satan wants you to own the thoughts that he plants in your mind. He knows that one thought planted at the right time is enough to bring defeat. This can be bad enough for any Christian but for those who are in ministry it is the hardest kind of pressure imaginable. Haunting is not too strong a word and the enemy of our souls knows it. For years we went on in this condition in Rugby and Porth respectively. It needs to be understood that for Dave he was at Bible College after being a Christian for only 22 months and in ministry full time within two years seven months, similarly for me within five years. By the grace of God we saw favour even though certain aspects of our lives were still in defeat. It is a tribute to the keeping hand of God that we came through those early years of ministry relatively intact.

During those years we hardly had contact with each other apart from a bit of chit chat at conferences and the like. We were suffering in ways that we can now help others to avoid. At that time we didn't know how to think in line with what God says about us and not the devil's version of what God says about us. You are likely to hear the latter and you receive it in relation to how your subconscious has been influenced and in some cases trained.

As young ministers we were handling truth in part because we had not yet fully gained our own freedom. Dave's experience was to change dramatically through a series of life events that like John preceded their re-connecting with one another. The following account from Dave describes the place where he and Sheila had arrived at just before re-connecting with me.

Dave

I love the attitude of Sir Winston Churchill. A man who knew incredible moments of failure in his life, yet somehow he maintained a positive outlook when he said, *"We are all worms. But I do believe that I am a glow-worm."* Indeed when his moment in history came he was found to be ready for the task. It is also believed that Winston had a model that was kept on his desk, a beautiful model of a ship made entirely from burnt matchsticks. The illustration being clear, in that God is able to construct beautiful lives from what is ostensibly, the burnt out remains of lives that in their own strength have literally almost blown themselves out.

There is no doubt that once we embark upon the road of faith, we begin to face resistance and opposition from without and from within. No wonder we are called into fellowship, it would be impossible for any of us to stand alone. This happened to us.

Paul the apostle knew what it was to face resistance from the enemy, yet he also knew what it was to experience conflicts within. When I say within I mean both within the church and also the conflicts of doubt, and fears within ourselves. I once remember a preacher saying, *"Goliath never bothered to spend too much time trying to verbally discourage David, he didn't need to, his 'brothers' had already done that."* The most painful and difficult conflicts to deal with are those that occur within the church. Satan takes a perverse pleasure in using God's children to do his dirty work. He will seek all kinds of ways to inflict as much damage as possible to a faithful one before making any kind of direct assault upon them. This softening up process often occurs through believers who are not being as alert in the spiritual realm as they should be.

There seems to be an attitude in the body of Christ (the church) that manifests whenever someone dares to start climbing high as it were. They will do one of three things; cheer them on to greater things, join them in the climb, or shoot them from below to bring them back down to their level. Paul the apostle experienced all three attitudes, but he did not make the mistake of allowing himself to become cynical in spirit. Neither must we. None of us are perfect, we are all in a constant state of learning (or we should be). That is what disciples are, learners, followers.

Jesus, when encountering even well meaning opposition to the purpose of God dealt with the spirit behind the words, He did not aim any salvos as it were at people. There have been times that I have preached very challenging messages that have stirred up responses that have not been entirely positive. Sadly, the recipients of such frustration, even anger have often been my wife or even my children. This can be one of the most difficult things for a Pastor and his family to deal with. Offence carries with it a 'bitter sting' that can lead to the defilement of many.

Some of us seem to live in a fantasy world where everything is wonderful all of the time. God's people always treat us as we want to be treated, our circumstances are always positive, and the enemy leaves us alone. If that is your experience I think you need to read the words of scripture again, *"In fact, everyone who wants to live a godly life in Christ Jesus will be persecuted,"* [2]

"We must go through many hardships to enter the kingdom of God,"[3]

Sadly, many Christians will settle for something less than what God has in mind for them. As soon as they encounter hardship of some kind they begin to allow themselves to be

[2] 2Timothy 3:12

[3] Acts 14:22

conformed to their surroundings rather than seek to change them through Godly confrontation.

We can be in danger of trying to find the path of least resistance. Jesus taught us that following in His footsteps would mean things like, (carrying our own cross, denying self, resisting the devil, being obedient, suffering for His sake, putting our old self life to death and the like.)

So many have lost their way, because they assumed that the correct path was the one that offered little or no resistance at all! Just before meeting up again with John, Sheila and I went through a time in our lives of prolonged resistance, attack, opposition, and criticism. Almost everything you could think of happened in a very short space of time. We had just moved out of the Church house and purchased our own home. Sheila's father had a prolonged illness, which had involved her visiting him everyday in hospital for many months. I had just recovered from a cancer scare resulting in a 'subcutaneous mastectomy' (partial removal of breast). I was to lose my other breast a couple of years later. On the same day both my wife's father and I had operations. Poor Sheila was in Rugby one minute visiting her dad, and in Nuneaton the next visiting me. When I came out of hospital, Sheila literally crashed emotionally. She was exhausted in every way, physically and emotionally.

Sheila's dad eventually died, and at the same time we had also experienced some fairly serious leadership problems resulting in various people leaving the church. I did not recover too well from the operation. The consultant had told me to take a minimum of three weeks off, however, I was well into martyr mode, and so after the weekend I was back into work. This resulted in me having to have my wound drained on three or four different occasions, which was a very distressing procedure.

Apart from the normal pressures of pastoral life, we were also suffering financially after a number of unexpected costs hit us all at once. We didn't share this with anyone, because so often a Pastor's motives can be suspected when he shares his family's needs.

Sheila and I began to experience a loss of confidence in all kinds of ways. You begin to ask a lot of questions, Gods faithfulness, relationships you thought were rock solid are shaken, the absolute confidence we thought we had regarding our calling was also severely shaken. By that time we were both, to an extent, looking for potential ways out.

We were angry, hurting, and confused, yet also still hoping that God would change things. We wanted God to simply make things better for us, to give us a protracted time of peace and blessing. The irony is that even with all these things taking place, when asked how I was I would just say, fine! I would discover positive things to relate, I would speak positive things for that is what I thought was expected from me, spiritually.

I was also burying my true feelings, which is what I had learned to do over many years - to seemingly adopt my new identity.

The following year began with the news that both my parents had been diagnosed with terminal cancers. I also developed a virus that kept me off work for a period of five weeks.

Moving into the year we had our daughter's wedding in the April which brought a number of stressful problems we had not banked on, including some personal attacks on members of our family that proved to be very difficult to deal with. Our finances were also hit again at that time with some more unexpected costs.

We sank even lower, yet at the same time sought to maintain a brave face and a 'business as usual' attitude. We were almost staggering towards our holiday, almost seeing it as the change that we needed, fooled into believing that afterwards everything would be better. There was additional conflict in both of our hearts, as we were talking between ourselves very much about a possible new ministry, not realising that in truth we wanted a 'way out.'

We took a holiday in the June and on returning found our car had been broken into and seriously vandalised, it was subsequently written off. We lost quite a lot of money on that. A week later our home was hit by lightning causing utter devastation, and requiring us to move into a hotel for two weeks and then into rented accommodation for about six months. It was a total mess. The gable end wall was damaged, many of the ceilings had fallen in, and our son's bedroom was totally wrecked, as a fire had started, most of the electrical appliances were destroyed and the roof was damaged. We were just numb, yet also trying to be a good example of a Christian. The press in particular enjoyed reporting this, trying to bring an angle to the story. BBC2 had also expressed interest in covering the story but it meant we had to be willing to be seen in a somewhat negative light. The sad part of it all was the reaction of some Christians. Some just wanted to be able to take the position that we had obviously done something terribly wrong to receive this.

We were told that it must be the 'judgment of God' for living in a 'panelled house,' actually it was a simple end of terrace. There were encouragements too, the first thing the Fire Chief said to Sheila when we returned home to find our home destroyed was, *"you must be Christians, normally when this sort of thing happens, people go to pieces."*

Sheila had been marvelous, and although her home lay in utter ruin, she maintained a positive disposition, believing still that in some way there was purpose in it all. However, just like me she was, to an extent, putting on a brave face. I would worry how much of that she was doing for my sake. Although we were both still 'praising the Lord' deep within there were questions developing concerning God's faithfulness. I had awareness that there was something much deeper going on that I simply could not see.

Of course we both still had parents to look after as well. Sheila was visiting her mum almost daily, and had been since her dad died, (and still does). I was daily visiting mum and dad as they both went through their respective treatments. Radiotherapy and Chemotherapy, and although they were both so brave, it was horrible seeing them suffer as they did. Eventually they both decided enough was enough, they were ready to meet with the Lord and decided they would have no further treatment.

Almost immediately another problem in the church began to develop which could have caused major difficulties, and resulted again in more people leaving the church. Both of our children had stopped attending church, disillusioned by the attacks they had experienced from Christian's. My son had turned to drugs, it began to seem as though our whole world had been turned upside down. We thank God that only now that he is through this and going on with God, have we been made more aware just how serious his situation had become. We were reeling. I had also been struggling with inner conflicts from my past and so I was coming closer and closer to a burn out experience. I would lay awake at night worrying about our children they weren't bad kids, and they were sincere in their attempts at living the Christian life. It seemed so unfair that they had received so many knocks in life. Where was God in all of this? The more I asked questions like that, the further away He seemed to be. The more I sough to gain control, the more it seemed our lives went out of control. My daughter had a very bad experience at work, involving someone threatening to rape her; she had been experiencing a problem for some time through sexual harassment, and now it was getting very nasty. The company she worked for did nothing to help or protect her in anyway. She came under terrible attack. For some reason the whole work force turned against her, leaving messages like, *"sack the vicar's daughter,"* daubed all over the toilet walls.

The person who had perpetrated the sexual harassment was seen as the victim, after all, it was just 'a bit of fun.' Constantly telling her what he would like to do to her, showing her pornographic images. Sharing with his friend's things he had downloaded from the internet. Although she made all the correct approaches to the company to have this matter resolved, she was hindered at every point. Her doctor, who was very concerned for her, as we were ourselves, signed her off work for over six months, due to her suffering with a terrible bout of depression. Normally our daughter was so bubbly, gifted and full of life, now it seemed as though all the life had been knocked out of her.

Her confidence was affected; she would once be working in the church regularly, now she was rarely even there. On the odd occasions she came to church again, an insensitive comment would knock her back. It seemed as though one moment we were positive, the next confused, at times we were simply going on. The holiday had been the best we had ever experienced; yet the benefits it seemed were lost as soon as we returned. The whole thing seemed so cruel.

I failed to recognise at the time how demanding I was becoming in my prayer life. All I could pray about were the problems; it was almost all I could see. I must confess I was also angry with Christians. Sheila and I had spent so much of our lives 'being there' for others and now it seemed to us as though few were really interested in what was happening in our lives.

Finally at the end of the November I broke. I was left convinced that I was finished, my ministry was over and people would never be able to respect my leadership again. I was leaning hard on Sheila, and I began to realise what this must have been doing to her, as she watched the one she loves slowly but surely going under.

At break down point I had to go to the church with the elders to write a letter to a couple I had offended. It almost seemed as though I was going to the office to collect my things and leave. I remember looking at the church building and thinking, "I wonder if I will ever go in there again?" It was a frightening thought. I collected a number of things for by that time my Regional Superintendent had already told me I would be having a break. It was a relief actually to know that now we were literally in free fall as it were. I sensed a bitterness arising in my heart that I was desperately trying to suppress, yet if truth be said not really succeeding.

I will never forget the look on Sheila's face as I left the home with the elders. My heart was almost bursting in distress as I thought back to the time I got the sack in my job as a manager. I couldn't help but compare the two experiences. I began to wonder if that was the simple truth, I was just a failure. Still, I simply pretended I was fine, I could not bring myself to bear my heart, my pain to those around me. I now try to imagine what it must have been like for my colleagues in ministry who had served with me for so many years. These were and are men who loved me and respected me. One of them had been to visit immediately on hearing the news and sat with us and wept and prayed over us.

People around us were, on the whole sympathetic, and supportive, yet, it felt as though we could sense they were confused, disappointed in me perhaps, and so I withdrew. I stayed away from the church completely for about five weeks, and avoided fellowship, even with those I was previously close to. My feelings, it seemed to me, were confirmed when I returned to work, and a member made it quite clear that in their opinion I had just enjoyed a nice five or six week break. That attitude hurt me deeply, and I worried that others perhaps saw things in the same way. After all, this person in particular was someone I had stood with during their own moments of perceived failure.

A few weeks later my mother died, it was an awful weekend, and, although we knew this time had been approaching you are never really prepared when that time arrives. Mum had grown increasingly weaker, and despite dad's valiant efforts in caring for her, one weekend she had to be admitted to hospital. She had begun fitting, and eventually it was discovered a secondary cancer had grown in her brain. After a struggle, mum passed into the Lords presence.

Recognising I was in no real state to take the funeral, I had already arranged for a colleague who knew mum to do the service. In fact he was held up on the motorway, which meant me taking the greater part of the service. He arrived in time to do the address, just as the tributes had finished. In fact that situation helped to restore some of the confidence I was now lacking. Because I was forced to face this, I discovered strength I didn't realise I had. I also realised that in truth my calling was still there, and that I definitely wanted to continue serving the Lord. A few days later we had to move back to our now restored home. And so we entered another year hoping and praying that things would get better. At this time, God also began showing me my heart. That is, I began to see how all I was ever asking God for was relief, a better life, and nicer circumstances. God had something far greater in mind. I could see the need to understand myself better. The 'life events' that we had endured in such a short space of time were incredible.

I spent the next couple of months trying to repair fences in relationships that had been damaged through my burn out, and eventually went on holiday exhausted. Sadly, another attack on my family ensued, and on returning from our holiday a few weeks later my father died, suddenly.

In all of this there were good things happening, but it was getting difficult to concentrate on them, and even at times recognise that God was still working for us. My son had a renewed experience with the Lord, resulting in him coming off the drugs and smoking, and finding himself a lovely wife. People in the Elim movement had also responded with kindness and generosity, we saw a lot of 'practical help.' Suffering, the bible tells us produces. What it produces will eventually be manifested in some way. My personal conviction is that if you are still pressing on, you are doing the will of God. Either we will press on, or be squeezed into the world's mould by being pressed 'out.' Pressing on is a proactive thing. Sadly today because of our culture of convenience, if something is costly; fewer people pursue it, especially if it means hard work. That is why there are so many 'cranky Christians' in the church today. They have chosen an easier road that does not require them to face up to issues in their lives, they settle into their personalities not realising the personalities are often the product of a diseased root. Every fruit tree has its own root.

I have discovered that at moments like these you need to discover who the Barnabas' (a close friend and companion to the apostle Paul) are in your life. They are the ones who stick with you no matter what flaws are exposed in you, as you face these things in your life. They do not become disillusioned with you, because they had no illusions about you in the first place. They are fellow travellers, realising there have been and will continue to be times in their own lives when they too will need a friend. Paul had a realistic view of himself when he said,

> *"Not that I have already obtained all this, or have already been made perfect, but I press on to take hold of that for which Christ Jesus took hold of me."*[4].

---

[4] Philipians 3:12

The key word for us here is 'press' Paul, speaking by the Holy Spirit, is saying that he is working through all kinds of resistance.

We do not just stumble into these things, we must press into them. He went on to say in verse 14, *"I press on toward the goal to win the prize for which God has called me heavenward in Christ Jesus."*[5]

Like you perhaps, I have attended the seminars, I have listened to the tapes, watched the video's, enjoyed the conferences, gone forward for prayer, read the books. I have come away sometimes thinking that on the intellectual level I have understood the truth, and in pride, at times, acted as though I owned it. I am learning still that knowledge is good, but the great test comes when it is time to apply that knowledge. One of my favourite verses is,

"Do your best to present yourself to God as one approved,"[6]

To press on into truth will sometimes require you to face the truth about your self. I want to make it very clear however, I do not believe it to be healthy to examine ourselves with a view to try and simply analyse. The only point in discovering an unhealthy root is in order to pluck it out.

As someone once said, "Get cut, get healed and get over it!" That remark was made within the context of Israel and the generation that needed to be circumcised.

John

One day, at our annual conference I wandered into the business session following a heavy lunch and nonchalantly

[5] Philipians 3:14

[6] 2Timothy 2:15

looked around for somewhere to sit. I saw a space next to Dave amidst the five hundred or so delegates. Dave and I greeted each other with the usual niceties of colleagues. That day would change both our lives. As we chatted, it was obvious that Dave was struggling; he had been through a lengthy period of negative events as he has just described.

He had suffered at the hands of some who had responded with discouragement to his first book that described these events. Knowing that I had also been in the navy he reached into his bag and gingerly gave me a copy of the book saying, "this might be interesting to you John." That night I read the book through into the early hours, I couldn't put it down because it was telling my story too. Here was a man who understood my own journey.

The next day we met up and I told Dave that I had read the book in one sitting and that it had ministered to me greatly. I then said these words, "Dave, you need to understand that though you may not get a positive response from everyone, this book has a constituency out there who need to read it." I knew because I was part of that constituency. That week we spent lots of time together and found that God had truly knit our hearts together. We talked and reminisced of our seemingly parallel lives – it was uncanny and we sensed that God was bringing the two of us together. I was ready for Dave's friendship due to my experiences in my previous years of ministry. In order to explain this I need to take you back.

On completion of Bible College back in 1989 Debbie and I were sent to the Welsh Valleys for our first pastorate. We arrived in Porth, Rhondda Valleys on July 17 1989. It was a beautiful summer's day as we took over the leadership of the small Elim Pentecostal church. It wasn't the best start as our predecessor was in prison having been sentenced due to fraudulent activity. Each experience in early ministry was a sharp learning curve as the whole landscape and culture was brand new to us. We were not only on that learning curve but also on a journey of discovery.

We were explorers in a new land performing a new duty. I started with a smile - thankfully it is still there - but it has surely been tested. Due to the circumstances of our appointment we did not have the usual start in the ministry, but nevertheless it was with a great love for God and people that we embarked on our new life. We had inherited a lovely group of people who had been through trauma. We held our first Baptismal service on August 14 1989 and we were underway. Domestically it was difficult, but eventually, having spent the first few weeks with our dear landlady, Lil Roberts, we moved into our own flat. At the time, it was a step-up from the one room we had lived in at Bible College for two years but looking back it was a bit grim. Due to the problems the church had suffered, it was in serious debt and so we earned a very small wage.

We had gone seriously downwardly mobile; yet, we were a couple deeply in love with each other, the Lord and His people. But like Dave, due to our catalogue of sin and inability to break free of some of it we could not accept God's unconditional love for ourselves. We have since learned that the people in God's church can be riddled with this insecurity and we write this for your attention. The earlier you can answer the following question the better your life will be. Who are you? Not who do you think you are but who does God say that you are.

Recently I had the privilege of spending time with tennis legend Margaret Court in her home city of Perth Australia. Margaret is now a very successful pastor leading a great church. However, in her younger days she was a tennis champion; incredibly she won a total of sixty two Grand Slam events, twenty four of them being singles titles. She won the Australian open eleven times, Wimbledon three times and the French and American opens five times. She is undoubtedly the most successful tennis player in the history of the game. The point is: Margaret's successful tennis career was achieved before she had a relationship with Christ and the subsequent transformation of her mind. Nowadays Margaret expressed that if she had known then what she knows now she would have been even more successful, in her own words, "I think if I had known then what I know now I would have won Wimbledon six times and not just three." She was of course referring to the transformation in thinking that is available to every person who gives their life to Christ. As we write this material we continually look back to those early years and struggle to take in our own transformation that is of course on going. It is truly awesome! We now look in more detail at the finer points of that transformation.

I Dave, smile, as I write these words as I look back to the first ever interview I attended on leaving school. It was in the RN careers office in Coventry, West Midlands. The question I was asked on filling out my application form was, 'previous employment'? I sincerely answered the question thus: 'Paper delivery boy.' I make mention of this as I now consider the fact that along with John, we have travelled all over the world and do so now as ambassadors of Jesus Christ. You would struggle to make this kind of story up, if you think about it; two broken and twisted lives that are still in process and have sprung seemingly from complete insignificance. We realise that everything we now have is due to the transforming power of the love of God. No one and nothing else could have set our feet on the paths we now take. Our message is: love never fails!

Chapter Seven – Early Days in Ministry

෴

When Sheila and I began our ministry, as mentioned, we had only been Christians for two years seven months. We started out as assistants at the Elim Church in Rugby as in those days it was buy one get one free. By that I mean that it was usually expected that a pastor's wife would work full time in the ministry with her husband, without a wage. I realise now that my 'fast track' into ministry was in fact going to bring me to a point of crisis which I have already described to you. However, the early days for us were wonderful. As assistants, we were to an extent protected from many of the pressures that come upon a Pastor and his family and it wasn't until the end of 1990 when David Khan left Rugby and we took over that we began to experience something different.

The early pressures were not overwhelmingly difficult and usually involved learning how to deal with a congregation that had become used to a certain style of leader. Of course we went through many amazing experiences when we learnt how to live by faith in terms of provision and we could write a book just talking about that. However, the pressures that come with leadership of a Church go way beyond these areas that are in a sense 'childlike' in comparison and in fact continue throughout the average Christians life.

I had inherited a leadership team that had been built by another man and so I had a number of conflicts to deal with in the early days. As well as eventually seeking to bring my own particular vision to a church that was still grieving the loss of its original pastor.

The interesting point for me is that my past at this time in my life was well and truly buried. I had spoken to Sheila and one or two others about the abuses that had occurred in my past but almost in a matter of fact kind of way, it was as though I was disassociating myself from the devastation these things had in fact perpetrated in my life. From 1984 when I was first saved up until 1995 when I first received my own unique sense from God for the future of our Church, we had, apart from relatively minor problems enjoyed a time of prolonged success and popularity. Now as the Senior Pastor I began to realise what that phrase, 'the buck stops here' really means. Like John I too began to see that there was a huge chasm between what the Bible taught and what actually went on in the local church, the body of Christ. I also had to face the fact that my own early passionate involvement with God had begun to wane somewhat. The true nature of spiritual warfare was at that time in my life perhaps something I only had a partial, intellectual understanding of.

One of the contentions in my own unique vision for our church was that as believers we only ever truly produce what we believe we possess. Any good vision is concerned with revealing to the people of God what they themselves have, it should not be about revealing what the preacher has, or the church has. For people to become keys they have to believe they are significant and will actually open something. Remember that faith is described as the substance of 'things' hoped for, the 'evidence' of things unseen. We are not talking about trying to bring into existence things that do not actually exist, we are talking about revealing what has already been given and does exist in reality. All that is happening is getting what exists in the spiritual into the soul and the realm in which we, at this time, are manifestly revealed. That is why I often talk about journeying.

As the book of Ephesians points out we have been lavished with every spiritual blessing in Christ Jesus. Our journeying here on planet earth is not about trying to get a reluctant God to give us what we think we need, or what does not exist, it is about revealing what we have already been given!! The book of Romans talks about the whole of creation waiting for the sons of God to be revealed, the sons are here already but they need to be made manifest, revealed to the creation that is literally groaning in anticipation for this to happen. Both you and I are potentially already little Christ's just waiting to be revealed in all of 'His' imparted glory. Both John and I are totally convinced concerning the love message and how our identities are actually meant to be - nothing short of Christ likeness. This is the manifestation that the whole of creation is awaiting.

We have discovered that many Christians do not really believe they are loved by God; this is also made evident in the fact that many do not love themselves. In not loving themselves they are not capable of loving others at the level God has commanded. John and I both believe that one of the major reasons Christians struggle to love themselves is because it is the wrong self they are trying to love. They are in effect experiencing an identity crisis. I had disguised the fact that for many years as a believer I in actual fact struggled with a self hatred problem. I had buried it, not dealt with it and it would be the pressures of ministry that would eventually expose my identity crisis and prove to me that I was not living in the new creation identity already won for me by Christ.

In 1987 Sheila and I were being interviewed by the Elim executive council, I had applied to become an Elim pastor. One of the questions Sheila was asked was, "What, in your opinion is David's best quality?" Sheila's response really sums up where I am at and what my passion is all about. She said, "His heart." This, I was to understand later, was what Sheila could see all along. This is what God sees and where God deals with us i.e. not in any given moment in time but rather with the core of our being.

For me personally, living from the heart is what really matters, to live from the heart means you cannot wear a mask. I remember saying to one of our senior men recently, "Structure alone cannot hold me, I need to be held and led from the heart." For me, this is why John and I have connected. It is not just that we have had similar backgrounds or that we can identify with one another's life experiences. It is more than that. It is because we are seeking to relate at the level that Christ Himself exhorted us to.

Pastors often teach that the heart is the well spring of life, yet so often fail to live from it. Jesus summed everything up by making it clear that unless we live by the Royal Law (The two love commands of God) we have missed "life." Life is found in the heart not in the head. Life is to be lived not contained. All of us know how to put on the 'glitz' but how many truly live from the well spring of life? I cannot recall how many times I have said to a pastor tell me about your wife's dreams, all goes quiet. Yet all I am really asking is tell me about the issues of your wife's heart. Surely if we are relating at that level we should know these things? Yet all we seem to know of one another is how many folks we have in our church, what kind of structure our churches have?

Living at God's intended level is not just a challenge, it is exciting. Being able to remove all semblance of the mask is so totally refreshing. Finding acceptance in the place of reality, the place you rarely allow another human being into is an experience that God wants all of us to enjoy. I say "enjoy" purposely for it truly is such a liberating experience to find our hearts and live from them. My relationship with John has been so liberating, as we have shared together at a level that has brought us both further freedom.

For many, life has become an exercise in projecting the right personality, doing all the right stuff, living, yet not living, simply existing from a context of religiosity that bears no semblance to the "life" that Jesus promised. This goes on to the extent that our true identity is lost beneath a plethora of conflicting personas. Many find they have a people centered ministry rather than a God centered one, simply because they do not know who they are any longer. Their unique Christ centered identity has been lost beneath the seeming endless list of expectations. The apostle Paul when giving a little more information about his Damascus road experience revealed quite clearly that he needed to be delivered from the people, before he could go and serve the people. You can only truly live this way when you know and realise who you are. Jesus is the perfect example of this - His humility arose from the knowledge of who He was.[7]

Until we recognise that there are masks that we are often living behind, until we are willing to either remove them ourselves or have them removed, we cannot live from our true identity. All of creation is waiting for the sons of God to be revealed.[8]

This kind of living is not for the faint hearted, it is not for those who simply want to play spiritual one up-man-ship, neither is it for those who live behind professionalism or pseudo spirituality. A new reading of the beatitudes shows us the kind of hearts that Jesus looks for in His children.

[7] John 13:3
[8] Romans 8:19

All these attitudes require a stripping away of all outward pretence.

In the Gospel of John there is a classic verse that we love to preach and teach from and indeed quote to one another.

"The thief comes only to steal and kill and destroy;
I have come that they may have life, and have it to
the full."[9]

Interestingly Jesus places these two statements together. We have an enemy who is intent on stealing, killing and destroying the life that Jesus promises us!

Heaven describes a place, a home if you like, where God is. Hell describes a place where God isn't. What saddens me is that I have met many who profess Christ as their Saviour and Lord yet seemingly lack any life! In fact some are miserable, passionless, lifeless and therefore, if they could only see it, - Godless. Others live a shallow, superficial kind of belief where everything has to be wonderful all time, where the life Jesus spoke of equates to happy, happy, happy.

Our journeys have led us on many varying paths, some pleasant, some very unpleasant, yet seemingly all leading to the same conclusion. What God has been teaching me all about is His heart. God's heart is good, His love is complete and His intention is that we learn to love at His level.

Almost every attack from our enemy into the regions of our souls has included the lie, the temptation to doubt the integrity of God's heart towards us. It is when the bad stuff happens that we have to face these kinds of issues. It is at those times that trite clichéd answers just do not work any longer. Even as we utter them they sound as though they are not authentic. Our minds tell us it is truth, yet our hearts experience something else. Somewhere deep within we

---

[9] John 10:10

begin to question God, we start to wonder about His heart towards us. "Does God really care about me? Am I merely a pawn in the great cosmic panorama?" Either we ask these kinds of questions or we repress them or even cover them over. Secretly we really do feel that God should be willing to tilt the whole cosmic scene in favour of us.

It has taken many of us a long time to get hold of the whole question, "Who do you think you are?" For that is where the problems all take place, in our thinking. My new identity is founded on the redemptive act of Christ on the cross; it is a finished work, yet some of us carry more baggage than others. If the baggage is not dealt with then the enemy finds "points of contact" where he can seek to establish strongholds, where he finds a degree of protection and from where he can cause us all kinds of problems. Now of course the baggage is dealt with in terms of our spiritual redemption, but our souls, which to remind you is our mind, will and emotions, sometimes take a while to wake up to that fact.

Jesus said to His disciples, *'that the prince of this world had no hold on Him,'*[10] there were no points of contact for the enemy to latch on to. How vital then that we live from our new identities in Christ Jesus, for only there do we walk in the stronghold of God. When we are tempted into a quick excursion into sin and we live from our old nature we are in big trouble. I have often had folks come to me and say, *"I have a spiritual problem,"* when actually they have a soul problem, especially if they are saying at the same time that they are born again. The old nature must continually be reckoned as dead, dead people do not sin. The resurrection life is the life of Christ in us.

A stronghold defines a mental fortress, sympathetic thoughts towards unbelief, thought processes that have not

---

[10] John 14:30

yet come under the Lordship of Jesus. These areas create footholds for the enemy, who will not be content to leave it there. His agenda will be to create havoc in our inner lives, our soul areas - how we think, how we feel and how we choose. The enemy's agenda is to coerce Christians into making agreements with him.

We are warned on many occasions in scripture about our thought lives for that is where the battle takes place. *"Prepare your minds for action."*[11] Of course another classic verse shows how *"the devil prowls around looking for someone to devour."*[12] We are also warned not to allow the sun to go down on our anger lest we give the enemy a foot hold. These warnings are there, because it is possible for our enemy to cause us problems in these areas. It is why we are given the armour of God. (See Ephesians 6 in the New Testament)

When I served in the navy, I worked as a communications specialist in the area of electronic warfare. Even then there were missiles that could home in on radar signals, or if the signals were infra-red, the missiles homed in on the heat. If we carry unresolved issues within our souls they attract spiritual attack. The enemy will home in on potential areas of weakness, areas where his endeavor is to form a foothold and turn it into a stronghold. The only answer is to get rid of anything that causes offence, don't play with it - crucify it!

This is why Jesus pointed out the enemy had nothing on Him. He must have nothing on us, no points of contact, and no areas of commonality. The old nature cannot put the old nature to death, it takes the new creation nature to put the old nature to death - that is where we must constantly live from, our new nature which is in Christ Jesus.

---

[11] 1 Peter 1:13

[12] 1 Peter 5:8

John

Looking back, it was during my early days in the church in Blackpool that I began to see the disparity between what the Bible teaches about love and how the church lives out that love. I think this was due to the fact that my coming to Christ was accompanied by an overwhelming sense of His love for me. I was soon to find out that the love of God towards me would not always be reflected by the love of the church towards me and that this was the general pattern. As time went on, I could see that if we didn't understand the gravity of this then the love of Christ for people would be undermined by the church. This has resulted in the church having an identity crisis as the love of Christ is interpreted and measured by the lack of love in His church. This is why I was drawn so much to the Henri Neuwen quote, 'you will never fully receive others until you know that you have been fully received yourself.'

It is very easy for the subconscious of man to mistakenly interpret the often lack of grace and mercy reflected by the church as coming from the Lord himself. As one who, because of my background, needed lots of ongoing grace I felt it was my duty to transmit it at the level that I had received it. For many years I couldn't articulate my thoughts in the manner that I can now in terms of love. Indeed it took an incredible journey, through much darkness and pain. It's true to say much of which could have been avoided had I known what I know today. That is a puzzling paradox: I would not know today what I do know had I not been through the necessary journey to get here but it was a journey I would not have taken had I known what I know today. It feels like, at some point, God took my hand for a season and said, 'follow me, you're not about to enjoy this passage but you'll be glad when you get there'.

Once, during the difficult times after my illness, that I will later describe, I sensed God said to me, 'you are climbing a mountain but when you get to the top you will have come to a place that not many people reach.' I have come to understand the inward journey of love and faith and the incredible relationship between the two. Faith is dependant on love, in order to have real faith one has to be rooted and established in love. God can test our motives; they are never hidden from him even though they can be misunderstood by man. The way of the 'heart man' can be very difficult at times as Dave and I can testify because we have both chosen to live from the heart and we have both faced difficulties because of it. This particular course can mean that one will go through feelings of forsakenness which at the time are mistaken for God's displeasure and ultimate condemnation.

The key to what I am saying is, whilst God will show displeasure toward our sin in His case it never leads to condemnation. Never! It is in knowing how much God loves us that we will set the course of our lives to love others. In other words this will determine our call in life and the decisions we make right down to daily choices. To know one is loved no matter what, sets one free to love others no matter what. It follows that in grasping this we will understand God's imperative that we can receive all the grace, mercy and love from Him that we need, during the course of our lives, as long as we will transmit it at the level that we have received it. The Bible says, *"those who have been forgiven much will love much."* It is true! Nobody can make you love but God commands it and promises to reward it. Some people substitute love for efficiency or for faithfulness or for a stance on faith. However, it remains that God's prime objective for us is to, *"love one another as he loves us,"* the **as** clause is not to be missed here.

As I write this I am once again purposely in Portsmouth to write the book. I am literally on ground that I have trodden on before some 30 years ago. It is 3:00am and from my room in the Holiday Inn Express again on the site of the afore mentioned old Naval establishment HMS Vernon now known as Gunwharf Quays, I can hear the late night revelers returning somewhere. How many times have I been there in that very position heading back to my ship or barracks, mindlessly drunk, facing a massive hang over as I 'turned to' (began work) early the next morning. It was a way of life then. I find myself asking, 'what was it all about?' is the course of our lives plotted out for us by God or is it a case that he will use the events of our lives for us to look back on and learn? Exactly as I am doing now! For us, there can be no doubt that God uses the events of our lives to help us understand Him. God's objective is love and love involves people in the ups and downs of life. Situations that we go through can either harden our hearts or soften them - we do have a choice. God loves us at each stage when we please Him and when we disappoint Him. I am reminded again as I am every time that we visit Gunwharf Quays of my days in military service where one was judged on performance not character. How difficult it is to reverse those two in our thinking.

As I relive the memories of a bygone life I can almost transpose myself back into situations that wounded my soul as I tried to stand up to those who would bully and undermine a person's worth. Words were definitely enough to do the job. Once having failed on the parade ground I was ordered by a GI (Gunnery Instructor) to tell everybody that I was a 'stupid c***' 'louder' he screamed until I was shouting at the top of my voice, 'I am a stupid c***'. We saw this as normal, part and parcel of military life and shrugged it off. But knowing what I know now in relation to the power of words it is damaging indeed. I bear no grudges to anyone from that period of my life but am simply making a point. The wounded soul is wounded because it gets wounded – "somebody" wounds it. How difficult it then becomes to receive unconditional love. The church should be championing this message, but how difficult we find it because we have not understood that we have received unconditional love. How can we then give what we don't know we have? This is how sin becomes a servant of God. It oversteps the mark. Grace accompanied by incentive is the greatest deterrent against sin. Grace is the knowing that you can still go on despite what you have done – with the incentive that if you abide in Christ (live righteously and in obedience) then you can *'ask for whatever you wish and it will be given to you.'*[13] Liberation awaits those who do understand this.

In the September of 1987 Deb and I entered Elim Bible College at Nantwich in Cheshire. I was a student and Deb worked first in the kitchen and then in housekeeping. It was the first year that the college had moved from Capel in Surrey to Nantwich in Cheshire and it was not finished. The site, on London road, was a former borstal and alongside the fact of me being a student for the first time we had to put up with conditions that were relatively harsh. For two years Debbie and I lived in one room and shared a bathroom with several others. The room was a former cell with just a tiny window.

As much as I loved studying the Bible full-time I struggled with accepting my new identity as a Bible college student and future minister. The contest was between the residue of the past and my present situation. So many things from my past life were still present in the new life particularly in my thought life. In simple terms I was dealing with guilt that secretly I couldn't match up to my newfound status. Failure seemed like the end of the world to me. Looking back I think I was so overawed at what God had given me that to fail him seemed utterly unacceptable. I could accept that God had forgiven me for all the bad things that I had done before I found His salvation but what about the sins I committed after I came to Christ. I now know that my Christian life was

---

[13] John 15:7

performance related - it is a hard habit to break. For years I walked around under the strain of unworthiness. It is a difficult burden to carry particularly when one spends his life ministering to others.

The truth is unconditional love drowns out all unworthiness. Sin is a power and so is grace. You are worthy because he made you worthy. In the same way that I was a 'sailor' because I was in the navy (even though I was never a particularly good sailor) I was in it despite my performance. In the same way I am a forgiven person because I am 'in Christ'. The analogy stands up even though the one is an institution and the other a person. As Christians we are clothed in the person of Christ which means His righteousness - therefore we are worthy. I couldn't grasp this for years even though I am a Bible student because it is an issue of identity not knowledge. Please understand that, having come to Christ, you are loved unconditionally despite your ongoing failures.

By the year 2000 I, along with Debbie and our two children, had been a missionary for over two years living in Tanzania, East Africa. My job was to oversee the East African operation for the Elim Pentecostal church. I covered Tanzania, Kenya, Uganda, Rwanda and the refugee camps housing the refugees that had fled from Burundi. My job was extremely stressful and demanding but with great variety. It all came to an end one night when I collapsed unconscious suffering from severe heart arrhythmias. I was quickly sent back to the UK for treatment. Having spent some time in Coronary Care I was stabilised through medication and was about to return to Africa, while I awaited a medical procedure in the UK. Then, I was wrongly medicated and ended up back in casualty. I was admitted with severe heart problems and after a couple of weeks underwent a heart procedure called Cardio Ablation. This involved instruments being passed into the heart through a main artery until the problem was located and then some of the wiring inside the heart being burned out. It was an unbelievable experience as I had to be fully awake whilst this was taking place – not even sedated! The procedure was effective but the aftermath coupled with the enormous stress we had been through led me into a very dark period. I couldn't sleep, couldn't digest food, would break out into sweats for no reason and for a season my heart seemed to pound around my chest (something I had been warned about). This coupled with the stress of being thousands of miles away from our home and kid's school was tantamount to torment.

I was convinced that God had abandoned me [due to my sin] and that I was dying [Godless]. I cannot in this brief account convey the utter darkness and torment that I was going through. I had been inwardly convinced that as God had now abandoned me there was no point in seeking his help! For months this went on until I took it upon myself to change my thinking. Once I changed my thinking my medical prognosis began to improve. I learned much in the days that followed about what God means by love. I was 42 years of age and this was the beginning of me sorting out my identity issue once and for all. I wrote these words at Christmas in 2000:

My beloved family how I love you all, and need you, I can't begin to tell you the torture and torment that is going on inside me at the moment. I have taken so much for granted and now it seems that I have lost it. How I plead with God to give me another chance to get back to normal living. My mind is in such turmoil. My need of sleep and rest is obvious. Deb you have been my dream girl from when we first met- how sorry I am that it has come to this! What a partner you have proven to be, God knows I never deserved somebody like you. Thank you for standing by me through these troubled days. How fortunate I am - I ask you to remember the real me and pray that we will have a miracle of restoration. How I wish I could be me and join in the Christmas festivities wholeheart-edly- my lack of sleep is dampening my enthusiasm because of the prospects of tomorrow. Only God knows if there is a way forward out of this mess? I need help and am so grateful to have a loving family around me. You have all been better than words could describe. The fruits shown by your mum and dad have shown them to be giants in my sight. Thank you Chris and Beth I plead with God that he will allow me to share in your tomorrows - you are fantastic my angels. Words cannot describe how I feel about you all I have been very fortunate as I look back and think about the amazing times that God has given us. Oh that he will give us more in the future. In the service on Christmas day as I sat at the back of the church I was so proud to see your ministry Deb - you really have something special in God and you looked so radiant. The hat makes you look very beautiful indeed (you have just told me to write good things - I was as you can see) it is a privilege to be your husband. You know that I have always felt that but certainly during these days of my illness I have so appreciated every touch - every chance to hold hands - every cuddle. Remember when we first met and went out, how precious every touch was, every look, every letter (where are they?). We can safely say that we have never lost our romance, have we? It has always given me a tingle to be in your arms - even the slightest touch has been precious to me always. And the shear joy of producing two fantastic children together - surely they are amazing (wouldn't any proud father say that?) Chris and Beth I just want to write the words, I LOVE YOU. Deb, I want to write these words, I LOVE YOU. I have to nip myself when I consider that I am married to you. I mean it from the bottom of my heart when I say that you are, to me, the greatest, most ideal woman in the world. That is how I have always seen it. Every parting has been a desperate time until we were back together again.

God grant us tomorrow and may our tomorrows be even greater than our yesterdays!

Chapter Eight – There is always a victory

✐

Many of the events that you are reading in this section of the book describe days that we have lived through and conquered. We write them for your consideration because we want you to pause right now and hear these words deep down inside. No matter what you have done and no matter what circumstances you find yourself in there is a way forward – we have both proved this! So, don't ever lose hope but instead find it…

"Have you spent too many normal days failing to prepare for the miracle days?" so said the American preacher T.D. Jakes. Well, we have spent many normal days but we have to say that we do so no longer. Once you realise who you are you start to consider what it is possible to achieve! It is imperative that you realise that sin will cost you – it will cost what could be yours. True prosperity is in the first instance: the security of eternal salvation, secondly, peace of mind and thirdly financial stability. Pleasure is not a bad thing. Legitimate pleasure has been paid for and results in no negative consequence; sinful pleasure has been paid for but results in major negative consequence. There is always a price to pay for sin! You cannot walk in a public church identity and a private identity that differs greatly. To experience the ultimate of God's blessing you must be consistent in character.

Don't believe the lie that you need certain things in order to be happy. You don't - know who you are in God and be it 24/7 - that is the pathway to happiness! Pleasure is what you receive during the event or the act, whilst happiness is what you receive after the event or the act and is determined by the legitimacy of the pleasure. It is time to take the leap.

God wants you to understand your identity and not to take a lesser option! Knowing your identity is the strength that will keep you in the dwelling place. If you stray into the domain of the evil one, your thinking will be messed up - you will not know who you are. Live consistently and you will gain consistently. You have an enemy who wants to reduce what you are. Each step you take in the right direction is a step into life *"As a man thinks in his heart so he is."*[14]

We used to think like archetypical sailors and we acted accordingly; but we also used to think like Christians who were not making it and acted accordingly. No more! You are everything that the Bible says you are but no doubt you have been reduced. You are reduced because the evil one can get at your thinking. You have to position yourself so that God can plant his thoughts in your heart and they will be received. God's thoughts are available in the atmosphere all the time - the problem is in the receiving. During the days when we were being fashioned into ministers of the gospel the place of reception was not right, therefore, we couldn't receive the fullness of what God says we can have in him.

Our past was definitely determining our future in a negative way when it ought not. The devil wants the moment so that you will always be searching. If you haven't arrived you never will. It is difficult to express Christ if you don't own the moment! The devil will take the peace of the moment by

[14] Proverbs 27:19

causing worry about the past or worry about the future. *"As a man thinks in his heart so he is."* We repeat this purposely - *"As a man thinks in his heart so he is."*

This is why we are told, *"Above all guard your heart for it is the wellspring of life."*[15] Preserve sound key thoughts based on your true identity for it is those key thoughts that in turn will birth endless other thoughts.

What are we saying? We're saying you have it all, you simply have to mature into the identity that Christ has died to give you. Make a decision to live in your true identity. Make a decision to finish the project - the real power is in the strength of the decision because the decision will be attacked during the process. A half-hearted decision is not strong enough to keep the devil at bay. You can only receive to the degree that you are able to believe for... if you can't believe for salvation then you won't be saved - the same is true of healing etc. In both our cases, perhaps due to the way in which we had exhausted life, our initial decisions for Christ were not half-hearted.

There is a result at the end of every decision. In a sense a decision contains the seed of your future. A righteous decision is the beginning point to a positive result. At the point of righteous decision you will have your "beginning point". This determines whether you are being influenced by *"The Law of the Spirit of Life in Christ Jesus"* or by, *"The Law of sin and death"*. The one brings life the other brings curse.

Now at the point of decision you begin a process. Each law has a beginning point and is universal it won't ever change and Jesus won't interfere except in response to you. The power is in your hands. The key to this life is in watering and nurturing the life of the decision. This is why it is absolutely vital that you get rooted in the right place. In our experience most people are not. The deeper you walk into the

---

[15] Proverbs 4:23

Law of the Spirit of Life the greater will be your results and the negative of this is true. That's why we are encouraged to keep a short account of sin…

> *"The promises of God are 'yes' and 'amen' in Christ".*

They are yes and amen but will remain outside of your reach unless you make the right decisions concerning them. Live in such a way that you will fall into the arms of a miracle, don't have too many normal days so that you won't be ready for the miracle days! What about this?

> *"With this in mind, we constantly pray for you, that our God may count you worthy of his calling and that by his power he may fulfill every good purpose of yours and every act prompted by your faith."*[16]

Be unmistakably who you are and act accordingly. There is no room for duplicity. Once you are in Christ, failure is dealt with by decision making. You decide. The proof of desire is in the pursuit. Abundant life is so all round good that even the best life outside of its means is poultry in comparison.

Every day you will have to defeat the enemy, so defeat him early in the day - take authority - confess who you are and confess your victory. Don't imagine that the best self-help books can bring you any where near what the Bible terms "Abundant life". They are very good and will greatly improve your life if you apply them; however, true abundant life is cosmic in comparison. It involves every area of your life. If you can see it then you can receive it but you don't initially see it materialised you see it in your mind's eye as it is influenced by the Spirit.

---

[16] 2 Thessalonians 1:11

Don't contradict the Bible in trying to justify your answer. Dwell in your righteousness and pursue love. The righteousness of Christ gives us our position or right standing. Our pursuit of love determines the strength of our anointing. You can determine the strength of anointing. Sin diminishes the anointing; disobedience diminishes the anointing; lack of faith diminishes the anointing. It is time to increase the anointing, for it is the anointing that breaks the yoke. Life is a process and the power of the process is in the depth of the decision. However, we didn't understand this ourselves for a long time.

Decide that you will no longer spend any normal days instead treat the normal days as mere preparation for the days of miracles. This means you need to live consistently! What treasure there is for the person who lives by these principles! Whatever it is that you need to decide then make that decision. If you follow on by making the right choices you can achieve anything.

"I can do all things through Christ who strengthens me."[17]

We are not settling for less if this is possible, neither should you. Pause for a moment and consider that you are reading the account of two men who began the way that we did. For us, in looking back far enough we can see that we have experienced a miracle. Albeit through process but nevertheless it is an incredible miracle. What latent talent is within you? What do you still want to fulfill? Have you reached your full potential in life? Again we say to you, identity is absolutely the key. Prince Charles, the heir to the British throne, reputedly pays himself some £13 million annually. It is a lot of money to pay oneself but the fact is: he is a Prince.

---

[17] Phillipians 4:13

His identity justifies his salary – at least in his own mind and it doesn't seem that others are protesting too loudly.

Your identity alters your thinking so when you become brand new in Christ you should no longer allow what you were to dominate your thinking and imprison your potential, you should start to think as God wants you to think. *"Be transformed by the renewing of your mind."* Transformed is translated from the Greek word "metamorphosis" which is the word used for the process that the caterpillar goes through in becoming a butterfly. It's true to say the most profound things that I (John) feel that God has said to me have been so simple. One day I heard the Lord say, "The charismatic church is trying to do **that** when I have commanded them to do **this** and if only they would do **this** then I would come and do **that**." He showed me that the **that** he was talking about was acts of power, healing the sick, delivering people, spiritual warfare, none of which are wrong, but our emphasis was on these things rather than on the one thing that he had commanded, "To love at his commanded level."

It was around this time that he said another profound thing to me:

"Your head is not the only place that you have eyes."

Together we have looked and learned concerning these things.

> *'Therefore, we do not lose heart for we are being renewed day by day. For our light affliction which is for but a moment, is working for us a far more exceeding weight of glory, while we do not look at the things which are seen but at the things which are not seen, for the things which are seen are temporary, but the things which are not seen are eternal.'*[18]
>
> *"For the things which are seen are temporary,"*

---

[18] 2 Corinthians 4:16-18

You can see from our account that we have both suffered affliction we know and understand it but you will also have noticed that our narrative has now taken on a new positivity as we relate to you what God has shown us with regard to His victory as well as His comfort.

There are obviously two worlds – one that we see and one that we don't see. The parallel is unseen but it is this unseen realm that post dates the seen realm and it also outlives it and can overpower the seen realm. We need to see the unseen realm and we need to experience it. So, let us ask, "What is really going on?"

We believe that it is in the following principles that you will indeed learn to see the positive nature of your future life and ministry from this moment on in a new light. We have prayed for you that it shall be so.

Now, how do we see what we don't see? You may or may not be familiar with the Old Testament story about a man called Elisha but it gives an understanding into seeing what we can't see.

*"So he answered, 'do not fear for those who are with us are more than those that are with them. And Elisha prayed and said, Lord, I pray, **open his eyes that he may see**. Then the Lord opened the eyes of the young man and he saw. And behold, the mountain was full of horses and chariots of fire all around Elisha."* [19]

We see how two men saw the same situation out of different eyes. Many things that exist are not seen with the naked eye. They can only be seen through the eyes of the heart. If you can see the invisible you can do the impossible so said Oral Roberts. We have learned the secret of this. If

---

[19] 2 Kings 6:16-17

you can first see it in that realm then speak it in this realm, then it shall come to pass.

"You shall have what you say..." Does this actually say pray or is the word "say".

The door is the word; behind the print of the word is the life of the word. It is *the living word of God*. God and his word are inseparable, they are one. Jesus is *the word of God*. You can only see it if your heart is in position to see it. Revelation comes through the heart.

"Open the eyes of my heart Lord that I may see from your perspective."

You will not know what you are seeing if you don't have perspective. It is his perspective that unravels the tapestry of what you are seeing in the spirit realm. He won't manifest his presence because we sing or pray or read - he will manifest his presence because of who you are leading to what you do: which should, of course, include the spiritual disciplines. However, the point is that it is not initially in the doing it is in the being. First it is being who you really are in Christ.

The real cosmic battle is not out there it is inside you, in your inner space. We should wage war against pride, rebellion, indifference, unbelief, a casual indifference to our own sin, and our unwillingness to keep the Royal law (The love commands of God). What are we denying ourselves by refusing to let go of certain things. Once the eyes of our hearts are opened we gain access to understanding both the universe within as well as the universe without.

Outside of God we will not have balance, our pursuit of understanding one will cause us to neglect and misunderstand the other. The eyes of the heart can look inward as well as outward it is they that can see the true state of our inner man; it is they that can see beyond the sky into a realm that exists, yet is beyond the reach of the natural. In seeing the one the other can be affected. What is your point of view - think about these words again: **point of view**, because what you see is determined by what you are looking out from. We must press into God until we can see through the eyes of our hearts. It is a question of perspective! Here is an incredible insight into Godly perspective.

> *"For my thoughts are not your thoughts, neither are your ways my ways declares the Lord. As the heavens are higher than the earth so are my ways higher than your ways and my thoughts than your thoughts."* [20]
> *"As high as the heavens are above the earth."*

That's a long way. So is it possible to understand God except through the eyes of the heart. The eyes of the heart interpret for the spirit; the natural eyes interpret for the soul. The soul is restored and our inner space is conquered by God when we draw close enough to interpret through the eyes (understanding) of the heart. The one key that gives access to all other keys is called the Royal Law - love at God's intended level. If you want to understand God and his communication to man you must grasp the Royal law.

> *"If you really keep the Royal Law found in Scripture, Love your neighbor as you love yourself, you are doing what is right."* [21]

This is God's will for your life, absolutely; unequivocally this has to take first place. It is this that is as high as the heavens are above the earth. If you want to know how God thinks then you need to understand and apply the Royal Law. It is above all application of the Royal Law that brings the presence of God and when the presence comes the symp-

---

[20] Isaiah 55:8-9

[21] James 2:8

toms will disappear. The question is: can we give him suffi-
cient of our inner space so that we can love at his level?
Remember: if you want to increase your treasure you have
to increase your measure. You act to increase your measure
of giving and God will increase your treasure. Real treasure
that comes with no regret!

Chapter Nine – Magnifying Moments

∂ℓ℘

We now come to the place in our lives where we look back to when it became apparent that something needed to happen in order to focus our attentions upon the lies and falsity in our lives due to the imposed identities. Most of us at various times go through some kind of crisis; those times are often opportunities to ask the important questions. A crisis itself asks questions of us. Who are you? Where are you? How will you deal with this situation? Why will you deal with it in that particular way? Just like Elijah - will you face it or run from it?

Pressure magnifies! There are moments in our walk with the Lord when He allows what is referred to in scripture as a time for "God's righteous judgment" to take place. In 2 Thessalonians 1:3-5 Paul writes again to a "model church" and indicates what it is he sees in this church, as they continue to develop in their persevering attitude during their times of persecution and trial. God's righteous judgment does not refer to either eternal judgment or indeed Bema seat judgment. Bema seat refers to the level of reward due to the faithful believer, according to what he has done. God's righteous judgment comes from the Greek words Dikaio

(Right), Krisis (judgment). Krisis is obviously where we get our word crisis from.

As we grow in Christ, there are often moments or times of crisis which because of the associated stress and pressure reveal to us our inner identity or condition. This can be a time of opportunity, where we recognise areas where we have indeed grown, or where we need to improve. Paul spoke in 2 Corinthians about conflicts on the outside and fears within, yet pressing on through the pressure. There is a danger when examining our inner world that we do not slip into making the mistake of judging our future by where we have been, especially if that point is a perceived place of failure, or imposed identity.

Those of us who have been Christians for some time have a lot of spiritual knowledge, but for that knowledge to become real it has to be applied to the soul areas of our lives. The crossing over from the spirit to the soul can be a painful journey and truly defines what it means to be a pilgrim. In this way the glory of God, His character is literally fleshed out from our spirit.

It is as though God is defining us, making us more distinctly His; by revealing our inner world and our core identity in Christ, during the course of our intimate moments with Him. However, the fact is that often those in ministry are more centered on their doing for God, rather than their being. So the Lord has to allow times of crisis to occur in order to get our full attention.

I wonder why it is that we seem to think that providing we are ministering effectively, this can be a good gauge as to where we are at personally. Jesus makes it abundantly clear that He is more concerned with identity than He is performance. A cursory reading of Matthew 7 ought to be enough to convince us that it is the fruit of our lives that comes from the inner being that is of paramount importance.

Both of us have been to the very edge during our ministries, certainly we have both experienced burn out. What caused the pressure or conflict was not as important as to what it connected to within us. During times of crisis we have both learnt incredible lessons in this whole area of discovering aspects of our inner lives and identities that needed to change.

Even when ministering to individuals we are always aware that it is pointless dealing with the fruit of something; you have to deal with the root that is internalised. Jesus placed loving God as of the greatest importance and then loving our neighbours as ourselves. To love yourself is only possible when you focus on the correct identity.

Our new identities in Christ are wonderful, growing from a renewed spiritual root. Thereby what is being produced in our souls is fantastic. We are not yet completed, but we are able to begin to appreciate what it is God is doing within us. That is where we find our strength, in our new identity in Christ Jesus. We have spent a lot of time describing the events of our past lives. We have sought to explain the various changes in our identities, the damage that was done through one identity being forced on top of another, until you do not know who you are anymore.

We can only genuinely begin to discover our real identities as we allow our minds (soul areas) to be renewed with truth. "Who do you think you are?" is a very important question, for as you think in your heart, so you are? The devil is still using the same strategy he used with Adam and Eve, causing us to doubt our new identity. He is tempting us to believe that we need to go on a journey to get what we already have deposited within us.

"His divine power has given us everything we need for life and godliness through our knowledge of him who called us by his own glory and goodness. Through these he has given us his very great and precious promises so that through them you may participate

*in the divine nature and escape the corruption in the
world caused by evil desires."*[22]

We have discovered during our walks with the Lord that
in truth we have often spent some time arguing internally
over the truth of God's word. Some learning curves have
lasted years. Most times it is up to us, whether we are going
to respond to the truth or not. We need to understand that it
is not just the truth that will set you free. It is 'knowing' the
truth that sets us free.

Are you going to accept that what God is saying is righteous judgment? We have known folks to make an appointment to see us simply because deep down they want an
argument. We rarely give a second appointment if that is
what we discern, it is simply too stressful. A person has to
come to a point of receptivity to the word of God, for that
is what being a disciple of Jesus is all about. You are teachable. We have to accept that God's judgment is right; otherwise we simply cannot be helped. God will often allow that
person to exist in a world of argument until they are sick of
it and really want to be helped and healed.

We have had to learn to be like Jesus if we want the
backing of heaven when bringing the Lord's counsel. Jesus
did not remain in an argumentative situation for long. He
could only help those who truly wanted His help. We have
struggled in the past when someone calls upon you to
minister to them with God's word, and then you discover
they are never at church, rarely in fellowship and they
honestly believe their own neglect of God's word will not
hinder their own situation!

We have always found that to bring anything to birth in
the soul, for any Christ like characteristic to be formed from
the spirit, requires a degree of travail. In other words we can

[22] 2 Peter 1:3-4

expect pressure, stress and discomfort. We can also expect at times a loss of dignity, a little like a woman giving birth to a baby. We would rather be wrong trying to be right than be safe. Giving birth is a dangerous time when you are very vulnerable.

A study of Revelation 12 gives an insight into "Christ being birthed". Jesus is not looking for those who want to sail through life never making mistakes, always in control or just wanting to be accepted as they are. Yes, we often say to non Christians "Just come as you are," and that is true, but we should also tell them not to expect to remain as they are.

You cannot have a moment in God without it involving all of you. When we are in a time of growth it is the fear of losing control, or losing our dignity, which often hinders that growth. We have lived in denial for many years in respect to certain life events, or attitudes within us. Change and the need for change is not about trying to prove something, it is about being willing to improve. That often involves the need for a breaking within us, similar to the breaking of a woman's waters when giving birth. Brokenness comes before releasing and it is often the crisis that brings us to that point of breaking. How long do you want to argue for? One year? Ten years? Forty years? We have discovered that sometimes God has allowed us to remain in our perceived place of "rightness" until we are sick to death of it. Then there is a breaking within us and we return in humility and discover a new facet of our renewed identity beginning to emerge.

Abraham was "credited" with righteousness simply because he believed God, but we wouldn't want him leading a seminar on ministering to your wife would we? This was the man who was willing for his wife to be used by other men if necessary in order to save his own skin. Fortunately for us God is not limited to seeing us in one moment of time. He sees the whole picture and can actually see us in completion. That is a good reason for us to persevere during our time of "Dikaio Krisis" ("Righteous judgement") because we cannot see the completed identity whereas God can. We take heart that God allows the crisis in the belief that we will come through it.

There are times we almost lose heart and are tempted to say, *"I can't see Jesus in me!"* That would be like a pregnant woman saying, *"I can't see the baby yet,"* - maybe not but the signs of pregnancy are very evident. To see the emergence we have to believe for it first.

Chapter Ten – Living in the reality of our new Identity

ᐃᑉ

The Bible is full of examples of people coming through various crises' or times of burn out. Elijah is just one of many good illustrations we can use to amplify this point, alongside our own life experiences. The great prophet Elijah took on the forces of evil in his day; he confronted the prophets of Baal and Ashtoreth and defeated them. We know, because the word of God tells us so, Elijah was a man like us, he had passions like ours and he fought in a spiritual war similar to ours, and although he faced up to evil personalities like Jezebel and Ahab the greatest battle that he would ever face would be with his own discouragement and with his identity crisis. You are not alone.

You see, as bold as Elijah undoubtedly was, he lived as a fugitive. Jezebel had murdered nearly all of God's prophets replacing them with dark, satanic, oppressive forces. Now when Elijah had faced up and defeated these false prophets he also prayed for rain to come, ending a three year drought. On one day both fire and rain fell from heaven at the words of this great prophet. However, contrary to Elijah's expectations, the nation did not repent. In fact nothing much changed; instead of the revival that

Elijah had hoped for an enraged Jezebel vowed to kill Elijah.

You may well be familiar with the story of Elijah's depression arising from his discouragement. (Told in 1 Kings 19) We see how the broken prophet literally lays down under a Juniper tree ready to die but he is given strength to go on a journey, not to send him back to battle, but to bring him back to basics.

If for instance we seek to fulfill the task God has given us, if we sacrifice our daily devotional life, our lives will soon become dry and desolate. In order to bring renewal to our "soul life" the Lord will bring us back to the basic essentials of spiritual life. Our first and highest priority is not to save our nation; it is to bring God pleasure. If we do not have that focus we actually live outside the reality of God. It is not enough to quote the fundamentals of the Christian life yet refuse to walk in those realities - for that is what they are - realities. If we do that we actually exist in the place - *"Having the form, but denying the power."* We need to understand that if we talk of spiritual warfare we are speaking of something very real.

Elijah is in great danger here, he has been in incredible battles and now his very life is in the balance but he is not dwelling and existing in the reality of God's love. We know this because of the state of his soul; we must understand he is so depressed he is almost suicidal; lying down under a tree to die!! This is why God leads Elijah to Horeb the mountain of God, interestingly the same place He took Moses, Horeb actually means desolation. It is possible that the place actually mirrored the state of Elijah's soul. Remember when God brought Moses to Horeb it was for two reasons; firstly to reveal Himself to His servant and to initiate a new beginning based solely on God's sustaining power in creating a new identity for Moses.

We have both been brought to this place, on more than one occasion. Take heart, for you will come through times like these, even though you are often left with feelings of exposure and extreme vulnerability. No wonder Elijah pulled his cloak over his head when God spoke to him.

Let's remind ourselves now of what transpires between God and Elijah. In 1 Kings 19:8-18 we see that Elijah first of all speaks to God about being very zealous for the Lord, but something that we have had to learn over the years we have been in ministry is that zeal that is not accompanied by wisdom eventually can become its own God, i.e. ministry becomes almost godlike in your life in terms of its influencing power. You see zeal on its own can compel you to attain to unrealistic expectations that can be outside the timing and anointing of God.

If you live on zeal without intimate encounters with God you can end up like Saul who later became Paul - he too was described as being zealous for God - but there is no point in being zealous for God and fail to know him! Jesus pointed to the last day when people would cite their achievements coming from their zeal for Him, yet Jesus will say, "I never knew you."

You see, it is not too long that Elijah is in the cave before the word of the Lord comes to Him and says, *"What are you doing here Elijah?"* Our primary purpose must always be to abide in Jesus otherwise we can become so consumed with other things, even the deteriorating condition of the world we live in that we fail to be aware of the deterioration of our own souls.

There is nothing that you are doing in this life that excuses the constant neglect of your soul. Do not count on having time to have a quick clear up before you go to be with the Lord, sanctification is a life long process that can only continue when you are abiding in the reality of God's love. God's love is meant to be a daily reality to you, not a theological concept that you quote to others in order to convince yourself or even excuse your lackadaisical attitude to your relationship with the Lord.

It may well be that we are going to need to pass through our own Horeb experience, to come back to the simplicity and purity of our devotion to Jesus.

> *"I hope you will put up with a little of my foolishness; but you are already doing that. I am jealous for you with a godly jealousy. I promised you to one husband, to Christ, so that I might present you as a pure virgin to Him. But I am afraid that just as Eve was deceived by the serpent's cunning, your minds may somehow be led astray **from your sincere and pure devotion to Christ.**"*[23]

Our belief is that Elijah needed to get hold again of his sonship; he had been so consumed with his service. You know it can be a crushing experience to give your best and still appear to fall short. Elijah's discouragement we see is in perceiving to have failed to bring revival amongst God's people. He withdraws into the cave at Horeb, his heart sick and as proverbs reminds us - hope deferred makes the heart sick. When we lose hope we also lose faith and faith is the substance of things hoped for, all we have left then is empty religion. No substance. People will eventually leave empty religion, but they will not leave **LIFE**, not if they have a heart.

The next step is to lose perspective; we feel we are responsible for the results or lack of them. But apart from the work of the Holy Spirit no man can change another person's heart, much less the heart of a nation. Clearly Elijah's distress arises from his own false expectations upon himself, this is seen from his own words, *"I am no better than my ancestors" (in other words, I have failed...)* that leads to self pity - *take my life Lord, I alone am left and they want to kill me etc."*

---

[23] 2 Corinthians 11:1-3

We have existed in that place also, saddened discouraged by our own inabilities or failures to achieve what we believe God had called us to achieve. Even mocked by some who have left us, derided for having a vision that was just too big for us! But when you come back to your identity and exist there you begin to see what He is able to do.

We see that Elijah needs a new revelation of God and as he steps out of the caves of darkness, the Lord, we are told, was passing by. A strong wind that tears apart mountains, an earthquake and a fire - and then the sound of a gentle blowing.

All of these powerful symbols would have been well known to Elijah who was well acquainted with mighty manifestations. Sometimes God has to set us free from our previous experiences of Him. You see in the past these kinds of manifestations had become signs of approval from God to Elijah, but a new experience which in fact would lead to the double anointing, was coming - the still small voice of God!

God will not fight for our attention; God must be sought after! God will not startle us with some great manifestation; He must be perceived. You see it didn't take any special discernment to see the earthquake, the fire or the storm, but to sense the Holy quiet of God, our other activities must cease. To be strong in the reality of our identity requires attention to our relationship with God.

This has come home to me (Dave) again recently as I have stood down from all ministry activity for about 10 weeks in order to more fully seek God. That has been a humbling time for me as I sit in the pew once again and listen as others take the platform.

We all live in a world of constant pressure and distractions, the attention of our heart must learn to ascend to the invisible world of God's spirit, we must learn to see Him who is unseen. We must simply learn to be still in the presence of God, to abide in the reality of God's love.

Elijah did not personally bring revival to the nation but he certainly prepared the way. Through his Horeb experience Elijah began to get a new understanding of his ministry. His ministry was not to establish, his ministry was to go before, to prepare the way for greater things to come.

In fact he was so successful at this that his spiritual anointing was apportioned to John the Baptist who came as a herald to Christ's first coming. Elijah is also destined to prepare the way for Christ's second coming as well.

It may be that some find themselves in a place of desolation and discouragement, but if you run to your Horeb - the reality of God's love, your desolation will actually be transformed to your place of preparation. You will rediscover your true identity and as a result your true purpose in Christ Jesus. Listen to the promises of Jesus here:

> *"He who loves me shall be loved by my Father, and I will love Him, and will disclose myself to Him."*[24]
> *"If anyone loves me, he will keep my word; and my Father will love him, and we will come to him, and make our abode with him."*[25]

That is why and how Christians sang their heads off (literally) when put to the sword for their faith, when stoned, persecuted, forsaken, humiliated, tortured, raped, sawn in two and the like - they sang, they loved, they hoped right into eternity itself, because they knew their God and their God knew them. They walked with Him in a spiritual reality that was made manifest in their identity and which marked them out as one of His own.

---

[24] John 14:21

[25] John 14:23

This is what impacted Saul when he witnessed the martyrdom of Stephen and when he himself met with the risen Christ on the Damascus road. This is what defines the reality of God's love.

Just to know that you are loved by Almighty God is enough! Just to know that He dwells within you and never leaves you is enough! Just to live for His pleasure, His purpose and His will is enough! (This is not the path for most Christians suffice to say whatever God calls us to do He will give us the grace to endure it. Ultimately we are all victors whether that victory is lived out on earth or prematurely in heaven!)

As Stephen fell under the storm of rocks he looked and saw the Lord seated at the very right hand of God - that's living in the reality of God's love. Only someone rooted and established in God's love and sure of their identity could possibly have gone through such an ordeal. That is living in the reality of God's love, being sure of your identity in Christ Jesus.

As Jesus prayed, knowing that not only was He about to experience death and hell (that is separation from His Father) and utter humiliation at the hands of those He came to save, mocking, torture, He knew His body would be subject to the powers of this world, He also had joy set before Him, that is the reality of living in God's love. It is not treating God like some kind of lucky charm, hoping to go through life with no disasters, experiencing all the good things in life as opposed to anything that could remotely be perceived as bad.

When you live your life from the reality of God's love you will cry out like the Psalmist constantly did for the very courts of the loving, living God. It is not a place for only the privileged; it is a place for anyone who will dare to call Him 'Father God'. This reality has now been opened up for anyone who will name Jesus as their own Saviour. You see, to discover this abode where Christ literally floods us with

His life is not just an interesting concept within a book; it is the object of our existence.

Does God love me? If I performed better would God love me more? Does God love one person more than another? Do I really know the rich inheritance I have in Christ? These kinds of questions trouble every defeated Christian or a Christian not experiencing the love of God. Paul is addressing these kinds of questions in this letter to the Ephesians, (3:14-21) modeling how we should pray for the saints - and perhaps for ourselves.

There are many in the body of Christ who know all kinds of things, they can quote scripture expertly having an answer to almost every problem it would seem and yet they do not intimately know the love of God. Comprehending the love of Christ requires us, Paul explains, to go beyond knowledge. You see God loves us not so much because we are loveable, for so many of us cannot believe that we are loveable, rather God loves us because it is His nature to love. The love of God is not dependent upon its object, which is why the love of God is unconditional. It is absolutely vital that believers know that God loves them and why. Otherwise we can so often get into this performance mentality which stops us being perfected in love.

Some Christians become stunted and only know God through doctrine, now it is a good thing to have sound doctrine but all knowledge should lead us to an encounter, doctrine should draw us into His presence. The Lord desires that we pass through knowledge as it were into an encounter with Him.

> *"...and to know this love that surpasses knowledge - that you may be filled to the measure of all the fullness of God."* [26]

---

[26] Ephesians 3:19

Can you imagine what our community would be like if those words were true of us? That in fact we had become lovers of God to such an extent that we have moved through knowledge to the extent that we are filled to the measure of all the fullness of God.

Because we are in Christ Jesus we have the capacity to love as He loves because we are participators in the divine nature. Because of the presence of God in our lives we should have the capacity to love even the unlovely, because remember the love of God is not dependent upon the object of God's love - that is what it means to love at God's intended level. As we grow in Christ, our nature should take on more and more the nature of love, and our capacity to love others should increase.

As we now look back over our lives, as we called them, "the confused pastiche of varying conflicting identities" we are able to more fully appreciate exactly what it is that God has done in us. The lonely, frightened, sensitive confused young men have and continue to be firmly established in their new identities in Christ Jesus. We are not completed in the time and space world we exist in, however, in the heavenly realms we are seated with Christ. It is from there that we now have the right to choose to live from.

God has and continues to do what only He can do. He removes all the damaged and damaging traits that have existed in our souls and transforms us daily into the image of His son Jesus. We are still travellers, the song says, "Sailor, stop you're roaming," no need to now for we have found what we have been looking for. More than most we have come to realise that we have a big say in our futures. Your future is not random and it is not fatalistic. Yes, we were on that path ourselves but no longer. God never meant it to be that way. After all it is He who says you can have the desires of your heart. If you could live your dreams and truly list the desires of your heart knowing that they would be fulfilled what would that list contain? Read on because you can and you ought to have the desires of your heart!

Chapter Eleven – You Decide

Before we go any further imagine if God said to you, "you can decide your future." What would you decide? Surely it would be to be blessed, to be a success at what he gives you to do; perhaps it would be to influence many for good. Maybe it would be to have *abundant life*. We have put this to the Lord:

'Lord show us what is going to happen concerning our future.'

We got an answer but it is not the one we was expecting. God said, "You decide!" Now, at first, that seemed far fetched, we have felt like saying no Lord that doesn't seem right but then God reminded us of some Scripture...

*"Commit **your** plans to the Lord and they will succeed."*[27]

Now we quote this Scripture often but on this occasion the Lord highlighted the word **"your"**!

---

[27] Proverbs 16:3

*"Commit **your** plans to the Lord and they will succeed."*

That means we have got a say in it. However, first you have to have some plans. You cannot commit something that you don't have! So what do you want out of life? What do you want to succeed at? To commit is no light thing it means you are going to have to cooperate with God. Then God showed us the power of remaining in Christ where our true identity is identified.

"If you remain in me and my word remains in you ask whatever you wish and it will be given to you."[28]

Let us break this down: For you to "remain" in Christ is imperative to your success. Secondly for the "word" to remain in you is also imperative to your success.

"The whole world is under the control of the evil one". Note: *"the whole world"* but not the whole universe. Here lays our key to understanding:

"But to each one of us grace has been given as Christ apportioned it. This is why it says: When he ascended on high, he led captives in his train and gave gifts to men. What does he ascended mean except that he also descended to the lower earthly regions? He who descended is the very one who ascended higher than all the heavens, in order to fill the whole universe. It was he who gave some to be apostles, some to be prophets, some to be evangelists and some to be pastors and teachers, to prepare God's people for works of service, so that the body of Christ may be built up until we all reach unity in the faith and in the

---

[28] John 15:7

knowledge of the Son of God and become mature, attaining to the whole measure of the fullness of Christ."[29]

Whenever we need a faith boost we look at the word Universe. Jesus ascended in order to fill the whole Universe – imagine that! And this same Jesus wants to fill you with his life, which determines your identity. To be filled with Christ is to be filled with what is superior to this world and it's God - superior on every count. Be filled and enlarge your overwhelming superior identity. So, if you get the full measure, you will get the full treasure – the treasure of all that it means to have abundant life.

When we were in the navy we worked with Radar and Electronic Warfare (incredible scientific inventions) but we have learned that there is something far superior to science. It is a great mistake to think otherwise. The Universe is bigger than our world. Satan is the god of this world but he is not the God of the Universe. To overcome the world you have to live above it. To live above it is to live in God.

We achieve this by living in love - that is why we are commanded to love at God's required level and that is why the Old Testament is a portrait of the dire, extreme consequence of not obeying God's commands. Sometimes whole nations died because of one man's disobedience. One thing is absolutely clear, the Old Testament has a certain message; there are drastic consequences for the human race in not obeying the commands of God. Inadvertently nothing has changed it is just that the church has become so used to low life living that we are not aware of what we have lost and the mediocrity in which we become accustomed to.

This is the startling truth: more people die and perish today as a direct result of the people of God not obeying the

---

[29] Ephesians 4:7-13

commands of God than ever perished in the Old Testament. The consequence then of disobedience was felt by relatively small people groups, in a localised part of the world. The consequence now is at a global level.

If you don't obey God's commands today, then untold people will suffer the consequence of your lack. God's people are meant to have dominion over the earth that God created, but there is an alien being on the throne and he will have to be dislodged! There is an identity battle taking place here, namely, whose glory will fill the earth? If obedience to the love commands of God is the highway to success, prosperity, authority and anointing that breaks the yoke then what are we denying people if we believers fail to walk in our birthright and live in the identity we are called to be.

Prosperity buys food, healthcare, education; it provides opportunities, enables equality and advances industry. Gives jobs, advances the gospel, influences politics, diminishes worry, supplies the kingdom of God, raises buildings, gains finance, changes things, has a knock on effect and demands a hearing. Because we have grown up taking most of these things for granted we relate the word prosperity with greed and opulence. That is because wealth has often been in the hands of the ungodly. Wealth in the hands of God's people, who have God's heart, is a totally different proposition. God's people will only ever produce what they believe they possess, especially with regard to their true identity. It is God's will to succeed or prosper you if you do the following:

> *"If you pursue righteousness and love you will find life, honour and prosperity."*[30]

---

[30] Proverbs 21:21

That is your position, your birthright as a believer and in order to maintain it, you will have to walk in authority. It needs to be made absolutely clear that your authority will be in direct proportion to your understanding of your identity in Christ Jesus. We might say that we will have to bring the authority of the throne of the universe into the domain of our world.

Jesus said, *"take heart I have overcome the world."*[31]

Because Jesus overcame the world you too can over-come the world. As we have previously seen we achieve this by not violating the love commands. To live in love we have to live in God, to live in God is to live in love. God is love!

One of the jobs that had to be done on a Guided Missile Destroyer was "Lifebuoy Ghost". This involves standing on the quarter deck of the ship (the Stern) and watching the wake of the ocean, ready to sound the alarm if anyone was to go overboard. It was quite a spooky job as one was isolated just looking out over the vastness of the ocean. Most warships had legendary stories about ghosts, particularly if people had died on board ship. It was amazing what one could see because of the imagination and isolation on the quarterdeck of the ship. A similar task was undertaken when the ship was passing through fog – this time sailors would stand on the port and starboard side of the bridge to give an eye witness report of what the Radar couldn't interpret. In a spiritual sense, what is it possible to see beyond what we see?

"Therefore, we do not lose heart for we are being renewed day by day. For our light affliction which is for but a moment, is working for us a far more exceeding weight of glory, while we do not look at the things which are seen but at the things which are not

---

[31] John 16:33

*seen. For the things which are seen are temporary,
but the things which are not seen are eternal."*[32]
"For the things which are seen are temporary,"

There are obviously two worlds – one that we see and
one that we don't see. In our experience we have both
concluded that as we have moved through the crisis' we have
experienced in our respective walks, it has had the effect,
without fail, of drawing us into a deeper understanding of
God's love. This has been followed by a greater revelation
of our true identity which, despite the potential debilitating
effects that any storm can produce, has in fact led us into a
greater, more stable and consistent practice of our authority
which stems from our identity. The Centurion soldier understood this when meeting with Christ. *"I too am a man under
authority."*

We have further learned that faith and love are intrin-
sically linked – there is no real faith without love. By the
summer of 2007 the Sporting Marvels community transformation project that I (John) am a founder and trustee of has
raised almost £850,000 running costs since the operational
side of our vision began in 2003. We began with no finance.
However, recently on a Sunday morning at the Gatehouse
Church (The Elim Church that I John pastor) God spoke to
us with regard to the fact that He lives within us by His Spirit
at the same time that He has ascended in order to fill the
whole Universe. Are you aware that a planet has recently
been found that resembles the earth – its distance from us is
105 Trillion miles. Can you begin to get your mind around
the vastness of the Universe and its billions of Galaxies? It
is so big that it is beyond the human mind to comprehend it.
This means that our earth is minutely small in the scheme
of things, yet, the creator and sustainer of the universe lives

[32] 2 Cor 4:16-18

within us believers. What does that say about our potential? No wonder the apostle Paul said, *"I can do all things through Christ who strengthens me.* Philippians 4:13. On the particular Sunday morning in question God said to us, 'I live in you but you cannot release me at times because of your small thinking. Therefore, you must swap your thoughts for my thoughts and plan accordingly despite your circumstances'. When we take any vision of faith forward we are constantly challenged to make decisions on the future based on what we feel God has said, as opposed to what our circumstances reveal. Know where you are going and God will give you creativity and invention on how to get there.

"I pray that the eyes of your heart may be enlightened..."[33]

As I said previously, "your head is not the only place that you have eyes." What a revelation! You see even the best eyes in the world can only see so far –

I.e. - As far as the naked eye can see. However, the eyes of the heart have unlimited vision – they can take us beyond the horizon of this dimension into the influencing sphere and realm of the Spirit where our identity is sourced - remembering that we are already seated with Christ in heavenly places.

Let us examine, *"The eyes of the heart"*.

What are they?
What can they do?
Under what circumstances can we use them?

It is a right heart that is a wise heart and only a wise heart is fit to see the invisible and handle deeper truth. The eyes of

---

[33] Ephesians 1:18

the heart are spiritual eyes – they enable you to see beyond the seen. We all have them even though many may never use them...

"Lord, I pray, open his eyes that he may see."

In turn they show you things that cannot be understood by mere intellect.

Paul says, *"that you may"*

Know the hope...
Know the riches...
Know his incomparably great power for those who
    believe...

Do you?

The eyes of the heart give you understanding on who you are and what you can do! If the Lord is your righteousness how much righteousness has He imputed to you. Is it unlimited righteousness? Does His righteousness mean His righteousness? Yes, because His righteousness is 100%. The eyes of your heart reveal to you that you are completely covered – they help you to see truth that disarms the arguments and pretensions of the evil one; they enable you to walk free of the snare of his lies. Truth changes the way that you see yourself and lifts you beyond the boundaries of your imposed limitations.

"This is the name by which he will be called: the Lord our righteousness."[34]

If the Lord is the strength of your life is that strength limited to human potential? Does His strength mean His

----

[34] Jeremiah 23:6

strength because He is pretty strong - much, much stronger than you are, surely, His strength is unlimited. The eyes of your heart give you revelation of the unseen realm which delivers wisdom. They enable you to see out of your spirit which is not limited in the manner that your soul is.

> *"I keep asking that the God of our Lord Jesus Christ, the glorious Father will give you the Spirit of wisdom and revelation."* [35]

The eyes of the heart are the window into wisdom. How do we use them?

We use them by understanding that our real enemy is not in the seen world but rather in the unseen world. The responsibility of Christian leadership is to be "heart led" relegating even essential politics into second place. The "heart led" leader will build big people. It is impossible to be a little person if you develop a big heart. The heart must lead and needs to be seen. Transparency is a prerequisite of true greatness! Trust that God promotes heart. The condition of the heart is linked to the delivery of *words*. When you talk about people in the negative it is a sign that you are dealing with things in the flesh or the seen. The negative tongue soon becomes a tool of the devil! It demoralizes the recipient and it weakens the deliverer. When you deal with things in the spirit you deal with it using positive words. This is a sure sign of growth because, *"Our struggle is not against flesh and blood, but against the rulers, against the authorities, against the powers of this dark world and against the spiritual forces of evil in the heavenly places."*[36]

In other words our real enemy is not in the seen world but rather in the unseen world. You learn to see behind what

---

[35] Ephesians 1:17

[36] Ephesians 6:12

you see and when you do it breeds tolerance even in the face of stark human weakness. This is what was taking place when Jesus saw behind the words of Peter and rebuked the spirit behind them. He looked beyond the identity of Peter and saw the source or identity of the words coming out of his mouth. Perhaps if Peter had been seeing with the eyes of his heart at that moment, he could have taken captive the thoughts that initiated the words.

Seeing the unseen through the eyes of the heart enables us to love the unlovely and carry out the commands to love even in adverse circumstances. Watch your words as they relate to another who has been accepted by God and stands in the righteousness of Christ. Look through the eyes of your heart and you will see that they are a trophy of grace and covered by the righteousness of Christ. God examines you through the eyes of the heart. He does not see your disgrace, He sees grace and that you are robed so fully in righteousness that your sin has been completely covered. Let's face it how could we (the writers of the material you are reading right now) ever have made it this far having failed in life so miserably. The truth is: it is by grace followed by obedience in what we have learned to be the right way! When we look through the eyes of our hearts we look through His eyes.

How clear this has become to us over the course of our journey because of the lifestyles we led, we would have been disqualified of ever coming to Christ and finding forgiveness. Likewise, we would never have been able to stand having come to Christ were it not for the above truth; and our gradual and deepening understanding of it. Quite simply a person can receive all of the grace and mercy from the Lord that they themselves need along life's journey, as long as they understand that they simply must transmit to other people grace, mercy and forgiveness at the same level that they have thankfully received it themselves. We are sure that your reading thus far of our previous way of life, coupled with our experiences of failure, burnout, inner struggles and the like validate the above statements and the following teachings. Thus, our contention that we must learn to transmit the love, grace and mercy and forgiveness at the same level that we have received! This reiterates what we said earlier, in that we can only produce what we possess ourselves.

Yes, by all means make observations and have your opinions but be heart led; yes, be constructively critical but be heart led. The heart led person sees through the eyes of their heart, therefore, they see through the eyes of Jesus. The way to solve problems is to see the invisible and hear the voice of the Lord. Then act...Here is some great instruction:

> *"Why do you look at the speck of sawdust in your brother's eye and pay no attention to the plank in your own eye? How can you say to your brother, 'let me take the speck out of your eye when all the time there is a plank in your own eye? You hypocrite, first take the plank out of your own eye and then you will see clearly to remove the speck from your brother's eye."*[37]
> *"Then you will see clearly..."*
> *"First take the plank out of your own eye then...*

When you remove your own plank you will see clearly to remove the speck from your brother's eye and know how to remove it painlessly. Is what you are trying to remove from another much smaller than what you need to remove from your self? Removing the 'plank' helps you to see the situation from the eyes of your heart. The eyes of your heart help you to see what mitigating circumstances have made a person act in the manner that they have. Pause for a moment right now and imagine a church that really believes this and

---

[37] Matthew 7:3-5

practices it consistently. Picture Noah lying drunk and naked in his tent and ask yourself, how would the church have dealt with him? Would we be like Shem and Japeth and cover over his nakedness or would we expose him like Canaan did?

Learn to see the invisible forces that are at work. Accountability outsmarts the enemy of our souls and links the invisible with the visible. Have the sense to realise that accountability means making sure your *ability* reaches your *account.* If you want to make it in life, one of your greatest fears ought to be that nobody will get close enough to you to tell you the truth that you need to hear about yourself. Without doubt this is the greatest obstacle to the realisation of our potential which of course stems from our renewed identity.

> *"…speaking the truth in love we will in all things grow up into him who is the head."*

Here is the link...

It is no use taking on the invisible obstacles and leaving alone the visible obstacles. Binding, loosing and *ignoring* is that how we are instructed? We don't think so! The two must go hand-in-hand but in reality we charismatic Christians have tended to major on the one. We have sought to solve our problems by majoring on spiritual warfare. Character has become secondary.

The seeing of the invisible reveals the weaknesses behind the visible. We deal with the invisible then bring to account the visible. When Jesus cursed the fig tree (what it represented from the invisible) he then went on to cleanse the temple the visible outcome of the spiritual situation.

The fig tree was metaphorically representing the invisible problem that was seen in the temple. Namely: the Jews (Israel) were not representing God in the manner he wanted them to.

Jesus had twice looked at the result of invisible forces as it pertained to Israel and as demonstrated through the life of the temple. He visited there at the beginning of his ministry and at the end. Twice in three years he gave them a chance to change. Invisible forces are at work, they affect our lives every day. It behoves us to understand them and by learning to see the invisible.

Let us pray, 'open the eyes of my heart Lord that I may see behind what I see.'

Michelangelo said: "The greater danger for most of us is not that our aim is too high and we miss it, but that it is too low and we reach it."

To conclude this chapter, seeing through the eyes of the heart essentially means we are seeing from the right identity, we are seeing what Jesus would see, because we are looking out from the place where His Spirit resides within us. Elijah, when in Horeb, was reconnected to his sonship and no longer a slave to his service to God. Elisha had learnt the key of seeing the invisible with the eyes of his heart, if you recall, when he followed Elijah and asked for the double anointing he was told, "If you see me when I go." If you see what the prophet sees you will receive the prophet's reward. In both cases we have a clear picture of what can be achieved out of the realisation of true identity. Elijah had simply forgotten who he was, Elisha in remembering who he was saw things as they truly were and was able to communicate this truth to his servant whose eyes were also opened. Let's not take anything away from Elijah, for every revelation that comes, someone has taken the journey to discover it.

Chapter Twelve – The Dwelling Place of God

We are writing the final part of H.M.S Life in Dar Es Salaam, Tanzania. It is a great backdrop for us to conclude our journey thus far. We want to help you to find your true identity then to remain in it and this is achieved by dwelling with God. Before we understood the revelation of the Royal law we would describe our lives as ascending the hill of the Lord but not dwelling.

> *"And in him you too are being built together to become a dwelling in which God lives by his spirit."*[38]
> *"So that Christ may dwell in your hearts through faith."*[39]

So, if the key to remaining in life and victory is in the dwelling place of God, where is it? It is where the heart of God and the heart of man meet. It is where man is finally at one with the demands of God's love. It is when the heart

---

[38] Ephesians 2:22
[39] Ephesians 3:17

of man is meeting the obligations of the love commands; when the nature of a human being ceases to commit sins of commission and sins of omission.

Where does God live? Well the Bible says, in the lofty places but also with those who are humble and contrite of heart. God lives in a place where there is no darkness where there is no violation of the love commands. We dwell in that place when we obey God and obedience may be explained as non violation of the love commands. For some time it seems like the body of Christ in general have been convinced that obedience is whether we pray or witness or travel as missionaries or suchlike. We have been further convinced that this obedience is not affected by our lack of love, unforgiveness, or the bad use of our tongues. However the two of us now believe the secret of Christianity is in recognizing the leap from being a believer to being a follower.

> *"Who may dwell in your sanctuary? Who may live on your holy hill? He whose walk is blameless and who does what is righteous, who speaks the truth from his heart and has no slander on his tongue, who does his neighbour no wrong and casts no slur on his fellow man. Who despises a vile man but honours those who fear the Lord who keeps his oath even when it hurts, who lends his money without usury and does not accept a bribe against the innocent. He who does these things will never be shaken."[40]*
>
> *"....and has no slander on his tongue, who does his neighbour no wrong and casts no slur on his fellow man."*

You may think that that is too hard but we want to ask you, what kind of environment would you like to live in?

---

[40] Psalm 15

Here is something to note, if you want to dwell, not only can you do no harm, you must speak no harm. This may be another opportunity to pause, as we the writers have just paused to consider this truth afresh.

As we have said earlier, the enemy sends a thought so that it will connect with something from our past lives. For years we didn't realise that in the dwelling place of God the enemy's thoughts are taken captive - they are exposed and seen for what they are. He thought he had us because of our past but grace sustained us, truth exposed his lies and love enlightened our understanding. Love has grown within and liberated us.

You can never fully realise who you are until you understand just what God means by unconditional love. As we said earlier the Catholic Priest Henri Neuwen once said, "You can never fully receive others until you realise that you have been fully received yourself." What wisdom we have here. The unacceptable part of us has been received along with the acceptable part. This is only achieved where unconditional love reigns.

For years the pair of us could not accept that what we perceived to be the unacceptable part of us (previously described as the baggage) had been accepted and absorbed into the unconditional love offered by the Lord. It is only in our understanding of this that one can begin to offer unconditional love to others. Jesus said, *"Love one another as I have loved you."* The power of this is in understanding the clause, *"as I"*. Can you see how this connects with what we said earlier pertaining to Noah? Until we begin to deal with one another in light of unconditional love, we will never walk in freedom. We are not only talking about sins committed as unbelievers, but sins committed as believers, because of the aberrations. We speak as two who have sinned before our conversions but also after our conversions and we have found equal forgiveness on both counts. Ask us, 'what sins have you committed since coming to Christ?' Ask God what sins have they committed since they came to Christ? This is what he will say, 'I cannot tell you, as they are in the sin of forgetfulness. I have put those sins in a place as far is East is from West, if you need to see them you will have to take a journey that will last for the rest of eternity, you will never catch them up. So great is my love for them and for you!

The third part of our story has taken place post the year 2000, post many years in full-time service, post years of inadequate understanding of the gospel message. It is there-fore, this third part of our book that carries the power of our message to you.

Jesus said, *"The prince of this world is coming but he has nothing in me."*

This is what he meant! Satan could not send a thought that could connect with and trigger any sin from Jesus' past. Jesus knew that Satan had nothing on him. Perhaps as you read this you are one of those believers who has sinned on purpose. What is the answer? Repent on purpose, having forgiven those who have sinned against you with the same zeal that you have asked God to forgive you.

John

I recently went into a Cathedral just to sit and pray and sensed that God said to me, you can criticise the structure of any church or denomination but don't criticise the heart because of the structure. I prayed, repented, committed myself to his Lordship and experienced Him. I decided to pick up the Bible and open it at random. I didn't recognise the book that I had opened to and concluded that it must be the Latin for Isaiah. I read chapter two wondering if there would be something in it for me (there wasn't) before real-ising that I was reading the Apocrypha. The Apocrypha is an addition not normally found in the recognised Canon of

Scripture. I pondered whether the Lord was saying something to me before my eyes rested on the top of the page where it said, **truth is strongest.**

I realised that truth is stronger than external practice. Anybody who grasps the truth about love and applies it will enter the dwelling place regardless of the structure of their worship and service to God. You are not required to take your shoes off, as Moses was; you are required to take the old man off - all of him. Appear naked so to speak. If we do he will deliver life. It will be abundant life - life that does not need agreeable circumstances.

It is life that exists beyond knowledge because real love surpasses knowledge. Real love keeps no record of wrongs. It always perseveres; always protects, always hopes. It is the seat of power, the doorway to power, the expectation and indulgence of power. It always delivers and never fails.

Dave

I remember this moment as though it was yesterday. It was whilst John and I were in Portsmouth together working on this book. John was carrying some hurt due to a situation we had both been involved with in different ways. We had talked together and found a degree of empathy and care, however I could tell my dear friend was still struggling as he went on his customary run. On his return, I could see he had found peace and the dwelling place of God.

Ironically, it was to be my time during this trip to Tanzania. I too was carrying hurt and even anger and needed once more to find that place in God, that in and of itself provides the shelter we so desperately need...

The dwelling place of God is a place of unconditional love...

"He who dwells...*rests*; he who dwells...*stands*; He who dwells...*need not fear pestilence or plague;* he who dwells...

lives long and strong; he who dwells...*finds refuge*; he who dwells... *gets answered prayer.*"

In the dwelling place you live in him and he lives in you... You dwell then carry out the good works that were prepared for you to do before the creation of the world. Church without love becomes what you might call the system. We want to affect the system, work through the system, model life to the system but we can't submit ourselves to the system. Because the system is not led by the heart of God it is led by the politics of man – albeit often well meaning men who have found salvation.

A colleague once said to us, "I am firstly a man of God who serves a movement, not a man of a movement who then serves God." You see, God comes first, heart comes first, and love comes first.

Because of our past and our journeys, coupled by our desire to stick around serving God we have been forced to ask questions of our faith. Why does the Bible promise so much but appear to deliver so little. In a nutshell the message of the gospel is: *how to have abundant life and enjoy it forever.* It is patently obvious that whilst one receives salvation at the point of coming to Christ one does not receive abundant life instantly. We were ministers of the gospel but we most certainly were not enjoying abundant life – today we are! Sadly, however, it appears that the majority of Christians never enjoy abundant life throughout there earthly lives.

We have many dwellings but we must question did God build them or man, seemingly on his behalf? Only those who are heart led can enter God's dwelling place. Only those who are heart led can continue to dwell there. The dwelling place is the only place where perfect love exists. When we come fully to Christ we are elevated to where perfect love exists. *"Seated in heavenly places."*

Our standing then faces an onslaught as it is attacked by the three pronged attack of the world, the flesh and the devil.

We have come to realise that all of that then is about all of this now. It was to lead us on the longest journey to love, so that we can now set people free in love.

When we were boys we were pitched into a world where metaphorically speaking every time we looked for love we got raped and abused then we got raped some more; then we were "gang raped" until we could no longer distinguish between love and lust - that is what can happen - eventually the abused and maligned begin to abuse and malign and so the cycle of life goes on until it is broken. Only in Christ can it be broken! The churches task is to lead people into the place of perfect love. Alas, how can we if we don't know where it is or how we find it – our search has to begin somewhere. Just maybe, like us, your own search began when you were a child. As boys we even looked for love among the prostitutes – we were willing to pay but in reality sex was not the primary need, love was. Neither of us could accept that their interest in us was purely business!

In the place where perfect love is, the gap between here and eternity barely exists. The wall is so thin there that death doesn't exist; one simply walks into the next life. It is a mere passing. In perfect love there is a total absence of fear. It is the only place where fear cannot exist, it is driven out. We have understood God's greatest revelation that is: everything in life is found in love. Love at God's required level. We cannot emphasise enough that it is love at God's required level, his commanded level and not the best of what man can do with what he imagines is meant by love. The dwelling place of God is a place that is absent of negatives, negative action and negative words. It exists for you and you can dwell there.

"He who dwells in the shelter of the most high will rest in the shadow of the almighty. I will say of the

Lord...he is my refuge, my shelter, my God in whom I trust."[41]

Every promise has to have a plan of fulfillment. Therefore, the promises of God will not be realised until you work out the plan of fulfillment. The way that we are trained in this is to be coached. Coaching is different in the sense that it deals with the areas that teaching doesn't reach. Coaching deals with characteristics that are obstacles to us making it. One aspect of coaching acts on the general view of, *"why doesn't someone point that out?"* We are in need of being coached in unconditional love. This is the master class. You need to be coached into abundant life and the road to it is love. We often hear the term "original sin" but seldom hear the term "original glory." Original glory is the state that man is in as he was created to be; as he indeed is when he is in Christ and functioning to his full potential, this is man's true identity.

It was in this state that Adam was able to fulfil the incredible task of giving names to all the animals and creatures of the earth. Man was destined to go from glory to glory. Man, untarnished was incredible because he could live to his full potential as one who is made in the *image of God.* Then came the fall and mankind lost his incredible benefits of being God's crowning glory.

Man was lost! But God immediately declares his plan of redemption. First we are redeemed then we should be restored. Redemption is primarily a spirit thing whilst restoration is primarily a soul thing. Both are linked to giving: we are to give love, kindness, forgiveness, long-suffering, material possessions, healing. However, these things are not contained in the spirit they are issues of the soul. God has a particular way of dealing with us in these matters.

Do you consider that the following is true?

---

[41] Psalm 91

*"And my God shall supply all of your needs according to his riches in **glory** in Christ Jesus."*[42]

"His riches in glory".

The problem is we have interpreted glory to be just another word for heaven. We have made it future when it is very much present. God's interactions with his church can only work at their optimum level when his church understands how great God is and just what he has wrought for us in Christ. The world is blown apart when it realises the unsurpassed giving of God and his people. We have fallen short of the glory of God in these matters.

It began this way, *"For God so loved the world that he **gave** his only Son that whosoever believes on him shall not perish but have eternal life."* [43]

The evidence of love is giving. The Bible declares if you give, you will get. It is the fool who only looks to get money. If you look to get only money you will not get from God all the things that money can't buy. Good relations, peace, health - all- round success. We will see fruit in our lives as we enter the glory of giving so that we can enjoy the glory of *living* at God's intended level.

If you first give the required love then you will follow this by giving extravagantly in all other avenues. Extravagant giving is in our hands to achieve. It is giving what your heart says and not your head. In terms of giving, the journey from the heart to the head is a long way and usually results in a great reduction. In other words an idea to give drops into the heart and the heart says, *"Go on give that, you can do that,"* then it arrives in the mind and is quickly told *"you can't."* We call this being sensible or good stewards - God calls it stupidity.

---

[42] Philipians 4:19

[43] John 3:16

You see if you give you receive and when you receive it is a pressed down measure. Which means the amount you have given gets condensed so that your container can hold more. If you want to be loved then love, learn to follow the heart. Do you trust God's word on economics? You give out of this economy and God gives back to you out of his economy. *"Pressed down, shaken together and overflowing"*. How are we going to know this? Simply by doing it and doing it to an outstanding degree. God is an outrageous giver lets be like him. If you doubt that God is an outrageous giver then doubt no more.

How many of you would give up your son to the cross. Come on now...God so loved that he gave... To live in glory you have to live in glory. Faith is about giving. When was the last time you gave something that you couldn't afford? The return of the glory is linked to giving at God's level of giving. His church must match his generosity then the world begins to see his generosity and character through his church, they will have the evidence that Jesus is alive.

We are to match his generosity in love, grace, mercy and materially. The glory cannot be created outside of the glory. You cannot give at a glorious level if you have not received at a glorious level. To receive at a glorious level your thinking must be at a glorious level. Then your giving must be at a glorious level! This is achieved in the dwelling place of God and is a result of restoration. You cannot be restored until you have been transformed *by the renewing of your mind*.

What we can learn from the early church is that there is always enough to bless if only it is released. Now listen to the next point carefully: there is always enough to bless *everybody*. But it must be released.

You see glory resides in your thinking. *"As a man thinks in his heart so he is."*

Small thinking leads to small talking which leads to small living. Hear this: God wants to restore you to original glory. And this will affect every area of your life. The day that we realised the following was a great day, yesterday ended last night this is now today. Failure is not a person it is an event. This is now today and this is the day the Lord has made I will rejoice and be glad in it.

Move on and take advantage of every opportunity to get coached in the area of your soul. Remember, promises are delivered through process; you will only get the promise when you have a plan of fulfillment. Determine today I am going to get weaknesses coached out and my strengths coached in.

To conclude, the dwelling place of God is evidenced through the life of the believer in a way that is commensurate in manifesting the true Christ like identity which is borne out of an understanding of love at God's intended level. Remember we are only able to receive more if we are willing to transmit to others at the level we have already received at. Begin to give more of everything and you will set up a very bright future. Because we learned these principles, at least, to the degree that we have we know that we have stored up a great future for ourselves – the best is yet to come. The giving heart will experience endless blessings.

Chapter Thirteen – You can because you are

ঔ৶

Now back to that word that you will never hear in the
media, sin! To sin is to fall short of the glory of God.
When we allow sin to trespass in our lives we need to understand that all kinds of darkness will accompany it. Sin is
attached to the demonic, to oppression, to depression to sickness and infirmity. Sin is attached to the kind of weakness
that will attack your resolve and undermine your high status.
Sin will take you into the arena of the curse. Sin is never just
for the moment it always leaves a trail of consequence.

Due to our sin in attitude and actions we live in the arena
of defeat. Our lives become a continual reliance on the grace
that has been afforded us rather than the victory that has been
afforded us. It is time to make the shift.

The sin you enjoy today you will be dealing with
tomorrow. So, how do you overcome it? By living at the
level that God intended for you - don't lower yourself to the
level where you need sin's pleasure to gratify you. There is a
higher plain to live on. It is a place where guilt does not exist
and where sin is beyond some distant boundary. It is the very
dwelling place of God but you will not dwell there until you
know who you are and live a life of love. Remember, once

we dwelt in Brothels and now we are speaking of such high things. It may seem strange for you to understand that just like today, we were, in those days simply searching for love. What has changed is that internally we have understood that a human beings search for love has to undergo a transformation in what we understand love to be.

As soon as you know that you were made for love and to love, you will start to understand the mind of Christ. Outside of love at God's commanded level it is not possible to understand God's thoughts because God does not have any thoughts outside of love. God is love and that is not describing one of his characteristics - it is describing his essence. So, logically how could he think outside of his essence?

As previously stated, you see the invisible when you look through the eyes of love which are located in your heart. This is how we truly understand God and the unseen realm. This is how we live as, *"more than a conqueror"*. Love is more powerful than power - it was love that devised the cross. It was because, *"God so loved the world"* that Jesus came. How can God love the world when he tells us not to? Maybe it is because only God's love is strong enough to love that which is fallen.

We have realised in recent years it is not so much the devil who has wounded us over the years but rather a lack of love in the church. This ought never to be but alas it will remain until we start to root new believers in love at God's commanded level. We will remain short sighted and partially blind to the things of God. If God is the strength of your life then his strength is applied by love because God is love and love is God. There are three ways that we activate love:

- Through our prayers.
- Through our actions.
- Through our words.

Most Christians pray and do acts of kindness but it is on the third issue where the breakdown occurs. Words have the power of life and death; it is difficult to find someone who is not a gossip. Why? Because we enjoy gossip it fills our lives. On any given Sunday you will find numerous Christians doing the devil's job for him. I mean the post-gathering slander and slurring that goes on behind people's backs. What we fail to realise is that in God's presence no slander exists. It is a slander free zone. So, if you want to dwell with God you have to deal with the tongue. We think that it is time to create a new norm' in God's church by real-ising afresh the very high status afforded us in Christ then treating one another accordingly. We are in need of a 'new wineskin'

We normally try to deal with the faults we see in others by criticising the faults and weaknesses out of them. There is a better way to deal with problems and people's faults. *"First take the plank out of your own eye"* (and this bears repeti-tion). If you remove the plank then you will see through the eyes of your heart and deal with the problem in love, how God's children are meant to. Do unto others as you would have them do to you.

The potential of your high status is only realised when you fulfil the requirements of your high status. The maximum and minimum requirements are to love God and man at the commanded level.

"If we confess our sins he is faithful and just and will forgive us our sins and purify us from all unrighteousness."[44]

In God the deal is *all*. All is the outgiving nature of unconditional love. Therefore, if you give all - you get all. If

---

[44] 1 John 1:9

you want everything, give everything - that is the kingdom of God. You have every right to speak it out. *"He forgives all of my sin"*, even the ones that the Devil or people won't allow you to rest from. You are in a Covenant that is so good that it proclaims: Today you can have a brand new start and if you fail, well tomorrow you can have a brand new start. You just have to give all and then you'll get all.

So you must not let this book of the law depart from your mouth, the question is have you used your mouth to speak forth its truth. This is how we establish truth in this domain; a domain that is governed by lies. You have to gain a beachhead!

Now you ask is there a link between the forgiveness of all my sins and the healing of all my diseases - even the one that you currently have. Of course there is a link because sin creates the barrier between God and man.

So we must remove the sin. Well how?

1) By forgiving others *all* of their sin.
2) By confessing our own sin.

Here's the Scriptural pattern.

"Forgive us our debts as we also have forgiven our debtors".[45]

Why is the word debtors used here in the Lord's Prayer? Because sin leaves us in debt to love - all sin is a violation of the love commands.

"Let no debt remain outstanding except the continuing debt to love, for he who loves his fellow man has fulfilled the law."

---

[45] Matthew 6:12

The barrier between you and the promise of God is sin. So we remove that barrier through paying a debt of love by forgiving others *all* their sin against us. Then we confess our sin. Repentance is the foundation for confession. This is how the word of God lives for us and this is how we walk in the authority to speak to mountains and remove them by words. Those who instruct you are meant to lead you into the abundant life spoken of in the Bible. You will never grow bigger than your heart. Your heart is the wellspring of life.

Christ's identity was such that no sin could be found in him. As we reminded you earlier when Jesus warned His disciples, *"The prince of this world is coming, but he has nothing in me."* The new identity that we can live in has the potential of living at the level God intended us to live at; as we seek to do this we will find fewer opportunities being offered the enemy of our souls. He can only ever have what we give him through our failure to live in the dwelling place of God. Remember: whatever your past has been, it need not determine your future. And that means you. Pause now and make a decision that you are going to make it.

Chapter Fourteen – More than a Conqueror

S o, you can make it because you can conquer and over-come present circumstances. You can conquer, we know because we have. Conquered what you may ask, well the sexual habits that we have described that once dominated our lives for one thing.

> *"No in all these things we are more than conquerors through him who loves us."*

In all of what things? Trouble, hardship, persecution famine or nakedness or danger or sword! Why will you be more than a conqueror?

> *"Neither death, nor life, angels or demons; neither present nor the future nor any powers; neither height nor depth nor anything else in all creation, will be able to separate us from the love of God that is in Christ Jesus our Lord."*

Truth in love is the answer:

- Would you rather go to hell or have truth?
- Would you rather waste your life or face the truth?
- Would you rather be dished up false hope or face the truth?
- Would you rather be left alone and underachieve or be challenged and reach your full potential?

You can be *"more than a conqueror."*

To conquer is to first realise that because there is a God there is also a devil and that he lives up to his Biblical description. *"The devil comes only to kill, steal and destroy."*

To be more than a conqueror means to have within you the ability to deal with whatever obstacles the enemy places between you and your experience of abundant life. The continuance of this means having the ability also to deal with the obstacles that the enemy places between others and abundant life. God communicates the end to us so that we can work toward it. In effect we must become what God says we already are. But are not yet in practice!

We can realise this potential by faith that can only exist within the revelation of divine love. You live at the level of your identity. You were meant to live in the boundaries of divine love. Therefore, if you choose not to live in the boundaries of love you will always underachieve and most definitely fail to live to your potential. The dwelling place that we repeatedly refer to is that place that exists within the boundaries of God's love.

What lies have you subconsciously believed to the degree that they have entrapped you in low level living? By far the greatest test is to overcome the lie that you can be successful as a Christian even if you ignore the commands to love. It is a lie that is buried so deep within the body of Christ that it almost precipitates the need for deliverance. The Biblical definition of success is that you are blessed in every way.

The definition for success needs to be clarified. Success in Christ means to be living every area of your life in the abundant life that Christ has prepared for us. It is not success at the expense of relationship or marriage or parenting or social awareness. Neither is it financial prosperity that comes at the expense of soul prosperity or relationships. Success is modelling what it is to be a whole person.

How we have fallen into worldly thinking, by determining that success in the kingdom of God can be interpreted by worldly standards. The beginning point is love, which is to be, *"rooted and established in love."* It is during the rooting and establishing that the transformation of our minds takes place. This is where your new identity is forged and it is at this point that you understand the following:

"No eye has seen, no ear has heard, no mind has conceived what God has prepared for those who love him." 1 Corinthians 2:9

Note - **for those who love him...**

During the rooted and established in love phase, the transforming of the mind phase, you get understanding on the issue of how you unlock the promises of God in your life and walk in the abundance that God has prepared for your life. Furthermore, you understand that truth is passed on by revelation knowledge and not through the senses. Look again:

"No eye has seen"
"No hear has heard"
"No mind has conceived"

In other words the senses have not understood God or the understanding that he wants to impart. Why? Because they can't, God never meant for them to.

"But God has revealed it to us by his Spirit."

It is the Spirit that reveals to us what God has prepared for those who love him. Here is the crux: in order to know what God has prepared for us for this life and the life to come we have to know him through love which reveals identity. Whatever identity you have assumed if it is not fashioned out of the foundation of unconditional love it is going to be flawed.

It is in receiving and giving love that we understand what God is like and what he wants us to be like. But we have to change what we think love is. Here is a hard pill to swallow: the more you love at God's intended level the more likely you are to be unpopular in this world - including amongst Christians. This is because love is compelled to be truthful but the worldly system would teach us to hold back truth in the name of maintaining peace and a surface relationship. *"Speaking the truth in love"* will always decimate surface relationships and bring about, in the first instance, fracture. However, it is God's means of progress that the same thing that fractures is the same thing that heals. The one and same ingredient will fracture the soul but bring lasting healing to the spirit. It is just not instant!

One of the greatest problems we face in God's church is that we lack the maturity to resolve the fractured stage and we lack the maturity purely and simply because we have not been rooted and established in love at God's intended level. Any Christian leader worth their salt will be willing to face unpopularity from the devil, the world and the church in order to bring truth. The hardest unpopularity one faces is from an immature church.

The answer to the sin issue is *identity*.
The answer to the abundant life issue is *identity*.

If ever you are uncertain that the greatest thing you can possibly do is to keep the Royal Law, by loving God with all of your heart and your neighbour as yourself, you will not walk in your true identity. It is only when you walk in your true identity that you will achieve things through faith and ultimately speak to mountains, to the degree that you become a walking answer to your own problems and the problems of others.

Therefore, it is time to ask the following question again, "Do you know who you are?" Seriously! Once you know who you are you will walk free of sin; once you know who you are you will have abundant life. You will! Love has a purpose it is not abstract. We are to walk as Jesus did. You will never be able to stand if all you have done is sit. In order to stand you have to walk. This is why we refer to it as, "my personal walk with Christ." It is in the walking that we form our new and true identity. You need to be on your way to somewhere. Allow me to make an analogy: Portsmouth to Rugby, Portsmouth to Rhondda. From boy sailors in the Royal Navy to Senior ministers in the church.

"Since then you have been raised with Christ, set your hearts on things above, where Christ is seated at the right hand of God. Set your minds on things above, not on earthly things. For you died and, and your life is now hidden with Christ in God. When Christ appears, then you will also appear with him in glory. Put to death therefore, whatever belongs to your earthly nature: sexual immorality, impurity, lust, evil desires and greed which is idolatry."

You can't put to death what belongs to your earthly nature if you are not living in your new identity. You overwhelm the old to the degree that you walk into the new. The truth sets you free but not if it lands in your old identity. The reason that this is so, is because, the old man tries to solve the issues of sin by trying to keep the law in a legalistic way. In other words avoid doing it. However, this is impossible because you cannot keep the law. It is only when you get a new identity, realising who you are and live accordingly that you will "put to death". You achieve it by living above it! The law keeps you under the problem; grace lifts you above the problem. You live on a higher plain than where sin exists! This is truly how you conquer the old nature as it pertains to your sexuality – you make a covenant of love.

You live in the new realm by doing what is necessary to live in the new realm, namely: loving at the commanded level. These commands form boundaries and not legal requirements therefore, God's commands are not burdensome." This is where truth alone will set you free but truth in itself has an outworking through love. Listen, here is that Scripture again:

"If you obey my commands you are really my disciples then you shall know the truth and the truth shall set you free."

It is not the endeavour of the old man that will set you free; it is the character of the new man that will set you free. It is a matter of where you dwell...

"Do not let this book of the law depart from your mouth but meditate on it day and night being careful to do everything written in it, then you will be prosperous and successful."[46]

---

[46] Joshua 1:8

The process of life is determined by the depth of decision. Decide to act on the information that you are given. Satisfaction comes only from enough action *satis* meaning *enough*. Don't be afraid to use human resources that help to explain and empower principles that have their origin in the word of God. The Bible is the superlative self-help book in the history of the human race. All other resources that work can somehow [albeit often inadvertently] be traced back to principles first found in the pages of the Bible.

The Bible includes the following encouragement:

"Whatever you turn your hand to will be successful."

It then provides a thesis on how to achieve it. In a nutshell here it is: if you want to be a successful person then find out what God really wants - do it, then make it a habit so that you don't stray from it.

This is what the book of proverbs means by, *"The fear of the Lord is the beginning of wisdom."* We are not the only people to write a book but it was so far removed from our thinking and our perceived capabilities that it has to be a miracle.

Decide to build your life on what God really wants and you will be a success. A definition of success is the progressive realisation of a worthy ideal. If a man is working toward a predetermined goal and he knows where he is going, he is a success. If he is not, he is a failure. If you see that every decision is a seed and that inside every seed is the potential that is determined by the depth of the decision. How incredible is that? The uneducated person can decide to get an education! The unfit person can decide to get fit? The unforgiven person can decide to get forgiven. The poor man can decide to get rich. The single can yet find the love of their dreams.

The sick can get well. It is in this knowledge that our own lives have taken off.

The proof of desire is in the strength of the pursuit. When the Bible speaks about success, it means success. Are you getting the message? You can change. You can find success in areas that have eluded you thus far. Right now numerous people in our churches and in the general population are determinedly changing their shape. Some are determinedly pursuing business ideas. Others are not accepting sickness. Still others are planning unescorted mission trips for the first time. Some are determinedly coming out of debt.

Without doubt you have the power to positively change your life. You simply decide and the outcome is determined by how seriously you make the decision. First you make a decision...

Secondly, you water the decision by the daily choices that you make. The decisions and the choices that you have made in the past are what brought you to the place that you are at today and that means the same is true of your tomorrow. You can't lose because what can't be achieved naturally has the possibility of being achieved with supernatural assistance.

"The prayer of a righteous man is powerful and effective."[i]

Transformation can only be born out of the transformed. You can do it and what is more you can guarantee it. How do we know? Well the Bible tells us so.

"Those who wait upon the Lord shall renew their strength, they shall mount up on wings like eagles; they shall run and not grow weary."

How?

"Delight yourself in the Lord and he will give you the desire of your heart."

You can't delight in someone if you don't spend time with them. Furthermore, "delighting" is not abstract it means positive action in desiring to please the object of the desire. If you struggle to find time you simply decide to make time. Potential is ceaseless. If enough of us change our character then eventually we will change the character of our community.

Transform your life then; set a goal to win and nurture at least one other person in the good things that God has done (is doing) in your life and we are on our way to community transformation. Future generations can be inspired by your testimony. Meditate on these things. Meditation allows your focused imagination to create the outcome before it has been formed. Imagination has an uncanny way of acting like a magnet in attracting what you think about and making it a reality.

Imagine the day coming when you will have enough money to lie in bed each night and plot who you will be blessing the next day. Seize a negative moment by meditating on the assured outcome and you will find that the joy of the Lord is your strength even in the midst of darkness. Don't spend time, invest it! Time is the most precious commodity that there is so don't spend it invest it. There is not a day goes by that we don't improve our lives in some way.

People will accept you as you are but they won't seriously invest in what you do if there are no signs that you are willing to change. For this you must exhibit that you are teachable and accountable to others. You must be a work in progress, you are accountable. In the midst of our human weakness there simply has to be hope that we are working to eliminate those weaknesses. You owe it to God; you owe it to others and you owe it to yourself. The power in decision is truly astronomical. Decide now to improve your life and fulfil your potential. You can because you are! Remember we are talking about a new identity that is already yours; you will always produce what you believe you possess. Your true and great identity in Christ is not outside of you waiting to be grasped, but rather it is inside of you waiting to be released. The whole of creation is awaiting its emerging.

William Shakespeare said, "our doubts are traitors and make us lose the good we oft' might win by fearing to attempt."

Thomas Edison said, "If we did all the things we are capable of, we would literally astound ourselves."

You can definitely achieve your goals. The reason for certainty is because the laws of the Universe are inflexible. It is the knowledge of this that will make you more than a conqueror. The greatest power of our words in this chapter stands in the fact that we began our adult lives as boy sailors. You have read the account of our formative years; it truly is a miracle that we have come to the place that we are now at.

Chapter Fifteen – You are perfect

The Bible declares that you are perfect. You only 'can' because you 'are.' The way to succeed is to set goals, for the moment you set a goal a light comes on in your future. You can because you're perfect. On the surface of things that may be very difficult for you to believe, but that is just the surface, as I, John, look at my tattooed body I can still see the surface scars that speak of the lives we have described to you. However, that is only surface, the point is, it is the part of us that lies deep within, the very core of a person that can find perfection. We find it through an understanding of love and by walking in our true identity.

> *"Because by one sacrifice he has made perfect forever those who are being made holy."*[47]
> *He has made perfect forever...*
> *Are being made holy.*
> *"So do no throw away your confidence; it will be richly rewarded. You need to persevere so that when*

---

[47] Hebrews 10:14

*you have done the will of God, you will receive what
he has promised."*[48]

Here is our pattern - if you do the will you get the
promise. Your decisions are seed. The promises of God are
not usually contained in a miracle they are processed through
a way of life. In other words, they are released gradually into
our lives as we continue to obey God. We might say they
have a delayed release. The reason we write this book with
confidence is because we know that whatever we prove in
our lives we can replicate in the lives of others. Turn your
inner man into your inner coach.

*"These were all commended for their faith, yet none
of them received what had been promised. God had
planned something better for us so that only together
with us would they be made perfect."*[49]

Why are you perfect?

If the result of perfection hasn't come then you can't
walk in it. But it has now come so you can. It comes in
Christ who was first our substitute and is now our life. Satan
can't get at that which has been eternally established so he
attacks that which has not yet been eternally established - in
order to nullify that which has, he attacks that which has
not. You have received impeccable, imperishable seed. 'He
didn't examine the man he examined the Lamb.' (Bob Gass,
UCB)

Having the seed is your guarantee of eternal life but it is
not your guarantee of abundant life. Be sure God wants to
fashion abundant life in you. The reason you can is because
you are and the reason you are is mind blowingly because

---

[48] Hebrews 10:35-36

[49] Hebrews 11:39-40

you're perfect. If you improve and progress you advance in life until you pass into the next.

"With long life will I satisfy him and show him my salvation."[50]

All of this has already been paid for. God has given you all that you need to find abundant life but it is not automatic. You have been *made perfect* past tense; you are being *made holy* present continuous tense. What you have not yet received you are able to receive through the process of being made holy and this is due to the fact that you now have a foundation that is perfect. Don't be put off by the word holy, being made holy is nothing more than coming into wholeness as God sees it. You have been made perfect now God wants you to come into wholeness. He wants you to be rooted and established in love so that you can draw sap from such a root.

This is why the keeping of the Royal Law is imperative, an absolute imperative to being blessed in every way. You can only begin to see how good *the good news* is when you start to obey the command to love at God's required level. If you live by God's principles the life that you will receive will mean that you barely need a miracle for yourself. We have focused on healing much more than we have focused on health. Living by the principles that Jesus gave us will result in supernaturally, sustained, naturally worked out, abundant life. Remember: the power in the process is in the depth of the decision. So, decide to change your life and walk into your future! You absolutely can because Christ has made you perfect.

The average person talks to himself 50,000 times a day, 80% of it is negative. Like, *I can't do that, they'll think I'm*

---

[50] Psalm 91

fat if I wear this, it's obvious he doesn't like me, I'd never be able to do that, the other team is going to thrash us...I'm not a speaker, I'm not going to lose weight. Thoughts affect everything including motivation.

Your greatest limiting factor is the way you think. Without knowing it you have been programmed.

The solution?

"Be transformed by the renewing of your mind."

Change you're thinking in line with your dreams, set goals, then exchange your habits. Realise the power of your perfection. It is already in place and enables the following:

"If you can only believe all things are possible to him that believes."[51]

You can because you are but we now believe, you won't if you don't get coached. We are about to give you your greatest ever reason to truly live the Christian life. You have already been made perfect, so get on and achieve your potential. Maximise your potential. You are a spirit, you have a soul and you live in a body.

"Teach us to number our days aright, that we may gain a heart of wisdom."[52]

One of the greatest things that could ever happen to you is that you gain a heart of wisdom. Because real wisdom is wisdom that has been around since before the world began. In other words before wisdom was tarnished and corrupted by the fall of man.

---

[51] Mark 9:23

[52] Psalm 90:12

"An ancient legend has it that there was a time when ordinary people had the knowledge of the gods. Yet time and again, they ignored this wisdom. One day, the gods grew tired of so freely giving a gift the people didn't use, so they decided to hide this precious wisdom where only the most committed of seekers would discover it. They believed that if people had to work to find this wisdom, they would use it more carefully.

One of the gods suggested that they bury it deep in the earth. No, the other said - too many people could easily dig down and find it. "Let's put it in the deepest ocean," suggested one of the gods, but that idea was soon rejected. They knew that people would one day learn to dive and thus would find it too easily. One of the gods suggested hiding it on the highest mountaintop, but it was quickly agreed that people could climb mountains. Finally, one of the wisest gods suggested, "Let's hide it deep inside the people them- selves." They'll never think to look in there." Let us take this a step further.

The Apostle Paul prayed,

"I pray that the Lord will give you the spirit of wisdom and revelation." [53]

Wisdom is linked to revelation. This means that you have direct access to the wisdom that comes straight from the mind of God.

"Where there is no revelation, the people cast off restraint; but blessed is he who keeps the law."[54]

---

[53] Ephesians 1
[54] Proverbs 29:18

It is blessed to keep the law. The law is to love at God's commanded level. If you do this you are blessed, the more you do it the more blessed you are. Let's look at a familiar example of wisdom that is born out of revelation from God:

"Do not judge and you will not be judged? Do not condemn and you will not be condemned. Forgive and you will be forgiven. Give and it will be given to you. A good measure, pressed down, shaken together and running over, will be poured into your lap. For with the measure you use it will be measured to you."[55]

You can choose the measure! *"The measure you give will be the measure that you receive."* This applies to every area of your life.

The moment you give to God it leaves your present and enters your future. We need to trust the wisdom of a person's soul; not simply your spiritual prowess and capability. Your soul will not disqualify you from love but it may disqualify you from ministry and from what is rightfully yours. Don't allow your soul to assign you to a lifetime of low returns. Every believer must have character, competence and a sense of community if they are to fulfil all that God can do through them.

- A love foundation.
- The development skills of core genius.
- An attitude of servanthood.

In order to grasp the extent of God's love we have to first realise that it is there to be grasped at the degree that God says it is and secondly that there is an enemy who seeks to

---

[55] Luke 6:37-38

keep you from what that kind of love will deliver into your life. Thirdly, that you need power to overcome the enemy from keeping you from all that love, at that degree, will deliver into your life.

Do you exude confidence in your competence? You can never make a first impression twice. Being of good character is not enough. If you want to reach your potential you will have to be discipled (coached) in order that competence can be formed out of your good character.

"Without a vision people perish". [56]

In other words their perfection depreciates. One becomes less than God made you. Without a vision we descend rather than rise! We will always fail to defend what we don't really believe we have. When we come to Christ our lives should be continuously on the rise; you should be experiencing a perennial forward momentum. But be warned, if you do not put in place the right foundation then you will have to contend with less than God intended. Foundations are imperative! If you are not on a solid one, replace it.

We are talking about building here; do not suppose that this is an overnight, quick fix ideology we are propounding. However, as we have said in an earlier chapter once a correct foundation is established then even the crisis' we face are interpreted differently and indeed serve the process by acting as a springboard into a better future. If you think of these things within the context of relationship, any good relationship is established within love (passion) and results in production. You will produce what you believe in terms of a real love relationship with your heavenly Father. Get rooted and established in love (at God's intended level.) It is

---

[56] Proverbs 29:18

not too late; we didn't understand this for years even though we longed for it in our subconsciouses

Your character is nurtured but your competence is achieved through a process of discipline. Get your soul coached. Your body and soul will put obstacles before that which your spirit has seen. However, if you have been able to see God's plan for you then you simply have to bring your soul into line with your spirit and you will achieve what has been revealed to your spirit. You need the power to grasp the things that are rightfully yours, that stand beyond the obstacles that Satan has placed in the way.

Everything that unconditional love delivers is there for you waiting to be grasped. Love is not abstract, the activation of love, on our part, delivers all that love contains. Love is the platform from which you are *"made holy"*; become a whole person. If your words promise love then your actions should deliver on it. God's action does deliver that which he has promised but you have to grasp it. Deliver your love in such a clear way that people can grasp it! Love delivered has a pay day.

"Consider carefully what you hear, he continued. With the measure you use it will be measured to you - and even more. Whoever has will be given more; whoever does not have, even what he has will be taken from him."[57]

The measure of what you use will be measured to you.

Whoever has (used what he has heard/received) *will be given more;*

If the sum total of your Christian experience was simply about turning up half awake to a church service, then that

---

[57] Mark 4:24

is your measure, it is futile to think that what you are going to receive will far outweigh what you are in fact giving – or should we say, not giving. As someone once said, "If you always do what you usually do, you will only get what you usually get."

It is possible that you have used a great measure but you have little return because you haven't learned to grasp. Corrie Ten Boon once said, with regard to some suffering missionaries, "They have given all, but they have not received all." God reveals his plan to your spirit. You are more likely to do what is right before God by pursuing a God given dream than you are by keeping rules. The keeping of rules is not enough of a deterrent from stopping you from doing wrong. You have to realise your destiny is a great one – the prize in this life and the life to come is astronomical if you will reach your full potential. Spiritually, you have been made perfect, so it behoves you to live out of the spirit first. In so doing you are living out of the perfection of Christ.

Is your soul lagging behind what God has placed in your spirit? In order to get where you are going you will have to take advice on the things that you don't see about yourself. The length of your journey determines the price of your ticket. How far do you want to go?

We would walk or even crawl to get the information that we need to enable us to reach our potential and cause us to be blessed in every way just as Abraham was. God wants to take you to where you should be going - you have a destiny. If you are in the grip of sin you are paying massive interest on it. If you can realise today what can be yours; if you let go of that sin; this could be one of the best days of your life. **Decide!**

The abundance of your life on earth will be in direct proportion to the restoration of your soul.

"The Lord is my shepherd I shall not want, he makes me lie down in green pastures, he leads me by quiet waters, he causes me to walk in righteousness for his names sake, he restores my soul."[58]

Your soul is the container of abundant life. It receives from the spirit and fuels the life of the flesh. That is if we allow it to...

We are not called to walk in the spirit to attain something we don't yet have but rather to maintain something that we have already. Church is by virtue of its ongoing task, an arena of warfare, a cessation of war comes only through surrender of some kind. Don't surrender, move forward, and take control of your destiny! If you are in Christ then both the answer to your problems and the route to your destiny is inside you. Develop what is inside you then enquire within. Brain researchers estimate that your unconscious data base outweighs the conscious on an order exceeding ten million to one. This data base is the source of your hidden, natural genius. In other words a part of you is much smarter than you are. The wise people regularly consult that smarter part.

---

[58] Psalm 23

Chapter Sixteen – How big is your God?

⟨flourish⟩

How do you see God? Is he just big enough to get you through or big enough to help you to live your dreams? This should be our approach; my identity is in Christ therefore my inheritance is huge! We can draw on that inheritance now but we have to find some way of getting it from heaven (where it is stored) into the earths atmosphere for our benefit now.

> *"Praise be to the God and Father of our Lord Jesus Christ. In His great mercy he has given us new birth into a living hope through the resurrection of Jesus Christ from the dead and into an inheritance that can never perish, spoil or fade kept in heaven for you..."*[59]

The senses don't deliver heaven's blessing into the earth's atmosphere they are there to decipher and to enjoy the blessings. In our scientific world we cannot believe in God if our senses cannot find him or work him out!

---

[59] 1 Peter 1:3-4

The truth is they were never meant to. Our senses can see the result of creation but they cannot introduce us to the designer. Our senses cannot find him! It is ongoing revelation from the designer that gives us the means to access our inheritance now. The missing link is not a monkey it is revelation knowledge - a peep into God's universe. The Bible is the only book ever written that brings the revelation of God to man. The Bible is the revelation of the Royal Law, that the keeping of which is the doorway into the fulfilment of the promises of God.

God is love so the DNA that flows from his being will reflect this in our lives once we have been genetically modified through regeneration and renewal in the Spirit. Once we are born again and placed "In Christ" we have a choice to draw from the DNA of the old man (Adam) or from the DNA of the new man (Christ). The DNA of the new man draws from the river or passage of love i.e. love at God's intended level. This is what makes it possible to move from what we were in essence to where we are now in essence.

Faith is the substance that will bring heaven's inheritance into your life now. However, faith cannot operate outside of love. Faith is acting on the information that you get from heaven. The emphasis is on "acting". Information must be acted upon. Now, God will not reveal relatively minor details that pertain to the happiness and welfare of our lives if we are ignoring the major issues that he has already revealed. Particularly the not so minor issue that he commands us to love at his intended level. This is why your new identity is to be rooted and established in love so that you can be "transformed" by the renewing of your mind. If you don't understand love how then can love guide you into the wisdom that only it contains?

It would be good to take a further reminder of what we mean by love. As two men who once thought that love could be found in a bar or a nightclub, it is important to stress that whenever this book uses the word love as it pertains to God and from God, we always mean love at the intended, commanded level. It is love that is way beyond man's natural ability to achieve. It is love that comes from God and must first be received before it can be transmitted. The whole point is this, for much of our journey we have seen that the body of Christ largely will express a love but usually it is at a level that is far less than God requires. Think again on these words of scripture. John 15 – *"My command is this; you must love each other **as I love you.**"* In other words, Jesus is speaking about levels that we cannot love people at a level which is way below how Jesus loves us.

Love is God's character; faith is his mode of operation. Once we are rooted and established in God's love we can then be transformed.

> *"Therefore, I urge you brothers in view of God's mercy to offer your bodies as a living sacrifice holy and pleasing to God. This is your spiritual act of worship. Do not conform any longer to the pattern of this world but be transformed by the renewing of your minds."*[60]
>
> *"As a man thinks in his heart so he is."*

Identity determines thought. Gate keeping thoughts are torn down and replaced out of our new identity. This has been our journey and we have come a long way. We have learned that behind every key thought (Stronghold) lies millions of thoughts that will be born out of the key thoughts. It is imperative then that we replace the key thoughts. Like, "one day I might arrive", with, "I have already arrived by the grace of God".

---

[60] Romans 12:1

The pattern of this world has programmed us according to our nurture, nature and experience. We have been programmed to think a certain way given certain circumstances. The pattern of this world forms strongholds in our minds. It is only as a person comes to Christ that he breaks free of the old creation thus allowing the new creation to be formed. In Christ we are supposed to move from the certainty of being conformed, into the certainty of being transformed. The fact that many don't should tell us that we must undo deceit...we are gripped in one lie or another. So the issue becomes truth. Truth, however, must land in the right soil.

The fact that we came to Christ and found salvation was just the beginning, that fact in itself did not transform our thinking. If we had not gone through the process of having our minds transformed then our past would definitely still be determining our future even though we are now seasoned Christians. The emphasis therefore bears repetition; we must continue the process of renewing our minds so that we can first understand then live out of our new identities.

"If you obey my commands you are really my disciples then you shall know the truth and the truth will make you free." John 8:32

It is all in the genes the truth is to be found in that most famous of Scriptures:

"For God so loved the world that he gave his only begotten Son that whosoever believes in him shall not perish but have eternal life."[61]

The clue is in the Greek word *monogenes* which is translated "only begotten". When we break the word down we

---

[61] John 3:16

get *mono* meaning one of a kind and *genes* where we get our English word "genes."

It follows, that when we are born again our spiritual genetics change and we now have the potential; to transform our minds and break the strongholds that keep us in the prison of the *"Pattern of this world"*. In order to do so we must draw from the genes of our spiritual Father who is no less than God. Truth isn't words alone truth is either genetically modified through our new creation or it passes through the maze of *"The pattern of this world."* Truth will either confuse *you* or it will set you free. This is why there is veiled understanding of Biblical truth. It can only truly be comprehended through a mind that has been genetically modified so to speak. It is the spirit in a man that gives understanding.

Truth is understood and applied as we walk in the, *"Law of the spirit of life in Christ Jesus."* This is what it means to *"Keep God's Commands."*

Until our spirits are secure in perfect love we will not know what faith can achieve for us. Our senses will always create obstacles to faith until perfect love removes the possibility of obstacles or blockages. We fear that our understanding of love is limited to the five senses. The senses can no more understand perfect love than we can understand what is beyond our galaxy.

The spirit alone can understand perfect, unconditional love. *"It is the spirit in a man that gives understanding."* Love will forge our identity so that we can walk into our destiny. It is this that takes you into the category of being more than a conqueror.

"No, in all these things we are more than conquerors through Christ who loves us." Rom8:37

How fragile and immature we are at times. In reality we should feel super-human. Christ lives in us and we have access to his mind. The truth is, when we were born again our limited potential ceases because we are created brand new and we move from that limited potential into having His potential. We no longer rely on our potential but rather, through pleasing Him, lean on his.

We are continuing to ask the question," Who are you?"

From the text we can see that the believers in Corinth were taking one another to civil courts. So Paul reminds them:

> *"Do you not know that the saints will judge the world, are you not competent to judge trivial cases? Do you not know that we will judge angels? How much more the things of this life?"*

This ought to tell us something about our identity. Who are we? Who are you? If you were to judge the world or celestial beings would you be ready? We make a suggestion; could it be that we have been deceived and are not walking in the potential that our new identity has afforded us. At what point do we inherit our identity?

> *"Therefore, if anyone is in Christ he is a new creation; the old has gone, the new has come!"* [62]

At the point of our new birth we received our new identity. As we became, "In Christ", it was immediate. What came with that new identity?

- Sin was no longer counted against us. All sin...
- We moved from being *"under the law"* to being *"under grace"*.
- We became children of God.

---

[62] 2 Corinthians 5:17

- We became the seed of Abraham.
- We became joint heirs with Christ.
- We became more than conquerors.
- Christ's ambassadors reconciling the world back to him.

All this and more was credited to us the moment that we accepted Christ. So, our identity and our position in Christ are secure before our journey begins. Therefore what happens on our journey does not affect our identity or our position. It cannot because it was never meant to. Satan's master plan against you is to try to get you to use all your energy in trying to become what, in fact, you already are. You will never reach your potential if you don't know who you are already. You were created in God's image to be like him and to manifest him in human form. We are in God's class of being! Anything less than this is to underachieve. Isn't that amazing? No matter how we began life, this is what we have become by the grace of God.

Both of us have been in the place as Christians – even as Christian ministers, where we felt we were almost at the end. We have alluded to this earlier in this account. We were, at times, physically, mentally and socially burnt out. It was a place that we do not recommend, a place where one feels that he is thinking straight, but due to a lack of understanding is actually thinking out of a lie implanted by the evil one. The reality of this condition in the believer is that our old imprinted identity is having too much sway on our present condition. This in our experience was utterly devastating and is even worse for those who are in Christian leadership because of the sense of feeling we are letting God down and God's people. Our respective positions, you must under-stand, were worked out publicly, before an entire congre-gation. The embarrassment of standing in a pulpit before a people who were aware of all that you were enduring can only be born when you know you are loved by God and by those you are continuing to serve, despite your pain.

We both endured depression that was so dark, it seemed almost impossible to overcome. Both of us faced what we had hitherto imagined the stigma of being put on medication, the profound sense of failure, of being one of those who had broken down, these feelings were devastating. Can we remind you that both of us had experienced extreme stress during our time in the armed forces? John has already made mention of his experiences in Northern Ireland – David had his own journey through frightening times during fishery protection duties in the stormy environment of the Icelandic Cod wars.

But whatever stresses we had experienced during those situations and others, none had had the effect that we experienced during our times of burn out in Christian ministry. This is because we are partly aware as Christians of what we are supposed to be. We have discovered the distance between our presupposed position in Christ and our actual position in Christ is measured by our understanding and indeed our receptivity to the amazing love of God. Our healing therefore did not, with respect, come only from taking the right medication, (though we submitted ourselves to professional people, who were seeking to stabilise our physiological condition). Rather, our complete healing came through embarking on the journey we are now describing to you. All truth requires a journey to be undertaken, though we believe in the power of confession, that does not mean you can just name it and claim it, you have to walk it.

Right now if you feel that you are spinning out of control or you are not making it, please understand that with the right kind of help and instruction you will definitely make it. We know because we have and can speak clearly and with confidence about victory in Christ over these very matters.

Our greatest advice to you is alongside any medication that you have been prescribed, take the greatest medication of all which is to understand God's love for you and His requirement that you love others and transmit His love at the level that you are receiving it.

It wasn't long before I (John) was having serious doubts about my ability to lead a church. It was the haunting of my past life and the stark realisation that being a Christian (even one who has passed through Bible College) does not necessarily set one free from the consequence of the past as it pertains to our minds. In short some old habits die hard - at least in one's thinking. What a battle it is for the relatively immature man of God who is setting out to minister to the people at the same time as he is warring against his own internal battles. About two years into pastoral ministry I was so stressed out and remember thinking, at the time, 'I feel more stressed out now than I did during my service in Northern Ireland.' One of the symptoms I had was intrusive thoughts that seemed to come from nowhere and were totally unrelated to what I was thinking at the time. Was I going mad? I seriously thought that I might be, after all I had never before been troubled in such a way. On occasions it seemed like another entity was living in me. Unwelcome thought after unwelcome thought flooded my mind. I was overwhelmed and felt that the nature of my problem was so unusual that I daren't tell anyone what I was going through. Was I mad? Was I demonised? Had I had a nervous breakdown? Either way I was not in control of my mind. The deluge was incessant at times and it caused me to fear for my future.

I was ministering in public out of a private hell, even Deb had no idea how bad I felt - nobody did. I researched books on the symptoms of a nervous breakdown and found myself in the pages I also researched the affects of demonic oppression of the Christian and found myself in that. On top of it all, due to my performance related past I struggled with false functional guilt and particularly I struggled to accept God's love for me when I felt my behaviour let Him down. Many nights I laid awake unable to settle my tormented mind. Still week after week I filled the pulpit and on most occasions preached my heart out hiding my private torment and simply trusting that one day I would find release and break free. As the months went by into years I struggled on knowing that the area we worked in coupled with the nature of our work would always lead to stress.

I realised eventually that anyone going through what I have just described must have a coping mechanism. I began to refer to this as having something in the cupboard. One thing was St. John's Wort the herbal medicine used to brighten the mood. Another would be literature that dealt with the symptoms that I was feeling. Writing this now I realise that the Devil was pushing me around and getting away with it due to my lack of knowledge and weak understanding of my identity. In my so called cupboard were books such as, 'Why do I feel so low when my faith should lift me high,' by Dr. Grant Mullen 'Self help for your nerves' by Dr. Claire Weekes, I gained an understanding that most people's problems have an element of the following combination: spiritual, emotional and physiological. Hitherto I had probably focused on just the spiritual. I gained a great education!

Other authors I found very helpful were Dr. David Enoch the Psychiatrist and Dr. Neil Anderson of 'Freedom in Christ Ministries'. My life, at that time was full of fear and torment. Was this level of living normal for the minister of God who was doing his utmost to advance the kingdom of God? I didn't know and dare not tell which served to compound the sense of dread that I felt. What was happening? At the time I could see no way forward, I was hanging on to God and fulfilling my ministerial duties as best I could. From one degree to another, this went on until after my awakening following my physical illness and heart procedure. It was like an explosive war going on in the inside of me. There were times when I felt the Devil hated me, God didn't like me because of my shortcomings and some people were at war with me. Is this what the Bible promises concerning the *"abundant life"* spoken about in John 10:10? We can conclude that it is absolutely not but may well be the portion for the believer whose thinking is not straight on what God teaches about identity. We cannot live the new out of the old!

We have to move from the mindset of negative avoidance. What does that mean? It means reflecting to the world what we don't do and become proactive in what we do! That means circumstances are not allowed to get in the way and never allowed to affect the mood. We are constant in our families, our neighbourhood, our workplace, our world.

The Apostle Paul is appealing to the Corinthian church and to us by extension: why are you behaving like normal people when you have super human potential? It is time to let go of the small stuff and walk in our potential! Aged 15 and 16 we could never have dreamed that God would give us this chance. What we are communicating to you took years of disciplined learning and painful experience to understand. Learn it without hesitation, it is your birthright. God is for you. God chose you. God wants you to succeed. From this moment don't allow your past to determine your future.

Listen:

"The same spirit that raised Christ from the dead is dwelling within you, giving life to your mortal flesh."

There's a clue if ever I heard one. The moment you received Christ a divine exchange took place and before God you died, but in a millisecond you were resurrected into your new identity. The sin that was to kill you has already killed you. You were severely punished but felt nothing because one had already felt it on your behalf. Still you certainly came out of the old and into the new. Without knowing it you had shifted position: From under law to under grace for you had now died to the *"law of sin and death"* and were placed *under "the law of the spirit of life in Christ Jesus."* As long as you walk fully in your new and true identity you can remove any obstacle that comes naturally or any that is satanically inspired. Your new identity is 'loved in order to love'.

Whereas the law of sin and death condemned you to pay for your sin, the law of the spirit of life in Christ Jesus sets you free from your sin. Not only this but it kick started your potential for living. One law draws on your potential for dying the other draws on your potential for living. However, your potential for living is linked to your potential for loving. To live like one in God's family you have to love like one of God's family! You have to live in your new identity.

Your new identity will take you to a place of perfect love and where perfect love is in place, fear is banished and your insecurities are replaced by security. Insecurity is the thing that paralyses God's church more than anything. It causes us believers to sin. We sin because we fear that we will lose what we have if we don't defend it. This defense mechanism operates behind a camouflage that creates false reasons for our actions thus detracting from truth. Lack of truth in the body is reflected in our inability to reach our world.

So much truth outside of love has been leveled at us that we can no longer recognise the truth that comes to us in love. It is this truth spoken in love that God uses to cause us to grow up in all things, so the result is that we stay immature in our new identity when we should be reaching a potential that is nothing less than galactic. Other worldly, super human! Without realising it at the point of the new birth we move from our lives being energised from the soul to being energised from the spirit. In simple terms the new birth kills off the old you and the Spirit of God enters you to keep you alive.

"The same Spirit that raised Christ from the dead is dwelling within you giving life to your mortal flesh.")

Although you are now dead yet you live but it is not in the same manner. The new you now in your true identity is receiving life in a different manner. Your flesh is now being kept alive by the spirit of God who is living in you. You have been *made alive* by God. It is therefore possible to be born again yet starving the new life within – highly likely. Indeed from one degree to another it is a certainty.

The brand new you should be grounded in love until it is perfected in you, thus, eliminating fear and insecurity so that you can be launched into the positive of your new identity. It is in this place that you can overcome all things including weakness in the body because the spirit of God in you, operating out of the love of God, enables you to speak to mountains.

To maximise the benefits of the spirit, the new you must live your life out of the spirit. We are to, *"walk not after the flesh but after the things of the spirit."* This is a daily choice that you must make. Our call, as a group of people, is to prove life at this level. Our choice is to daily dwell on what we are and reckon ourselves dead to what we are no longer. This cannot be achieved as a one off. So, the apostle Paul is saying, 'Don't you realise who you are? Why are you then behaving as if you are not?

Can we level this at you? You will never live up to your calling until you realise who you are.

Chapter Seventeen – Moving the Core

꧁

A t any given time God is dealing with the core. The core is not to be determined by the outer skin or the peripheral. The peripheral is the everyday issues that surround our lives. Whilst these things are important to the individual they usually have no bearing whatsoever on the advancement of the Kingdom of God - they may, in fact, inadvertently oppose the advancement of the kingdom.

The everyday issues will come and go and these issues can deserve consideration. Nevertheless, they can neither determine policy, nor can they alter necessary ministry. A move of God is carried forward at core level - people come and go, situations come and go so one must minister to the core. Determine the core and minister at a level that will penetrate the peripheral.

At any given time we are all dealing with conspiracy theory planted by the devil. In short, this means, we can't hear what God is saying because we have been listening to what the devil is saying. It can go like this: "there's no love in this church any more, even the pastor doesn't care about the small things." "I'm ignored - no-one cares." "They're always talking about money." We all have to deal with the devil's conspiracies.

God focuses on the core - where the heart is. "Don't sweat the small stuff" was a best selling book because we tend to sweat the small stuff, we spend our lives dealing with the incidental - it is Satan's intention. Don't waste unnecessary time on small issues! It is difficult to minister positives if your mind is filled with negatives. You can do it but not in your present condition. So go to work on your condition and you will advance your position. Feed the core! The core is the life giver. The core determines the outer skins so don't be fooled by the outer skin, be it a person or an organisation; get close to the core or the character.

When we speak of peripheries we mean mood, feelings, circumstances, and habitual behaviour patterns - the things that govern normal, natural life. In the larger scheme of things God, through his word, does not deal with these things at all, he deals with the core. When you were born again, the part that was made brand new was the core, the spirit (the eternal part of you) it was this that changed and became your *enabler*. However, what you found was that you were still subject to the same moods, feelings, circumstances, habitual behaviour patterns and such. You now have the potential to free yourself from these limitations because you died in Christ.

> *"We always carry around in our body the death of Jesus, so that the life of Jesus may also be revealed in our body. For we who are alive are always being given over to death for Jesus' sake so that his life may be revealed in our mortal body. So then, death is at work in us, but life is at work in you."*

It is inward death that manifests outward life - a dying in the inner-self releases spiritual life through our bodies. The more you die inwardly; the more life will flow outwardly... We die to live! This is why we go through situations that cause us to die inwardly. Any death in Christ results in promotion. God deals with the core. Decisions in the inner man will eventually lead to the right choices in the outer man. Those are the choices that affect every day living. It is the decisions you make in the inner man that will determine your destination. The every day mix of life dominates us when it is largely insignificant to God. Core decisions determine destination. Daily choices determine the level of abundant life along the journey. You can choose.

God has put you out of the ordinary class. Are you living up to it? You need to be coached in the every day things or you will miss out on abundant life. How many overweight people wouldn't want to be slimmer? They just don't have the will power. They need a coach, a mentor. We believe that God's desire for you is that you will be blessed in every way! But, you can't have abundant life if you don't make the right choices that are being made out of right core decisions. The core has to swallow up the incidental.

The incidental only takes upon itself the imperative if you are not living on a higher plain. You are involved in God's work and it was completed before the creation of the world. So, don't allow the incidentals, along the way, to dominate your life. And don't speak the language of your emotions. Decisions determine destiny, choices determine life. That is they determine the degree that we enjoy the journey or not.

Here is the key!

Choices can be summed up in giving. Here we go again but yes it really is so important. Life is wrapped up in giving: *God so loved that he gave.* If you want abundant life you will be asked to give. It is in the giving that you find the living. God commands you to give not so that you can pay for your salvation. You can't pay for something you already own but rather because you are in debt to love.

When we obey God in the area of giving - the moment we give it becomes a seed of the thing we are giving. It turns into a seed. In the natural when a tree or a plant disperses seed it releases, in comparison, a tiny thing in relation to what the seed will produce. It seems innocuous for it is a tiny seed. But what is in the seed?

In the book of Exodus, God told the Israelites to give their best lamb. The lamb was a seed... What God tells us to do may not make any sense at all. When Israel had a need, God told them to give. Even when they were slaves in Egypt, when they were poor, their release came only after they had given. We have to understand that both a seed sown and a seed received are supernatural. A seed received from God comes from another dimension and a seed sown in obedience enters another world or dimension. Mike Murdoch said, "Nothing leaves heaven until something leaves earth."

The Israelites were to give a lamb - the giving of the lamb was a seed of salvation. It was a seed for their deliverance and also a seed for the deliverance of the whole of mankind. It was a picture, a pattern of the sacrifice or giving of the Lamb of God (Jesus Christ) *who takes away the sin of the whole world.*

God requires obedience and obedience usually involves giving. It involves, the giving of ourselves, the giving of our money, the giving of that which is not merited (love, mercy, forgiveness and grace), and the giving of our material possessions. The Israelites had been in the bondage of slavery for centuries they had just faced nine plagues without experiencing the promised deliverance, then God told them they had to give. What you give becomes seed it is sown natural but takes upon itself the supernatural. That is why it can be multiplied. The moment you release seed it changes dimension...So, if you want to walk in the supernatural, *"Offer your body as a living sacrifice...*

During the time that we suffered darkness and it was on more than one occasion, somewhere along the way both of us can identify the times where we were required to forgive those who seriously hurt us. Many times along the journey we have been called to give love, mercy, grace and forgiveness to those who naturally did not deserve it because of the harm they caused us. But, in our giving we were sowing seeds for our future healing and for the victory that we now live in today. The truth is: many people who have wounded us are no longer in our lives or in our thinking, what appeared to be a mountain at the time has now been removed. The same is or could be true for you.

Jesus was a seed planted from another world. *"He took upon himself life"*. The Son of God began life on earth as a seed just like you and me. The difference was he was seed from another world. But the seed he would sow would produce countless seeds. He gave good measure and he is receiving good measure. The measure you use will be measured to you. What did Jesus get for his giving? He got you and he got me and he got the millions upon millions throughout the ages who have believed. The Bible says, "We are his inheritance."

That means, he is our inheritance and we are his. God has always dealt with a seed group. That means his purpose is carried out regardless. The peripheral, ordinary, normal, natural, comes and goes. And as it is in the full scheme of things so it is with our lives. Don't make decisions based on the temporal or momentary - on the peripherals or on your feelings. Make decisions out of your core identity. Accordingly don't make decisions in the darkness that will affect the revelation you got in the light

It is this that determines your destiny. If you truly want to make it, then submit your natural life to being coached, find a church, a person, a group of people or contact us. You can make it but you need help. We want to minister to you in such a way that you end up being blessed in every way. Decide what you want then make the necessary choices on a daily basis.

Chapter Eighteen – Eating from the Wrong Tree

⚭

I **f you have read so far and are still not convinced that the gospel is true or that Jesus is who he says he is then, in light of what we have written we want you to consider the following:**

> *"….but you must not eat from the tree of the knowledge of good and evil, for when you eat of it you will surely die."*[63]

We are intrigued by the case of the judge in Italy who has ordered a Catholic Priest to prove the existence of Jesus Christ. This follows the priest's public criticism of an atheist businessman. So, how will the priest go about proving the existence of Jesus Christ as an historic person? Our advice would be to look at the result of his existence rather than trying to prove his existence. Being an atheist I would suppose that the businessman is an evolutionist thus believing that man has evolved over millions of years from less advanced forms of life. The theory is we all have a common ancestor who

---

[63] Genesis 2:17

was no more than a cell. If so, where did it all go wrong and who should we blame?

If there is no God and by extension no Son of God but only scientific naturalism, then we must assume that scientific naturalism has created (through a process of evolution ever since) all that we are and all that we see. This however leaves us in somewhat of a predicament, let's face it; a philosophy that deals only with means and not with ends has no basis for morality. In this is our point. You see, where did it all go wrong and who should we blame?

Is scientific reasoning simply a rationalisation of our wrongdoing? This is the pitfall: Science does not command *us to love other people as we love ourselves.* Therefore, if scientific naturalism is to replace God and set boundaries so that man can live together in harmony then it must better this command. It does not because scientific advancement is only safe if it is under the guidance and government of a being who is himself directed by the heights of unconditional love - under a maxim of, *"Do unto others as you would have them do for you."* Whatever government we choose to live under will determine this outcome.

Scientific reasoning cannot tame God although it attempts to do so. At its worst, it is a tool that can help us to rationalise our behaviour as it sets itself against God's moral code. In its final analysis this rationalisation allows us to do unto others what we would never want them to do to us. Information creating evolution states that genetic information mutates and therefore produces improvement independent of some external source. Thus, over millions of years man has been formed as a process - starting out as a cell, later to become a fish, progressing to some kind of amphibious frog and so on and so forth through the monkey stages. This argument does not allow for the possibility of their being an architect or great designer behind the Universe - all that we have become is as a result of a combination of natural law and chance.

The question is: did the information to create this process come before the chemical laws created the information that would evolve and improve itself in due time? Is it all down to chance and physical law or is it down to chance, law and a third factor? For the materialist (those who deny any interference from God) God is replaced by a mechanism referred to as, "natural selection." Well, can creative evolution take place based purely on chance and chemical law? Surely this cannot be done unless there is first "an intelligence" that sets that ball rolling. Has intelligence evolved out of nothing? If so, where did it all go wrong and who should we blame.

So let's look from another angle. We believe that there are two kinds of knowledge: one received through the senses and another kind received in the spirit as revelation from God. Is there a possibility that the foundation of human knowledge is shaky, therefore, our interpretation of all things is off beam resulting in that which is finite seeking to interpret that which is infinite through flawed human intellect, using inferior data based on science, when all the time a creator has determined that reality can only be understood through spiritual means. If this is so then surely the Italian businessman has bitten off more than he could chew. Could it be that unconditional love is an ingredient that leads to far greater understanding than the intellect of man seeking knowledge through scientific means? We think so.

We should question why we think what we think. Why do we interpret theory as fact?

The Bible says, Eve ate from the wrong tree, *"for God knows that when you eat of it (the tree of the knowledge of good and evil) your eyes will be opened, and you will be like God, knowing good and evil."*[64] Is it possible that secular thought has been eating from the wrong tree ever since?

---

[64] Genesis 3:7

Furthermore, is it possible that some of those minds that our world esteems the most are as far wrong as it is possible to be wrong? After all, intelligence or talent - even if it is devoid of character - will suffice in making you important in this upside down world. Scientific knowledge can benefit mankind but it cannot give us what we need the most, it cannot lead us to love our neighbour as we love ourselves.

A staggering 100 million people died in wars in the last century. Where did it all go wrong and who should we blame? Surely history will prove that nothing can lead us to love our neighbour as we love ourselves except some being that is capable of doing this, modelling it for us. Why then is there so much fuss about something that stands inferior to all that love at this level produces? Science does not affect the condition of the human heart - it is obvious that the Christian gospel can, does and is! Jesus Christ is the founder of the Christian faith (Christian means *little Christ*). In the final analysis we should really pity those who place more emphasis on what they know than they do on how much they love.

Even secular writers speak of a vacuum in today's world wide global village. They say there is a moral and spiritual vacuum that exists in every society on the face of the planet. What has gone wrong? Who shall we blame? Shall we simply continue asking these kinds of questions, or should we rather seek the one who specialises in filling voids. The creator of this thing we know as the universe, the one who spoke and filled the vastness of all emptiness.

We want to encourage anyone reading this book, that the God of Love that we are relating to you, as Paul Scanlon explains, is 'on the look out for emptiness.' In fact God is attracted to emptiness.' We have made mention earlier concerning those who wear masks; you see mask wearing in effect is pretending that you are full. Jesus had strong words for churches that said they had all they needed, when in fact in His words they were wretched, miserable and pitiful.

Earthly brokenness attracts heavenly openness. If we live according to the love commands, at the level God has always intended for us, in effect we build him a place of habitation in our lives. Our mission has become to build a "Spiritual House" that God is attracted to. A house where there is no mask wearing, no pretending and no adopting of identities that bear no resemblance to the identity we have in Christ.

Our belief is that God wants His church to create a collective hunger for Him, through understanding the need to live in the love commands, that can only be done out of the Christ identity. We have both expended great quantities of our lives taking on all kinds of identities just to survive. We are not talking of surviving now, we are speaking of living. Yet many believers still endure their Christian lives, struggling just to reach the perceived end and say, "I just about made it", yet failing to apprehend, let alone live in the abundance provided for us.

On more than one occasion, some brave soul was willing to put their hunger on display in order to stop the religious parade going on around Jesus. That hunger stopped Jesus in His tracks. What about you?

Our pilgrimage has taught us this much, we have both learned to be honest and open with God and with one another in seeking to live and experience the love of God. How do you think blind Bartimaeus felt as he shouted out with all his might, *"Jesus Son of David have mercy on me"?* How do you think poor shorty Zaccheus felt as he shimmied up the sycamore tree just so that he could catch sight of Jesus? Yet these men managed to stop the religious parade and drew the divine attention of the Christ. They received His intimate attention for they were unafraid to admit their desperate need.

Zaccheus in fact hilariously exposed his sin and everyone had a good laugh about it. He threw open his purloined bank account and gave back with interest all that he had stolen.

Everyone laughed with him as he found his deliverance because the saviour came to his home.

He prepared a place for divinity to come, he exposed himself so much so that he revealed, despite his prosperity materially he was totally aware of his poverty of spirit and wanted salvation, and that is what he received as Jesus full of joy and laughter declared, *"today salvation has come to your home."*

Putting your own poverty of spirit on display is very humbling; it means we stop pretending that we have it all together, God wants a passionate response to this kind of thing not a religious one. Emptiness is what makes way for fullness. Puffed up human knowledge leaves no room for the possibility of an emptiness that can only be filled by God.

You see we must beware of just becoming fact collectors about God. Some folks are compulsive collectors of second hand facts about God which creates a false sense of intimacy, but let us assure you, it is not intimacy with God you are experiencing. It is intimacy with your own pride. There is a difference that is revealed many times in Scripture between those who know about God and those who know Him. Aaron and Miriam had to learn a painful lesson because they dared speak against Moses who knew God in a way they did not. He had a level of intimacy that had been tested with the bread of adversity and the water of affliction; they had not experienced that in the same degree.

Have you ever sat in an intimate setting and suddenly, in the quietness of the room your stomach starts growling because you are hungry? So many times we have sat in that kind of setting, you try everything, crossing and uncrossing your legs, holding your arms across your tummy, coughing at crucial times hoping to obliterate the horrible squelchy noises coming from your insides.

Well, we can sense in ourselves a spiritual stomach growling that will not subside. That kind of hunger must be encouraged for when God comes, he will take us to the places that in ourselves we cannot attain to. You see, God's senses are actually dulled to humanities supposed strengths and virtues, but He takes huge notice, in fact He is drawn to the slightest hint of desperation in our hearts and lives for Him and His strength. Just as you wouldn't feed a child unless it was hungry, neither will God 'force feed' us, we have to be hungry.

We remember hearing someone once say that God is shopping for His next place of outbreak. It always comes to places where there is spiritual stomach growling taking place, where people are not only hungry for Him, they are not afraid to put their hunger on display.

> "*Now the earth was formless and empty, darkness was over the surface of the deep, and the Spirit of God was hovering over the waters. And God said,*"[65]

At the very dawn of creation when everything was still formless, empty, when all that existed was a void, when all was dark, God spoke and by His word created and sought to fill that void. God is attracted to emptiness – He is a creator therefore whenever he sees emptiness he wants to create something.

A vacuum is a place where matter is not. Space for instance is devoid of matter. It is in fact described as a place that has had all matter removed from it. There is much talk today of Britain being described as a spiritual vacuum, that is, all truly spiritual matter has and is being removed from our society.

This has happened to such an extent that our society is now described as the second most godless nation on the earth. There are all kinds of philosophies and religions that

---

[65] Genesis 1:3

are and will seek to fill this vacuum, and we who have light must awaken to realise our responsibilities to bring light and life where darkness threatens to overwhelm.

We have many who will oppose this message; we face in this time a plethora of ideas that threaten to intimidate, and to coerce Christians to remain inert with regard to their witness. Many are not even bothering to try anymore in regard to reaching out for they are intimidated by these forces, these strongholds that seem so immovable. Many of the mindsets of Western civilisation are proving to be impotent and contain no answers, relativism, romanticism, rationalism, consumerism, hedonism, materialism, secularism even religious syncretism. None of these mindsets are providing answers to people still trapped and desperate to know if it really is possible to know God. Our advice to the Italian business man and to all is at all costs, get to know Him!

Epilogue

⚘

As we begin this epilogue our location is Dar es Salaam (Haven of Peace), Tanzania, East Africa. We have spent several days locked away with our manuscript, in our attempt to complete in time for publication. The three years spent in writing this book have been in themselves a process of understanding, healing, and great excitement. As we have realised that even in those days when we were boy sailors, God had ordained our journey and brought us to this place of destiny.

We have most definitely relied upon His grace, leant on His strength and absorbed His love. We have travelled together far and wide, during times of wonder, awe, and incredible testing. We have a profound sense that God has prescribed the truths in our book to the wider body of Christ. We are aware of our human frailty and anonymity, yet also, acutely aware that all things are possible to those in Christ Jesus. We are convicted of the uniqueness of our account and sure that we will find the constituency that we mentioned earlier in the book. Today we are Senior Pastors, Dave is still in Rugby after 23 years, and John is still in Porth after 18 years. Here we are now together again in a place where our destinies in many ways, once again intertwined. John lived in Tanzania as a missionary for two years. David had come and lived here for just over two months. Since that time we have travelled here together, continuing our on going mission to live love and influence as many people as possible with this message; Proving that this truth above all transcends the boundaries of continent and culture.

We have a deep and profound sense of gratitude that God could take us from those degrading days of our youth, and supply us with wives who have journeyed with us throughout, despite the fact that our earlier lives were completely alien to all that they had themselves experienced. With patience, love and great grace they have allowed us the moments we have spent in putting into words our honest, yet disturbing account. We are aware that in sharing the facts as we have, we have laid bare ourselves and them to public scrutiny. As stated earlier we believe the details were necessary in order that you the reader might be more cognisant of God's incredible workings in our lives.

Incredibly, considering the start we had, we now can celebrate over fifty years of wonderful marriage between us. Four children have been produced as well as five grand children, what an incredible legacy from lives that were heading toward destruction. We are both aware that we have received at levels that we did not deserve or expect and the story still goes on and improves almost daily. It is true to say that both of us feel we are at the most exciting period of our lives and expanding ministries. The best is yet to come! We have come to realise that each part of our parallel stories has served to give us the insight we live in and teach from today. Only the complete picture can reveal the true grace of God, in the repairing of the broken, tarnished and totally dysfunctional aspects of our identities. We are aware that there are many in our world today that have also experienced tragedy and brokenness beyond that which we have described. However, the unique nature of our story is how God has brought together two individuals who have almost walked one another's story and come to the same inevitable conclusions.

Love never fails!

Junior radio operator second class D W Crabb D/121275N & Junior seaman second class J Bullock D/143004T.

Or now

Rev J Bullock – first class!
Rev D W Crabb – first class!

For other materials by Dave Crabb and John Bullock

Email: david@rugbyelim.org.uk

Email: johndeb@rhondda.fsworld.co.uk
crabb50@hotmail.com

Or visit: www.gatehousechurch.com

See also www.sportingmarvels.co.uk
www.rugbyelim.org.uk

i

Printed in the United States
201009BV00003B/118-525/A

9 781604 772050

SIX A[...]

On Soaring Sixes
and Lusty Six-Hitters

A meticulous researcher, Kersi Meher-Homji is a devotee of cricket 'with a predilection for its minutiae', according to David Frith, the former editor of *Wisden Cricket Monthly*.

This is Kersi's seventh book on cricket following his *Cricket's Great Families* (1980, 1981), *1000 Tests* (1984), *Parsee Cricket Centenary* (1986), *Out for a Duck* (1993, 1994), *The Nervous Nineties* (1994) and *Hat-Tricks* (1995). In *Six Appeal* he portrays cricket's great entertainers — the six-hitters — with flair, insight and humour.

Kersi freelances for the *Sydney Morning Herald*, *Australian Cricket* and *Wisden Cricket Monthly* (England) and is the sports columnist for the *Indian Down Under*. He has also contributed to *Cricket in Isolation* (1978), *The Oxford Companion to Australian Sport* (1992, 1994), *The Oxford Companion to Australian Cricket* (1996) and *Ray Robinson — Between Branches* (1996).

A scientist by profession, he comes from a cricketing family including an uncle who played Test cricket and once, in a first-class match in Bombay in 1935, hit the dreaded Harold Larwood for a six.

'Move over Wisden,' wrote David McNicoll in *The Bulletin*. 'If you've never heard of Kersi Meher-Homji, let me tell you that he has given me more enjoyment with his cricket book than any of the turgid tomes produced by our Test cricketers ... Kersi is the first person I have encountered who can make a cricket book interesting for a non-cricket fan. Quite an achievement.'

One of the heaviest hitters of all time, Australia's George Bonnor was called 'Bonnor the Basher' and 'Colonial Hercules'. (Jack Pollard Collection)

SIX APPEAL

On Soaring Sixes
and Lusty Six-Hitters

KERSI MEHER-HOMJI

Foreword by DOUG WALTERS

Kangaroo Press

Dedicated to the memory of

Norman Roy Halpin (1926–1995)

A cricket-lover and a sincere friend

Cover photo: A jubilant Steve Waugh raises his hand in ecstasy as he smashes the richest six in cricket history. His hitting of the Mercantile Mutual sign on the WACA with that shot on 22 October 1995 made him and his NSW teammates $140,000 richer. (West Australian)

Published in 1996 by Kangaroo Press Pty Ltd
3 Whitehall Road Kenthurst NSW 2156 Australia
PO Box 6125 Dural Delivery Centre NSW 2158
Printed by Griffin Paperbacks, Netley, South Australia

ISBN 0 86417 799 2

Contents

Foreword by Doug Walters 6

Acknowledgments 9

Introduction 12

1 Long-Distance Thrills 15

2 Give Me Six 17

3 Hellish Delights 21

4 Sixes in Court 26

5 Some Enchanted Sixes 33

6 A Jackpot of Sixes 44

7 Calling all Sloggers 52

8 Nugget's Towering Sixers and 'Ponders' 63

9 Vintage Six Symbols 70

10 Modern Six Smiters 88

11 Hurricane Comets 114

12 Hits and Myths 120

13 Minor Skyscrapers 125

14 Sixomania 135

Appendix 151

Index 158

Foreword

Kersi Meher-Homji has written many books and his writing style is unique as his books are read not only by cricket buffs but also by those who do not avidly follow or understand cricket. Born in Bombay, Kersi is the nephew of a Test cricketer, so cricket is certainly in his blood, and like his many other followers I look forward to reading this book. The first few chapters I have read, viz. 'Long Distance Thrills', 'Give Me Six' and 'Hellish Delights', have certainly whetted my appetite.

Hitting sixes and seeing the ball hit for six is to me what cricket is all about. When I was very young I was presented one of Sir Donald Bradman's books. In this book he explained how he hit a century in three overs. Of course they were eight-ball overs and it wasn't a particularly high grade match, but the fact that he achieved this feat in any match really impressed me. There were sixes galore scattered throughout his innings, and I immediately wanted to get a bat in my hands to try and emulate his wonderful accomplishment. I guess that was the first mistake in my cricketing career, because for anyone to go chasing records set by Sir Donald Bradman is ridiculous. The absurdity of it did not stop me trying and I am pleased that it has not stopped many other cricketers the world over. In a way, I am pleased that I did not read too many of Sir Donald Bradman's books while I was still playing, because I found out after I had retired that Sir Donald hit only six sixes in his entire Test career. I can understand his reasoning now that I have read other books he has written because he rightly claims that you cannot get out caught if you hit the ball along the ground. I am not sorry I did not know it until recently and perhaps a lot of spectators and other cricketers are happy that everyone did not try to imitate the champion of all champions. Hitting a six gives a batsman a tremendous sense of satisfaction because it means that he has done most things correctly.

My first six was probably on our side verandah and it crashed through a window pane, but I have very fond memories of a few since then. My favourite is probably the one I managed to hit off Bob Willis in Perth. Australia was playing against England in the 1974–75 Test series and I brought up my century in a session on the last ball of the day. I guess we all have a dream in life where we imagine that everything will be absolutely perfect for us at a particular moment. The moment I hit that six was probably when my dream came true. It was as if bowlers were aiming at the middle of the bat and hitting it — I would never have imagined they could be that accurate! Sixes are an amazing thing — people talk about them for years and years. In the years since my

And a sixer climbs the sky. Doug Walters shows the West Indians how it is done.
(Doug Walters)

retirement, that six has got bigger and bigger. At this stage it is just about on the rooftop, whereas in actual fact it only just cleared the roped-off boundary.

One of my earlier sixes, a much bigger one which is still talked about, was the one at the old Sydney Cricket Ground No. 2. That ground has now disappeared, so nobody will ever hit a bigger one there. The match in which it occurred was a NSW colts game against Queensland and on that occasion, a wrong 'un and a good piece of willow connected at the right time. The ball sailed over a brick wall, and the experts say it vanished in Kippax Lake — quite some distance from the wall. Admittedly the ball was wet when it was retrieved, but I maintain that it must have had a couple of favourable bounces off Driver Avenue to finish in the lake.

Another of my favourite sixes, believe it or not, came during net practice in 1981. Before anyone starts doubting that I really practised, let me assure you that I did practise, except on the morning of a match. The third six to which I am referring came about as a result of the infamous underarm bowling incident against New Zealand in 1981 when Trevor Chappell delivered the final ball in a limited-overs international in an underarm action. After thinking about that delivery, I came up with a solution as to how Brian McKechnie could have scored a six. Allan Border bet me it was impossible to hit a rolling ball for six as it would be classed as 'bumped'. To prove my point (even on the morning of a match), I attended a practice session. I took him to the centre of the SCG No. 2 ground and asked him to bowl a ball along the ground. I stepped down the pitch a few paces so that I could not be given out LBW and flicked the ball up with my foot. My bat connected with it at the correct time and it went flying over the fence. Allan Border shook his head in disbelief and returned to the nets. I am still waiting for him to pay up, despite what he will tell you about having settled the wager.

I hope thousands pay up for this book as I know it will be a book well worth reading and dipping into every time a Brian Lara, Michael Slater, Steve Waugh, Andrew Symonds or Jayasuriya skies one over the fence and into the crowd.

Doug Walters
June 1996

Acknowledgments

It is my pleasure to thank: Doug Walters for his entertaining Foreword; Gerald Brodribb whose book *Hit for Six* was my bible and his letters a source of inspiration; Stephen Gibbs, honorary library consultant, NSW Cricket Association Library, who dug out rare and interesting references for me; Ross Dundas, Colin Clowes, Erica Sainsbury, Marion Collin and Graham Clayton for supplying and checking some of my statistics; Keith Miller and Alan Davidson for sharing with me their precious six-hitting memories; Geoff Prenter for giving me details on Mercantile Mutual Cup's involvement with six-hitting; Tricia Ritchings for her word-processing expertise, her typing speed comparable to a whirlwind inning by Jessop, Alletson, Miller or Botham; Nigel Smith, Jack Pollard, John Wood, Dr Vasant Naik, Bob Lord, Vasant Raiji, Mark Kerly and Anandji Dossa for sending me their views and statistics on famous and obscure six-hitters; readers of the *Sydney Morning Herald*, *Wisden Cricket Monthly* (England) and *Australian Cricket* for submitting their six stories — along with clippings and score-sheets which are acknowledged alongside their contributions; everyone at Kangaroo Press, David Rosenberg, Van McCune and especially editor Carl Harrison-Ford; my wife Villie who bears with patience my cricket-writing obsession, although four books in four years must have been equivalent to be hit for four sixes in four balls or even worse with books and newspaper clippings everywhere!

For photographs supplied, I acknowledge Andrew Foulds of the *Sydney Morning Herald*, Ken Piesse of *Australian Cricket*, Jack Pollard, Patrick Eagar, David Taylor of the *West Australian*, Tony McDonough of *Newsline*, Geoff Prenter of *Mercantile Mutual Cup*, Doug Walters and Australian Picture Library.

Books referred to were: *Hit for Six* by Gerald Brodribb (Heinemann, 1960), *The Big Hitters* by Brian Bearshaw (Macdonald Queen Anne

Press, 1986), *Six and Out* edited by Jack Pollard (J. Pollard, 1975), *Caught in Court* by John Scott (A. Deutsch, 1989), *The Grand Old Ground* by Philip Derriman (Cassell Australia, 1981), *Wisden Cricketers' Almanack* — several editions (John Wisden & Co), *The Wisden Book of Test Records 1876 –77 to 1977–78* by Bill Frindall (Macdonald & Jones, 1979), *The Wisden Book of Cricket Records* by Bill Frindall (Macdonald Queen Anne Press, 1986), *The Wisden Book of Cricketers' Lives* compiled by Benny Green (Macdonald Queen Anne Press, 1988), *The Complete Who's Who of Test Cricketers* by Christopher Martin-Jenkins (Rigby, 1983), *Great Innings* by Peter Roebuck (Pan Books, 1990), *The Immortal Victor Trumper* by Jack Fingleton (William Collins, 1978), *Sir Donald Bradman: A Biography* by Irving Rosenwater (Batsford, 1978), *Bradman the Great* by B. J. Wakely (Nicholas Kaye, 1959), *Sir Gary: A Biography* by Trevor Bailey (Collins, 1976), *Sobers: Twenty Years at the Top* by Garfield Sobers with Brian Scovell (Macmillan Australia, 1988), *This Curious Game of Cricket* by George Mell (Unwin Paperbacks, 1983), *Curiosities of Cricket* by Jonathan Rice (Pavilion Books, 1993), *The Great Australian Book of Cricket Stories* edited by Ken Piesse (Currey O'Neil, 1982), *The Cricketer Book of Cricket Disasters and Bizarre Records* edited by Christopher Martin-Jenkins (Lennard Books, 1983), *The Cricketer Book of Cricket Eccentrics and Eccentric Behaviour* edited by Christopher Martin-Jenkins (Lennard Books, 1985), *Cricket's Strangest Matches* by Andrew Ward (Robson Books, 1994), *Cricket Advance* by Gary Sobers (Pelham Books, 1965), *Australian Cricket: The Game and the Players* by Jack Pollard (Hodder & Stoughton and Australian Broadcasting Commission, 1982), *Test Tussles—On and Off the Field* by D.K. Darling (1970) *Botham* by Patrick Eagar, John Arlott and Graeme Wright (Kingswood Press, 1985), *The Test Match Career of Walter Hammond* by Derek Lodge (Nutshell Publishing, 1990), *Green Sprigs* by Ray Robinson (Collins, 1955), *Great Days in New Zealand Cricket* by R. T. Brittenden (Reed, 1958) and *Give it a Heave, Lance Cairns* (MOA Publications, 1984).

Magazines and newspapers referred to have been *Wisden Cricket Monthly, The Cricketer, Playfair Cricket Monthly, The Cricket Quarterly* and *The Cricket Statistician* from England, the *Sydney Morning Herald, Cricketer,* the *Sun-Herald, Australian Cricket, Inside Edge* and *Hill Chatter* from Australia, the *Times of India, Sportsweek, Sportsweek's World of Cricket* and *Khel Halchal* from India and *Boundary* from New Zealand.

Every effort has been made to contact the owners of copyright.

This book would not have been written but for the variety of publications available at the NSW Cricket Association Library in the heart of Sydney.

Introduction

Yet even from the pedant what a deep ecstatic sigh
When a batsman jumps to meet one, and a sixer climbs the sky.

— E.V. Lucas

A six takes you right in the game, breaking all barriers between players and spectators. I recall watching my first big game of cricket when eleven. It was between a Commonwealth XI and the Cricket Club of India at the Brabourne Stadium, Bombay in January 1950.

The match was meandering towards a draw when Bill Alley, an expatriate Aussie with arms as strong as a blacksmith's, hit a towering six which soared in the sky and landed next to my feet. There and then cricket and I became bosom pals.

Six appeal is universal and is as important for maintaining cricket fascination as sex appeal is for species preservation. Mercantile Mutual in Australia have invested money by offering large cash to six-hitters and instant cash to a spectator who catches one during a Mercantile Mutual Cup match. The most precious six in financial term was the one hit by Steve Waugh for NSW v. Western Australia in a Mercantile Mutual Cup match in Perth on 22 October 1995. Just one tall shot which hit the advertisement signpost and it netted a jackpot of $140,000.

Yet the six which gave spectators — live on the WACA ground and watching on prime-time TV all over Australia — the greatest thrill was the one Doug Walters hit in the Perth Test against England to reach his hundred in a session off the last ball of the day, 14 December 1974. All those lucky enough to witness that soaring spectacle got the vicarious thrill as if *they* had hit the English paceman Bob Willis out of the ground.

The late Arthur Wellard of Somerset is considered the daddy of all six-hitters, although not necessarily the fastest scorer. He hit 561

A real all-rounder, Bill Alley was a blacksmith's striker, boilermaker, deep-sea fisherman, dance-hall bouncer, professional boxer, a left-handed hitter of cricket balls who scored 3019 runs for Somerset in 1961, aged 42, and a Test umpire. (Jack Pollard Collection)

sixes in his first-class career; 123 of them in only two seasons, 1935 and 1936.

Australia has had her six symbols in the gigantic George Bonnor, Joe Darling, Keith Miller (also a sex symbol with his movie-star looks and charismatic demeanour), Alan Davidson, little Johnny Martin and David Hookes to name a few. In recent times England's unpredictable genius Ian Botham and India's trojan Kapil Dev delighted onlookers with drives that bypassed the turf. Botham's most prolific season in England was in 1985 when he slammed 80 sixes in 27 innings, almost three sixes every innings. Then in 1995, the young exciting Queenslander Andrew Symonds eclipsed two major six-hitting records when playing for Gloucestershire.

In the batsmen-dominated 1996 World Cup in the Indian subcontinent, more sixes were hit in a month than you would normally expect in a couple of seasons. The Sri Lankan batsmen Asanka

Gurusinha, Sanath Jayasuriya and Romesh Kaluwitharana, India's Sachin Tendulkar, Australia's Mark Waugh, South Africa's Gary Kirsten and Hansie Cronje among others blazed the sky with sixes that landed among delighted onlookers.

The book does not claim to be an encyclopaedia on sixes; what could be more exasperating! Record-keeping on sixes has not been very accurate at first-class level — let alone in minor cricket. And distances measured — vertical and horizontal — in most cases have been guesstimates apart from Gerald Brodribb's immaculate research in England for some of the big hits. Rather, the emphasis has been on the appeal of sixes, the excitement they create, the thrills, the ecstasy... a moment to cherish.

The book is all about six-hitters and their sprees, their *modi operandi* and the reactions of their victims — the bowlers and the struck spectators. And when I say struck, I mean struck physically. A powerful hit can maim or kill an inattentive bystander but as long as there are sixes in the sky, cricket will remain alive and throbbing.

1

Long-Distance Thrills

*'What Doug Walters fan?' she screamed hysterically. 'You nearly killed me.
You went through two red lights and avoided a five-car pile-up by inches.'*

The WACA ground exploded with applause when Doug Walters
completed his century in a session in the Perth Test of December 1974.
I was then driving in my old Toyota on a busy Sydney street and the
reaction of the motorists amazed me.

It was incredible. They honked in frenzy and showed 'V' signs to
me. They really looked excited. If I did not know the background, I
would have said angry, even furious.

What an ecstatic moment, Doug's century thousands of kilometres
away provoking such a strong response in his home town. I honked
back, wound the window down and shouted back 'Good on ya, Douggie!'

Just then I heard the baby-sitter sob convulsively, 'I didn't know you
were a Doug Walters fan', I said.

'What Doug Walters fan?' she screamed hysterically, 'You nearly killed
me, *killed me*. You went through two red lights and avoided a five-car
pile-up by inches.'

I can imagine you lapping this up but demanding a 'please explain'.
Where does a baby-sitter fit in a serious cricket study, such as this book,
and what traffic lights?

That's the trouble with vicarious thrills. They linger and what your
narrative gains in dramatic effect suffers in clarity.

I had better begin at the beginning. Doug Walters was 3 not out at
tea in the Perth Test on 14 December 1974 and was blazing away on
resumption. All I wanted that evening was to see my favourite cricketer
bat but at 7p.m. Sydney time I had to bring home the baby-sitter from
Mosman to Artarmon, about a 15-minute drive, as we were going out
that night.

Doug Walters' famous six off the last ball of the day from Bob Willis in the Perth Test of December 1974 which brought him a century in a session. (Patrick Eagar)

Reluctantly I left, tuned in the car radio and enjoyed every stroke Walters played. He was in his nineties when we were driving along Falcon Street in Crows Nest and 97 when turning into the Pacific Highway. Now to the final ball every true-blue Oz-cricket lover claims to remember. As English fast bowler Bob Willis delivered it, Walters needed three runs for his century and a six to get his 100 in a session.

The commentators went berserk with excitement. So did I, among the thousands at the WACA, and perhaps among tens of thousands in Sydney homes. Willis bowled a short ball and coolly Walters skied it for a spectacular six.

As pointed out later by the baby-sitter to my wife in a tone as crisp as Walters' six: 'Your husband is crazy. He never spoke a word to me. Oh, he was miles away listening to the stupid radio, behaved like an animal, went through two red lights and luckily avoided a big pile-up. Ooh, the other motorists were wild at him showing obscene signs, it was disgusting — but he kept smiling and shouting back "Good on you, Douggie". Please look for another baby-sitter, I'm lucky to be alive to tell you all this.'

Everyone has a favourite six story — a selection is printed in a separate chapter. But Walters' six in Perth nearly killing ten in Sydney deserves top-billing.

2

Give Me Six

It starts a board game, finishes a tennis set
and holds spectators spellbound in cricket.

The number six has different meanings for different people. You cannot start most board games till you get a ::: on the die. Clocks tick over in multiples of six, 60 seconds in a minute, 60 minutes in an hour, 24 hours a day, and for the superstitious ones, 666 is the devil's number.

According to the book of Genesis, the Lord made heaven, earth, sea and everything in them in six days and rested on the seventh day.

In tennis there are sets of six games, a converted try yields six points in rugby league and in modern cricket there are six balls per over and six stumps hammered into the pitch, three at each end.

And of course the ultimate in excitement — a soaring, lusty, towering six which neutralises day-long tedium in a few slow-motion seconds when time appears to stand still. It is like a goal in soccer or a try in rugby — only taller, rarer and at times closer to your lap.

Interestingly, a hit over the fence/ropes/pickets/boundary line/ sightscreen was not always called a six. Before 1910 in England, a hit over the fence counted only four runs in first-class and Test matches. Only a huge hit right out of the ground (including the stands), which happened rarely, was awarded six runs.

A different practice prevailed in Australia. As in England, six runs were awarded only for hits out of the ground, 'an extremely rare feat in their big grounds with tall stands' to quote B. J. Wakely from *The Cricket Quarterly* (England), 1963. But hits over the boundary line were credited with five runs — and the batsman lost the strike.

The Australian team raised this point with its Board of Control for the 1905–06 Test series and the Board decided that 'owing to different arrangements on different grounds, it would be inexpedient to lay down any hard-and-fast rule that a hit to the boundary should count four and a hit over the boundary six'.

This is, however, going ahead of the story. The history of boundaries is rather complex. According to Gerald Brodribb in his *Hit for Six* (1960): 'Originally, all hits were run out, but it later became agreed locally that if a ball reached a certain object such as a tent or pavilion, the ball was "dead", and boundary runs were awarded. An early name for such hits was "booth-balls".'

But with more spectators attending matches and the possible danger of a fielder running among them when chasing the ball, it was decided at most grounds in England in mid-1880s that a boundary line be marked all the way round the playing area, and four runs were generally awarded for a hit reaching or crossing this line.

As mentioned before, only four runs were awarded for hits which pitched over the line unless the hit was so colossal that it carried right beyond the limits of the whole ground. This changed in the first decade of the twentieth century and the 'airy boothball' evolved into a six — also called in the past an overboundary and a sixer.

Joe Darling, former captain of Australia and an adventurous left-handed batsman (1657 runs at 28.56 in 34 Tests with three centuries) was quoted by his son D. K. Darling in *Test Tussles: On and Off the Field* (1970):

When I first went to England in 1896, the batsman only received 4 for hitting the ball over the fence, the same score as when it was hit along the ground to the boundary. In Australia the batsman received 5 for hitting the ball over the fence. To obtain 6, both in England and Australia, the ball had to be hit right out of the ground, and on many grounds this was a physical impossibility.

I can remember the first ball I received from Dr W. G. Grace. I hit it over the fence and received only 4. Again I remember hitting a ball from Townsend right over the pavilion at Crystal Palace and the umpire turned to Dr Grace and said, 'Well, Doctor, I suppose that is 6,' and the old man replied, 'No, only 4. The ball has to go right out of the ground for 6.' I asked Grace how much further I had to hit the ball for 6 and he replied, 'About another 100 yards.' These two hits of mine would have gone right out of the Melbourne Cricket Ground and yet I received only 4 for each of them.

In 1899 the Surrey County Cricket Club gave the Australian team a dinner and the President of the Club deplored the fact that the game was becoming very uninteresting as the batsmen would not take any risks and this made the play very slow and tedious to watch. When replying on behalf of the Australian Eleven, I urged that the authorities in England alter the rules to enable a batsman to take risks by giving 6 for every hit over the boundary.

My suggestion led to a lot of discussion with the result that I was asked to write to the Marylebone Cricket Club to agree to the suggestion in Test matches. The English authorities are well known for their conservative ideas and although it was not done in 1899, on my return to Adelaide, I moved at a meeting of the South Australian Cricket Association that the 5 for over the fence be deleted from the rules and 6 substituted in its place.

In moving the motion I pointed out that by allowing a batsman only 5 for a hit over the fence you really penalised him by forcing him to change ends and thus lose the strike. The South Australian Cricket Association was the first cricket body to allow 6 for over the fence and this was adopted by all the other States and England followed suit later on.

This confirms that before World War I there must have been many big hits which earned the batsman only four runs. Brodribb cites the example of Australia's Albert Trott who got only four runs for his famous hit which bounced on the top of the Lord's pavilion in 1899.

Now with most grounds having a boundary line of 75 metres, many sixes hit in the 1996 World Cup in the subcontinent — to give an example — would have counted as only 4 or 5 before 1905, or even have been caught by deep fielders.

B. J. Wakely's research shows that only nine sixes were hit in Tests between Australia and England in 32 years from 1876–77 to 1907–08. (This does not include sixes which included overthrows.) Those nine sixes were hit by six batsmen — all being Australians.

- The only one ever hit in Australia in that period was by Joe Darling in his 178 at Adelaide in 1897–98 when he completed his century with a huge pull to square-leg which went out of the ground.
- Six sixes were hit at Manchester in England, two by Darling in 1902

and one each by Albert 'Tibby' Cotter, Victor Trumper, Vernon Ransford and Albert Hopkins in 1909. 'It was and is rather easier to drive a ball out of the Manchester ground than out of other Test match grounds,' added Wakely.

- One six hit out the Nottingham ground in 1905 by Warwick 'Big Ship' Armstrong and
- One hit by Cotter at Birmingham in 1909 into the Pavilion — Birmingham then being one of the very few grounds where hits out the playing area counted six.

Six-hitting records at Test, first-class and limited-overs levels have been listed in the statistical section but if genuine pre-WW I hitters like George Bonnor, Charles Thornton, Gilbert Jessop and Albert Trott do not figure prominently in it, it was not because of their lack of firepower or their desire to uplift and entertain.

Footnote: In the Super-8 competitions played in Malaysia and Australia in 1996, a hit over the boundary was awarded eight runs and not six.

3

Hellish Delights

To hell with that kind of batting.
— John Jackson

A six zooming into the pavilion can be as much a health hazard as a thrilling spectacle. Kent batsman K. L. Hutchings' mother had come specially to watch him play. When she was comfortably seated at the top of the pavilion at Canterbury, 'a safe enough place at most times' — to quote Gerald Brodribb, an authority on six-hitting — Hutchings struck a huge straight-drive which landed on her fob-watch which was pinned to her dress. The watch was smashed but Mrs Hutchings escaped without a scratch.

Lieutenant Kenneth Hutchings was an outstanding batsman who drove and fielded brilliantly. He played seven Tests for England, the highlight being his century in the thrilling Melbourne Test of February 1908 which England won by one wicket. He was killed in action during World War I in 1916 when 34. The year of his fob-watch-smashing six is not recorded but it is presumed to be in the early 1900s.

Another lucky escape story concerns Warwickshire batsman John Henry Parsons who hit four consecutive sixes against the touring West Indians at Edgbaston in 1928. One of the hits landed in a cup of tea. The cup was shattered but left its handle — nipped off with surgical finesse — in the startled but unhurt owner's fingers. Parsons was ordained in the church the following year and retired from cricket in 1934. But for World War I, he would have represented England in Test matches. He died in 1981, aged 90.

Brodribb narrates two deckchair stories of six-escapism in *Hit for Six*. Just as a batsman or a fielder cannot relax on the field, neither can spectators — especially those lying comfortably on deckchairs. Lancashire's W. E. Phillipson hit a six at Bournemouth, England, in

1946 which landed with a hideous thump on the stomach of a man sleeping near the sightscreen. The dozing and dazed victim was miraculously unhurt but must have suffered psychological trauma.

Frank Woolley was one of England's most graceful left-handed batsmen but he could hit tall sixes to frighten the bravest. One of his powerful aerial drives cut right through the canvas of a deckchair. Fortunately, the deckchair occupier had just left to buy a scorecard. Imagination boggles as to what would have happened if he had been in the chair at that particular moment.

At Parks in 1930, N. M. Ford of Oxford University, while scoring a century, hit a six which landed almost on the toes of a baby sleeping in its pram but did not awaken it. In Worcester in 1953, a New Zealand batsman struck a six which landed in a lunch basket carried by a mother walking alongside a small boy. The ball missed the boy's head by centimetres and broke an empty bottle in the basket.

Not all victims are that lucky. For the touring Australians against Duchess of Norfolk XI at the picturesque Arundel on 7 May 1989, skipper Allan Border hammered a six which hit Mrs Susan Edwards on the face and broke her nose. Visibly upset, Border was out in the same over and rushed to the boundary to express his concern.

Four years later on 10 July 1993, Border was again in six-hitting mode. He hammered 111 runs (eight sixes and 10 fours) in 54 balls against Ireland in a non-first-class match in Dublin. He hit five successive sixes in an over from off-spinner A. R. Dunlop but none of these sixes made contact with a viewer.

Another great Australian, Keith Miller, twice sent spectators to hospitals during Australia's triumphant tour of England in 1948. The young men who were hit returned home safely having tasted possibly their only brush with fame.

As far as six-hitting is concerned, the year 1995 belonged to 20-year-old Queenslander Andrew Symonds. Playing for Gloucestershire against Somerset in August, he set two world records: most sixes in an innings (16) and most in a match (20) at Abergavenny, Somerset. In June that year against Sussex at Hove, his hits struck the same spectator, a woman from Bristol, twice when scoring 83. Having been struck in the face by a four, she returned from treatment only to be hit on the leg by a six. And it was back to the first-aid room for the lady.

In 1957 Sussex batsman D.V. Smith scattered spectators left and right during his whirlwind 166 (nine sixes; six of them over the pavilion) against Gloucestershire at Hove. As the boundary line was only 50 metres from the batting pitch, one can imagine the panic in the crowd. Apart from the sixes, the crisply hit fours also caused concern. One such shot struck a spectator a glancing blow on the side of his face. Soon a blaring ambulance was on the way and paramedics got busy.

Dr W. G. Grace, a kindly man despite his rough exterior, once went through torture thinking that he had badly maimed a child. When staying with a friend at a hospital, he decided to go for a bit of cricket practice. After a while, he hit a ball right out of the hospital grounds into an adjoining street. Rather than waste time looking for the ball, they abandoned the nets and returned to the hospital.

Imagine his anxiety when casualty rang a few minutes later with the news that a child had been hit with a cricket ball and was lying unconscious in a ward. Naturally, he jumped to the conclusion that his hit had caused this mishap. He ran to the ward to attend to the stricken child and found that the injury was serious and the case looked hopeless.

'I felt greatly distressed and felt very miserable,' wrote W.G. later on, 'until someone inquired where the child had met with the accident. It then transpired that the injuries had been inflicted on a cricket ground a mile and half away from the hospital.'

In March 1952, India's great all-rounder Vinoo Mankad (2109 runs and 162 wickets in 44 Tests) was playing in a festival match to celebrate the silver jubilee of Matunga Gymkhana in Bombay. As both the teams included Test players, a big crowd had gathered. Opening the batting, Mankad hit a six which landed on the forehead of a five-year-old. The boy fainted, the crowd went 'ooh' and 'aah' and Mankad rushed to the scene. When he saw the swollen forehead he prayed aloud for the boy's safety and refused to continue batting till a taxi was called and the boy moved to a hospital.

Clive Scott, a Herefordshire batsman, hit a six in December 1993 which knocked his wife Sharon unconscious as she was wheeling their baby on the boundary line. His response was typical of male chauvinistic pigs. 'She cost me a century as I had to go into a shell after this.'

It was a bad day for Walsden's bowler Peter Green in Central Lancashire League. He bowled a 'soft' half volley to Wilson Hartley of

Rochdale. Hartley gave it the treatment it deserved. But this was no ordinary six; it sailed over the crowd, travelled an enormous distance, crossed the nearby Strines Street, smashed an upper window in one of the houses and came to rest on a bed, the bed of bowler Peter Green. But minutes later Green had his revenge. Hartley tried to repeat another window-smasher and was caught on the boundary for 61, according to next day's *Daily Mail Reporter*.

Recalled Hartley, who was making a comeback after a spell in the 2nd XI: 'The first one was an easy one but I hadn't the faintest idea that it would finish up in Peter's bed. We'll be talking about this one for 20 years. The trouble is it couldn't have happened to a nicer fellow. I wish I had done it to one of the other bowlers. I hope we are still friends.'

'I knew I bowled him a bad one but I wish he had stayed in the 2nd XI,' replied Green. The story had a happy ending. The Walsden Club's insurance covered the £2 bill for a new window pane in Green's house.

It is not always the onlookers who get hit by sixes. At times it is the fielders; once even a batsman awaiting his turn to go out to bat. During his innings of 105 on 20 May 1995 at Kingshott School, Hitchin, in England, Dennis Barnard of Marshalswick Baptist Church team hit nine sixes. One of these hit team-mate Colin Martin who was standing in front of the pavilion — all padded and waiting his turn to bat — on the arm. After striking Colin, the ball flew up over the roof of the pavilion.

'It happened so quickly that Colin did not have time to feel the pain of the ball's impact for a minute or so', recalls his captain Bob Little who sent me this story. Although shaken, Colin scored 8 runs and later opened the bowling.

The *Daily Express* (England) reported another hit-and-fly story in its 'Just Fancy That' feature on 26 August 1970. In a league match near Oldham in Lancashire, Moorside batsman Chris Taylor hit a ball at fielder Alan Broadbent of Uppermill. Broadbent ducked and the ball bounced off his head and sailed into the pavilion for six and not the expected four. The extra two runs gave Moorside XI a win. It was just not Broadbent's day.

George Mell narrates a fiery six story in *This Curious Game of Cricket*. It involves Ken Barrington, a dour defensive English batsman, but paradoxically the first one to reach a Test century with a six three times. Once when playing a Sunday game at Reading Cricket Club's ground, he hit a six which landed on the pavilion roof and set fire to it. 'Presumably, there was an electrical fault and the six sparked it off', concluded the *Daily Mail* of 8 August 1964.

What sort of reaction do sixes arouse among bowlers? Glamorgan's Malcolm Nash, who is the first bowler to be hit for six sixes in a six-ball over from the West Indies great Sir Garry Sobers (playing for Nottinghamshire at Swansea in this match in 1968), told me: 'It certainly did not put me off the game. Rather, it put my name in the *Guinness Book of Records* the hard way!'

In a club match in Bombay in 1917, Dossu Bulsara was hit by Faram Pavri for a huge six which cleared the vast Azad Maidan, crossed the main road, touched the wall of the old Municipal Building and rebounded a long way. The batsman was naturally proud of his achievement but not half as much as Bulsara, bragging to one and all that *he* had created a record. 'Would Pavri have hit that shot if I was not bowling?' he asked. The next day he brought along several peons from the Bombay Municipality and had the distance measured.

Not all bowlers take such punishment so well. Jack Milburn, the father of aggressive English Test batsman Colin, was also a ferocious hitter of the ball at club level. Once Jack hit an off-spinner for five sixes in five balls. The bowler was so disgusted that he threw the ball at his feet and refused to complete the over.

John Jackson was a fast bowler in the 1850s. When two of his express deliveries were hit over the rails, he muttered: 'To hell with that kind of batting'.

4

Sixes in Court

When the bleeding was stopt outwardly he bled inwardly,
and when stopt inwardly he bled outwardly.

— Anon (1731)

You are thrilled when Ian Botham, Viv Richards or Andrew Symonds sends a ball flying out of the ground. But would you enjoy a six if it comes crashing in your backyard and hits you on the head when you are enjoying a cuppa or a cold beer, or smashes your glass window, dents your new car or lands in the fish pond, killing your favourite goldfish?

A big hit has sometimes resulted in injuries and property damage. At times it has provided easy money for solicitors and QCs as the six-hit victims have taken the 'offending' clubs to court, with appeals and counter-counter appeals.

In his book *Caught in Court*, John Scott cites examples of six-hitters being sued and fined but mostly acquitted on appealing. An early example of a six flattening out a man occurred on 7 June 1731. Mr Legat, a cooper and dealer in brandy and rum, was passing through a cricket ground in London when struck on the nose by an airborne ball.

'When the bleeding was stopt outwardly he bled inwardly, and when stopt inwardly he bled outwardly,' stated a contemporary press report. He died a month later from loss of blood.

There have been several instances in a first-class match when passers-by have suffered injuries when hit by a whirlwind six. The first chronicled case took place at Harrogate in England on 1 August 1901 when South African all-rounder Jimmy Sinclair hit English spinner Wilfred Rhodes out of the ground. The ball dislodged from his perch a taxi-driver enjoying a free view of the match from the top of his cab. A solicitor's letter was sent but it was ignored and nothing happened.

Scott mentions another such accident, the first one which was followed by legal proceedings. It happened in Scotland in 1908. Arthur Abraham, an elderly man, was playing cricket with three 12-year-olds at Cambuslang near Glasgow on 2 July. In a nearby row of houses, separated by a 1.7 metre high stone wall and by a lane 3.4 metres wide, lived John Ward and his daughter Mary.

Mary was sitting in her backyard that evening when she was struck on the head and badly bruised by a cricket ball hit by one of the four players. She brought an action against Abraham and the boys, claiming damages for the injuries sustained by her.

The case was first heard on 20 August 1909 and on behalf of Miss Ward it was alleged that the greens were not meant for playing cricket and the defenders —especially Abraham — should have known about the grave dangers of a ball hitting someone in the neighbourhood. The defenders pleaded that the Ward's 'averments were irrelevant' and the Sheriff-substitute acquitted them.

Miss Ward appealed and it was heard by the Sheriff of Lanarkshire on 15 November 1909. He also dismissed the case as irrelevant, his reasons being that the three 12-year-olds did not have the foresight to anticipate danger to their neighbours and therefore the case against them was dismissed. However, to acquit Abrahams was more difficult but he did it on the grounds that it was not known who had 'projected the ball which caused the injury'. Feeling exasperated and badly done by, Miss Ward appealed again, this time to the Court of Session two months later, and the court came to practically the same conclusion as the Sheriff.

Many such legal battles initiated by a lusty six have been cited by Scott in his book. To detail or even outline each would be beyond the scope of this slim volume which only claims to inform, amuse and entertain. Besides, I do not have the legal training to give you the finer shades of meaning apart from between 'negligence' (a single act of omission) and 'nuisance' (a continuing state of affairs), nor explain legal jargon like 'assolizing', which I am assured is not a dirty word but only means acquitting.

I will only delve into two fascinating court cases. Cheetham v. Stone (also called Bolton v. Stone) is regarded as perhaps the most discussed cases involving cricket —apart from the Kerry Packer - PBL v. cricket establishment of 1977–78.

On 9 August 1947, Miss Bessie Stone of Beckenham Road, Cheetham, Lancashire, was standing at her garden gate when hit on the head by a ball struck by a batsman on the nearby Cheetham Cricket Ground. The distance from the middle of the ground to where Miss Stone stood was about 90 metres and there was a 2.2 metre (7 foot) fence surrounding the ground. So it had to be a big hit by Denton St Lawrence batsman Leadbetter off the bowling of Cheetham spinner Geoffrey Topham.

Miss Stone sued the Cheetham Cricket Club but did not sue batsman Leadbetter or, except as a part of the team, bowler Topham. At the hearing of the case at Manchester Assizes on 15 December 1948, Mr Justice Oliver ruled in favour of the club who were not held responsible for the injury.

But Miss Stone, in her early fifties, appealed against this. By a decision at the Court of Appeal, the original verdict was reversed by Justices Somervell, Singleton and Jenkins in October 1949 and she was awarded damages of £104 19s. 6d. (which would be currently worth about £1500), as well as costs amounting to £449 (about £6300 in today's money).

The Cheetham Cricket Club did not take this lying down and, after consulting the National Cricket Club Association (NCCA) and the MCC, made an appeal to the House of Lords. This was no ordinary appeal; it was 'we the cricketers v. them' mega-appeal. With much financial backing, the club brought out big guns in the House of Lords, namely Sir Walter Monckton, KC (who had played cricket for Harrow in 1910 and later became president of MCC) and Bill Sime (captain of Nottingham) as its counsel. What a formidable array of legal talent as Henry Nelson, KC led counsel for Miss Stone.

The top-heavy legal eagles thundered at each other in March 1951 and delivered the judgment two months later . The Lordships considered the case 'fairly balanced' and 'borderline' but decided unanimously that the Cheetham Cricket Club had not been negligent. Costs amounting to £2000 were awarded against Bessie Stone.

Outraged by this, she was heard mumbling that if cricketers were real sportsmen, they would themselves pay the costs. In July that year, the NCCA debated the matter and advised the Cheetham Cricket Club not to claim the full cost. 'We regard the case as being conducted on behalf of cricket generally rather than on behalf of the Cheetham club only and so, we feel it is only right that cricket should pay for it,' the chairman of NCCA announced.

A fundraising drive was organised to pay for the costs and MCC guaranteed a three-figure amount. The rest was raised by club cricket all over the country.

Since this Cheetham v. Stone case, every club insures itself against causing damage to person or property. To quote Brodribb in *Hit for Six*, 'All cricketers (and club secretaries) owe a debt of gratitude to the unfortunate Miss Stone for bringing a case which proved not only very interesting but beneficial to the interests of cricket'.

And cricketers, in turn, proved to Miss Stone that they were really sportsmen by paying the costs. As a postscript it may be added that the residents of Beckenham Road now no longer run any risk of being hit by a six as the Cheetham Cricket Club ceased to exist in 1967 and the ground has since been built on.

Another famous court case involving cricketers v. residents occurred in the mid-1970s. The Lintz Cricket Club in Burnopfield, Durham, represented the typical English village green atmosphere. For 70 years the picturesque club ground had echoed to the sound of leather on willow as white flannelled souls whiled away a lazy summer afternoon.

It was all peace and quiet with the possible exception of a moo from the cattle and baah from the sheep till a developer bought the adjoining land from the National Coal Board and built houses on it.

This was when trouble raised it ugly head. Soon a house owner complained in the *Newcastle Evening Chronicle* that a cricket ball had landed in his fish pond and knocked out his goldfish.

A little later John Miller and his wife Brenda, both in their thirties, decided that zooming cricket balls and garden tranquillity cannot coexist. It reached a stage, they claimed, when they were frightened to go outside in case they were hit by a hard ball.

When the Millers bought their house in 1972, the distance between the cricket pitch and their house was about 80 metres and there was a 2-metre concrete fence which did not stop balls from 'invading' their garden. In response to their complaint, Lintz Cricket Club erected a 5-metre chain-like fence at the cost of £700. Still the balls kept coming and the Millers stated that one of them just missed a window of a room where their 12-year-old son was sitting.

The club responded by offering to place unbreakable glass and shutters to the windows and doors at the rear of the house. This offer was rejected and the Millers decided to sue the club, claiming negligence and nuisance because they could not enjoy living in their own property. They sought an injunction to restrain the club from playing cricket.

The case came up before Sir Trevor Reeve at Newcastle upon Tyne Crown Court in October 1976. A number of neighbours of the Millers gave evidence that they had also suffered from balls being hit into their backyards. Their next-door neighbour, Colin Craig, said that a ball had just missed him when he was picking raspberries. In a reserved judgement delivered on 3 December, the judge awarded the Millers £174 14p. damages of which £24 14p was for compensation for repairing the window and the roof.

But that was not all. He also granted the injunction as requested by the Millers. This upset the Lintz Cricket Club no end as it was not possible to erect a higher fence due to the exposed position of the ground. The injunction therefore meant that the club had to look for another ground.

The consequences were serious for other clubs throughout the country —especially for those where recent building plans could create endless legal wrangles. Therefore when Lintz Cricket Club decided to appeal, the NCCA and the Test and County Cricket Board agreed to underwrite the legal costs.

The appeal was heard in the Court of Appeal in April 1977 by Lord Denning; the counsel for the club being Michael Kempster, QC, who six months later headed the cricket establishment's team in the Kerry Packer case. The practical effect of the judgment was a victory for the Lintz Cricket Club.

In his summing up, Lord Denning opened with: 'In summer time, village cricket is the delight of everyone. Nearly every village has its own cricket field where the young men play and the old men watch. I am surprised that the developers of the housing estate were allowed to build the houses as they could for their own profit. The planning authorities ought not to have allowed it.'

After weighing various legal precedents, he decided in favour of the cricket club, saying: 'It is our task to balance the right of the cricket club to continue playing cricket on their own ground, as against the right of the house-holder not to be interfered with. On taking the balance, I would give priority to the right of the cricket club to continue playing cricket on the ground, as they have done it for 70 years. It takes precedence over the right of the newcomer to sit in his garden undisturbed.'

The two other judges, Sir Geoffrey Lane and Lord Justice Cumming-Bruce, did not wholly agree with Lord Dunning but in the final analysis also favoured the club. They lifted the injunction, although the club had to pay about £650 damages to the Millers.

Despite the fact that the club had won the case and were not required to do anything further, the members decided to apply for permission to build a new safety fence 13 metres high at great expense to the club. In fact so high — although rather ungainly — that both cricket-lovers and the Miller family could enjoy the pleasures of their summer afternoons.

I find it intriguing that no such legal battles have been reported in Australia between cricket clubs and householders. I consulted Robert Lord, a cricket-loving QC, on this issue. He wrote back: 'My research, by no means exhaustive, finds no comparable local litigations. I have no doubt the larger size of our grounds in Australia is one reason for this.'

Smashing car windscreens or denting parked cars is another occupational hazard for a batsman with powerful arms, strong shoulders and sweet timing. But on the whole they have been lucky as no-one has taken them to court as far as I know.

At Blackpool in 1958, P. Marner of Lancashire hit seven balls in an innings into a nearby carpark without damaging a single car. W. H. Sutcliffe, the son of the illustrious England opening batsman Herbert Sutcliffe, was delighted when one of his huge drives went zooming out of the ground for a six. Unfortunately, it dented his father's car but the proud dad readily pardoned this 'lapse'.

Trust Brodribb to provide the best car-damage story. Charles Lyttelton (later Lord Cobham) went through mixed emotions during a club match at Canterbury in England. He drove a ball right over the huge concrete stand — a very rare feat. Soon after the ball had vanished over the top, there were horrible sounds of shattered glass. He was highly elated at his achievement, only to discover later that the ball had smashed the windscreen of his own car.

5

Some Enchanted Sixes

Everything that deceives may be said to enchant.

— Plato

Bill Alley was a colourful character, a versatile workhorse, a professional boxer who won all his contests till a cricket ball broke his jaw, a hitter of sixes and one of the most exciting all-rounders not to have played Test cricket.

On a personal note, Alley means much more than runs and wickets. As an 11-year-old I watched spellbound as Alley (206 not out with a six and 20 fours) and Fred Freer (127 with three sixes and 12 fours) put on 343 dizzy runs in Commonwealth team's total of 5 for 587 against the Cricket Club of India at the Brabourne Stadium, Bombay, in January 1950.

Alley's six landed next to my feet which excites me as much now as it excited me then. Born in Sydney on 3 February 1919, Alley first played cricket when 11. He was a left-handed attacking batsman, right arm fast-medium bowler and a wicket-keeper. At 18 he appeared in A grade cricket for Sydney's Northern District; the moment to treasure was his scoring 265 runs (12 sixes, 24 fours) and taking 8 for 27 in one match. NSW kept their eyes open for this talented youngster but World War II intervened.

After the war he performed so well for NSW that he received an offer from Colne in the Lancashire League to play as a professional. He hesitated but Bill O'Reilly persuaded him to take the plunge. While with Colne, Alley toured the Indian subcontinent with the Commonwealth team of 1949–50 under the captaincy of another Australian expatriate Jock Livingston. Alley shone out as a batsman, scoring 1255 runs at 66.05 including two unbeaten double centuries and an unbeaten 168, finishing second only to Frank Worrell.

Alley started his county career (for Somerset) in 1957, when 38, and proved himself not only a worthy all-rounder, 'but a splendid man to have in the dressing room', according to *Wisden 1962*. After scoring 3019 runs at 59.96 in 1961 when 42, he was honoured as one of five Cricketers of the Year by *Wisden*, which wrote: 'Nothing daunts him and he breathes a spirit of confidence among his colleagues'.

A man of many roles, 'Bill the Conqueror' never received any coaching in cricket or boxing. At one stage he was a boxer of renown in Australia, having won all his 28 fights as a professional. He had set his sights on the world welterweight title when a cricket accident forced him to hang up his gloves. His jaw, which few pugilists could touch, was broken by a cricket ball. Twenty stitches were necessary and he never boxed again.

After retiring from first-class cricket, Alley took up umpiring and his Test debut as an umpire was at Birmingham in 1974. Alley was the first Australian-born to officiate in a Test in England since Jim Phillips in 1905.

He was as tense as the cricketers as England's fast-medium Geoff Arnold delivered the first ball to India's Sunil Gavaskar. Gavaskar snicked the ball, Alan Knott caught it behind the stumps and the Indian walked without waiting for an appeal or the umpire's decision.

'This upset Bill Alley', recalled Gavaskar at a recent book launch. 'He buttonholed me at lunch that day and said in his fruity accent: "This was my first f—ing Test, my first effing over, my first effing ball and you left before anyone could appeal and I could lift my effing finger".'

For all his 11 centuries in 1961, his proudest moment was the match against Middlesex at Lord's in 1957 when he opened both the batting and the bowling and also kept wickets — a true all-rounder with the sort of personality which keeps the game alive.

Another remarkable character was England's Ken Barrington. He batted as if his life, and England's Test fortunes, depended on it — and the latter often did. He was stockily built with features of considerable strength, notably a nose and chin which might have been carved from granite. Australian wicket-keeper Wally Grout once remarked that when he saw Barrington walk out to bat, he imagined a Union Jack trailing behind him.

Nicknamed 'Colonel', Barrington possessed a powerful array of shots but used them sparingly. He was like a millionaire who lived a spartan life, suspecting a share-market collapse. In India he was a crowd favourite despite his dour batting; he was both a clown ('shooting' barrackers with his cocked-up bat) and a hero. A run-machine, his Test average of 58.67 in 82 Tests was second only to Herbert Sutcliffe's 60.73 among Englishmen.

Despite his accent on defence he reached a Test century with a six *three times* — the first one to do so. In 1962–63 against Australia in the Adelaide Test, he became the fifth batsman to reach a Test ton with a six (see Appendix). Not quite satisfied, Barrington repeated this in the Melbourne Test against Australia in 1965–66 and against the West Indies in the Port-of-Spain Test of 1967–68.

His sudden death from a heart attack in the West Indies (when he was the assistant manager and coach of England) during the Barbados Test of 1981 at the age of 50 was mourned throughout the cricket world. He was more than a great batsman, he was a friend of cricket.

India's Vijay Hazare was another batsman noted more for his reliability than for six-hitting sprees. Yet he is remembered for a unique six. A man of few words, he came to India's rescue time and again. He was lying on the massage table to get rid of a spasm during the Leeds Test of 1952 when told that India had lost four wickets with no runs on the board. He leapt from the table, quickly donned the pads and went out to subdue debutant English fast-bowler Fred Trueman on a rampage and saved India from humiliation — although the Test was lost.

Previously, against Australia's super-quicks Ray Lindwall and Keith Miller, Hazare hit centuries in both innings of the 1948 Adelaide Test. He holds two world records, being associated in the highest partnership for any wicket (577 for Baroda v. Holkar with Gul Mahomed at Baroda in 1946–47) and scoring the maximum percentage of runs out of the team's total (309 out of 387; 79.84%).

The latter was a memorable match, between the Rest and the Hindus in the Bombay Pentangular final of 1943. The Hindus included 10 Test cricketers whereas the Rest (or Christians) had only one player of renown, Vijay Hazare. The Hindus declared at 5 for 581 (Hazare 3-119 in 52 overs). The Rest were asked to follow-on after totalling 133 (Hazare 59).

Trailing by 448 runs, Rest lost 5 for 62, when Vivek Hazare joined his elder and distinguished brother Vijay. The partnership between the Hazare brothers will rank as among the most heroic in the annals of cricket. They added 300 runs for the sixth wicket, cheered to the echo by 40,000 spectators thronging Bombay's Brabourne Stadium.

Younger brother Vivek's contribution was only 21 but the elder Vijay reached a magnificent triple century. He went from 295 to 301 with a tremendous six which landed on the sightscreen at the Churchgate end. He was the last man out, having batted 410 minutes, belting 31 fours and that one glorious six.

The Rest still lost by an innings, but what an effort by the asbestos man and crisis-specialist Vijay Hazare; 3 wickets out of 5 (60%), 59 runs out of 133 (44.4%) in the first innings and 309 runs out of 387 (79.8%) in the second. 'In future people will talk in terms of Vijay Hazare as they have done in the past in terms of Sir Donald Bradman', said Vijay Merchant, the captain of the Hindus and Hazare's contemporary in Test cricket.

Hazare's only six in a Test match came off a no-ball from Alec Bedser in the Manchester Test of 1946.

Australia's captain Jack Ryder, for Victoria against NSW in the Sheffield Shield match of 1926–27 in Melbourne, also tried to go from 295 to 300 with a six but holed out to Alan Kippax off Tommy Andrews.

This was the run-rich match in which Victoria amassed 1107 runs — still a world record. After openers Bill Woodfull (133) and Bill Ponsford (352) put on 375 runs, 'Stork' Hendry (100) and Ryder went merrily along. Ryder hit six sixes, the record for a first-class innings on the MCG. When 275, he hit Tommy Andrews for 4, 6, 4, 6 before attempting to bring up his triple hundred with a six, but was caught at mid-on.

English legend Wally Hammond was one of the greatest batsmen of all time. A contemporary of Ponsford and Bradman, he was more stylish than either. He was one of the most elegant batsmen ever to take field, a classical off-side player who did not know how to play an ugly stroke. To quote Sir Neville Cardus, 'He drove almost nonchalantly. The swift velocity of his late cuts seemed an optical illusion. The wrists were supple as a fencer's steel.'

To describe him as a six symbol would be a sacrilege; so smooth was his strokeplay that he glided the ball where he wanted it to go. No jumping out, no brute strength; just perfect timing from a genius. Yet he holds a Test record in six-hitting. His 10 sixes in the Auckland Test of 1932–33 still stand as a record.

This was the second Test of the series, and Hammond had scored 227 in the first Test at Christchurch. But this seemed only a warm-up, as he notched up an unbeaten 336 at Eden Park in Auckland four days later. 'He played the most spectacular innings seen in Test cricket to that date, Jessop and Bradman not excluded,' according to his biographer Derek Lodge. Hammond's hundred came up in 135 minutes and then he accelerated. His third 50 took only 38 minutes and after reaching 200 he went completely 'bonkers' and went on to 336 in another hour. His 300 took 288 minutes which remains the fastest Test triple century. His third hundred took only 47 minutes.

He gave only one chance, which injured the hand of fielder Eric Dempster who was forced off the field. Besides 10 sixes, he hit 34 fours. At one stage he struck medium-paced left-handed Jack Newman for three sixes in a row. He had broken Bradman's Test record and only 492 runs came while he was in, 68 percent of them scored by the Master. Besides, he had a series average of 563.00.

Hammond was the first batsman to have ended a Test with a six *twice*. The first time was in the Sydney Test during the Bodyline series as England beat Australia by eight wickets on 28 February 1933, achieved by the Hammond six. A fortnight earlier, team-mate Eddie Paynter had become the first batsman to win a Test with a sixer. This was in the fourth Test at Brisbane and the victory enabled England to regain the Ashes. Paynter had won over many hearts when he left a hospital bed to score a gritty 83 to save England in the first innings.

The second time Hammond won a Test for England with a six was against the West Indies at Bridgetown on 10 January 1935. This was the remarkable low-scoring match on a treacherous sticky wicket which produced a match aggregate of only 309 runs, Hammond scoring 72 (43 and 29 not out) of those, about 24 percent of the match aggregate — sign of a genius. England declared at 7 for 81, 21 runs behind the Windies who in their turn declared at 6 for 51, setting England 73 to win. The English lost six wickets but Hammond, unbeaten on 29, saw them through — climaxing with an epic six.

Hammond's record of 10 sixes in a Test innings looked secure until New Zealander Chris Cairns came close in January 1996 on the same ground. In the second Test at Eden Park, Auckland against Zimbabwe, Chris smote nine sixes in his 120 off 96 balls. The run charts of Hammond and Chris Cairns are shown next page. One six from leg-spinner Paul Strang lifted over the covers onto the roof of the stands, was memorable. His first 50 came in 58 minutes (49 balls) and his second in only 48 (37 balls).

Chris' father, Lance Cairns, was also a big hitter. Although primarily a medium-pace bowler, Lance was massively built and could hit the ball to vast distances with a blacksmith's might and relish. In 1979 - 80 he hit a century in 52 minutes off 45 balls for Otago against Wellington — the fastest ever in New Zealand.

The most ecstatic moment in Lance Cairns' career has been hitting Dennis Lillee for amazing sixes in a Benson & Hedges final on the Melbourne Cricket Ground on 13 February 1983. The New Zealanders were in deep trouble, 6 for 44 against Australia's 302 and Lillee was on the kill — cheered on lustily by a crowd of 71,393. Cairns was greeted by Lillee with a bouncer that hit him on the head. Commentating on Channel 9, Bill Lawry squeaked: 'Cairns' head must be going ding-dong, ding-dong inside that helmet'.

When the 'ding-dong' stopped, cavalier Cairns hit Ken Macleay for two sixes in the next over. Not quite satisfied, he smashed Lillee over wide mid-off for a big six.

'That was okay,' recalls Cairns in his autobiography *Give it a Heave, Lance Cairns*, 'but two balls later he fired another right at my toes. I tried to jump out of the way and I sort of swung my bat one-handed. The ball just took off. I couldn't believe it. Greg Chappell was on the fine-leg boundary and he was racing in. Then all of a sudden he stood and stared at the ball. It went miles over his head. He couldn't believe it either!' It was an enchanted six, no ifs, no buts.

At the other end Macleay was replaced by Rodney Hogg and Cairns lanced his first ball over his head for a six and repeated the dose two balls later. He reached his fifty in 21 balls with six sixes before being caught by a deceptively slow ball by Geoff Lawson.

One of the most extrovertly happy sixes was hit by Australia's all-rounder Greg Matthews. Australia was in all sorts of trouble in the

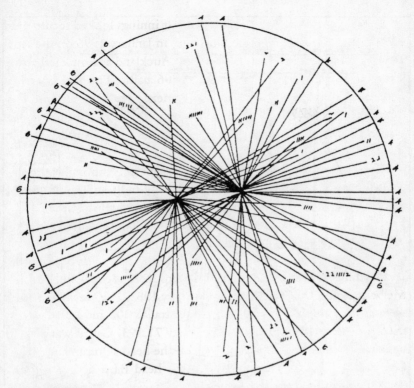

Wally Hammond's 336 not out for England v. New Zealand at Auckland in 1932-33 included 34 fours and 10 sixes — eight of them on the off-side. Scorer W. Ferguson made this chart of his strokes. (W. Ferguson)

Brisbane Test of November 1985, trailing New Zealand by 374 runs in the first innings. They were in a hopeless position at 5 for 67 in the second innings when Matthews joined skipper Allan Border. Both hit centuries, Matthews bringing up his in classic style with a sweep shot over mid-wicket for six from the bowling of spinner Vaughan Brown.

As soon as the ball disappeared over the fence, Matthews raised his bat in exultation, punched air and ran 30 metres towards the stand, waving to his girlfriend (now wife) Jillian. He then traced the letter M (for his mother) and after jumping his way back to the crease he slapped hands with Border and kissed the Australian coat of arms on his cap. It was a moment to cherish for the gregarious Greg Matthews.

Australia's Dean Jones was another quicksilver hitter of the ball whose one shot made a big difference in the fortunes of Australian cricket. It

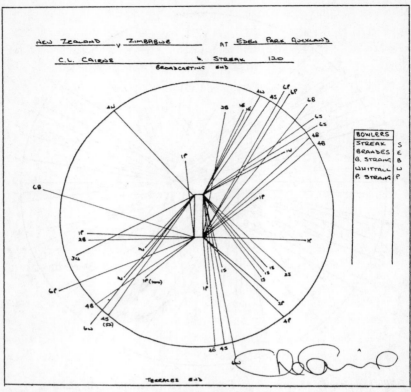

Chris Cairns of New Zealand hit nine sixes in his maiden Test century (120 runs) v. Zimbabwe at Auckland in January 1996 (Run chart courtesy *Boundary* New Zealand)

was in the Reliance World Cup match against India at Madras on 9 October 1987.

One of his two sixes had been signalled as four. But between innings, India's captain Kapil Dev showed sportsmanship of the highest order by concurring with the Australians that the ball had cleared the boundary. (There were no on-boundary cameras then, nor was there a third umpire.) Thus Australia's total of 6 for 268 was adjusted to 6 for 270. It made a crucial difference as India was all out for 269 and lost by *one* run.

Till then Australia was a diffident side but this narrow victory galvanised them and they went on to win the World Cup, beating England by 7 runs in the final at Calcutta, cheered on by a crowd of over 90,000.

Steve Waugh was the man most responsible for the one-run victory over India in Madras. In the final over, India needed only six runs to win but 'Ice-Man' Steve restricted them to four runs and sent Maninder Singh's off-stump flying. On the contrary, the Benson & Hedges World Series Cup match against Pakistan at Hobart was depressing for Steve. Pakistan needed a six off the final ball to tie the match. Amazingly, left-handed batsman Asif Mujtaba, already 50 not out, hit Steve's last delivery, a slower ball, over the mid-wicket boundary to force a tie.

Another Pakistani to hit the final ball of a limited-overs international for a six was the majestic stroke-player Javed Miandad. In the final of the first Austral-Asia Cup at Sharjah on 18 April 1986, Pakistan needed four runs off the last ball. Cheekily, Miandad hit India's Chetan Sharma for a six to ensure a win. Miandad's Man of the Match performance of 116 included three sixes. He was rewarded very handsomely for his last-ball six which enabled Pakistan to beat arch-rivals India. According to a source, he took home 18 big packages of gifts — duty free.

It was in fact the fear of a six off the last ball which was the reason for the notorious underarm incident of the third final of the Benson & Hedges World Series Cricket match between Australia and New Zealand in Melbourne on 1 February 1981. New Zealand had won the first final and Australia the second, with three matches to go in a best-of-five series.

When New Zealand needed six runs to tie the match off the last ball, Australia's captain Greg Chappell instructed his brother Trevor to bowl an underarm grubber to New Zealand tailender Brian McKechnie. This caused a mega-furore in the Australian-New Zealand relations and is still not quite diffused. The incident will be forgiven one day. But forgotten? I doubt it!

McKechnie blocked the grubber and threw away his bat in disgust as Kiwi captain Geoff Howarth ran on to the field to protest because he mistakenly believed underarm bowling to be illegal in Australia. It was not then for one-dayers, but is now certainly illegal. Greg Chappell later said, 'I regret the decision which was made in the heat of the moment. It is something I would not do again.' He claimed he was mentally exhausted and wanted to leave the field after 40 overs but Rodney Marsh insisted he should not. Marsh also pleaded with Greg not to instruct Trevor to bowl underarm.

Greg was chastised by just about everyone, including the Australian Cricket Board chairman Phil Ridings, Sir Donald Bradman, elder brother Ian, Australian Prime Minister Malcolm Fraser and New Zealand Prime Minister Robert Muldoon who called the underarm 'an act of cowardice appropriate to a team playing in yellow'.

It was the biggest stir in public opinion since the Bodyline series of 1932–33 and the Packer breakaway in 1977. And all this to block an unlikely six by a no. 10 bat not known for his hitting potential.

One of the most heroic matches in the annals of Test cricket was played between South Africa and New Zealand at Ellis Park. Johannesburg, on Boxing Day 1953. The Kiwis in the end lost by 132 runs but showed courage in mega-doses. The stylish left-hander Bert Sutcliffe and all-rounder Lawrie Miller retired hurt before scoring — struck on the head and chest by balls from Neil Adcock, the 6 foot 3 inch Transvaal terror bowling on a green top — and were taken to hospital. Both bravely resumed their innings.

When Sutcliffe was hit the crack was heard all around the ground like a gunshot. A crowd of 22,000 watched in horror as a stretcher came to lift him; many thought he was dead. He fainted on the way to the hospital, his busted left ear bleeding profusely. After receiving treatment he insisted on returning to the match and went in to bat with New Zealand on their knees at 6 for 82 in reply to the opponents' 271. He played like a champion to hit seven sixes and four fours in his unbeaten 80 out of 105 in 112 minutes. His second six saved the follow-on which at one stage had seemed inevitable.

But the real hero of this dramatic Test was fast bowler Bob Blair. A day previously (on the Christmas day) he had heard about the death of his fiancée, Nerissa Anne Love, 19, in a train crash in New Zealand. So heart-broken was he that nobody expected him to play in the Test but, inspired by Sutcliffe's gallantry, he came out to bat. The crowd gave him a standing ovation, his team-mates cried unashamedly and Sutcliffe hugged him on the pitch. It was a moving moment. Wiping tears every ball he faced, the valiant Blair helped Sutcliffe to add 33 runs in 10 minutes. World-class off-spinner Hugh Tayfield was hit for 6, 6, 0, 6, 1 by the rampaging Sutcliffe. Then Blair got into the act by lifting a six himself as 25 runs were plundered in an eight-ball over.

The circumstances under which Sutcliffe and Blair batted made these sixes the most sensational and enchanting ever. 'This was indeed triumph from tragedy, a great and glorious victory over misfortune and despair,' wrote New Zealand author Dick Brittenden in *Great Days in New Zealand Cricket*. Johannesburg writerVivian Granger described Sutcliffe's innings as 'the greatest 80 ever made in Test cricket'. Added Ray Robinson in *Green Sprigs*:'Until Sutcliffe played it, such an innings did not exist outside schoolboys' dreams'.

6

A Jackpot of Sixes

Not even a cricketing gun-layer from the garrison artillery could achieve
such pinpoint accuracy with a shot requiring such a whole-hearted heave.
— Ray Robinson

These contrasting criteria were met by Steve Waugh during the
Mercantile Mutual Cup match at the West Australian Cricket Association
(WACA) ground in Perth on 22 October 1995. Unfortunately Ray
Robinson, the most entertaining of all cricket-writers, and a friend of
cricketers in five continents, did not live to see this six; he passed away
thirteen years ago. I am sure he would have borrowed a tape from
somewhere and measured the length and height of the hit pronto; not
forgetting to work out the mathematical probability of it happening
again.

That Steve Waugh is so far the only batsman to hit a Mercantile
Mutual Cup sign in the four-year history (involving over 70 matches)
of this popular one-day national competition would suggest how difficult
it is to combine power with pinpoint accuracy. Batting for NSW against
Western Australia, he unleashed a thundering straight drive from the
bowling of tall medium-pacer Tom Moody and hit the sign hanging
from the left-hand side of the sightscreen. The distance from the pitch
to the sign was 80 metres, according to Charles Bull, the WACA
honorary statistician.

Normally, Steve Waugh shows little emotion on the field; his
expression seldom changes — whether it is a double century against
the West Indies or a duck against the Indians; whether he takes a blinder
at gully or drops a sitter (very rarely) at point. No wonder his team-
mates call him 'Ice-Man'.

But after hitting the Mercantile Mutual Cup sign, he lifted his hand
in ecstasy and, for once, smiled visibly because he knew he had won

the $140,000 jackpot. His colleagues were equally jubilant when Steve announced after the match that he would be keeping the jackpot in the team kitty. (He also donated a portion to the Children's Hospital in Sydney.) Later that evening a happy Steve said, 'They [the NSW teammates] are all being nice to me in there now. I don't expect to be buying another beer for the rest of my career while I'm playing with NSW.'

The prize reverted to $10,000 for the next match between Queensland and South Australia in Brisbane. At the time of writing (September 1996) the amount has jackpotted to $100,000 and will further jackpot by $10,000 per game until it reaches $250,000 when it will be locked in until claimed again.

Mercantile Mutual has also increased spectator involvement in Australian domestic cricket by offering $100 instant cash to anyone in the crowd catching a six during a Mercantile Mutual Cup match. So far over 20 watchers have been lucky to have been in the right place at the right time to catch those sixes; a majority of these catches have been snapped up by alert spectators outside the small and picturesque North Sydney Oval.

Many happy faces as a spot-on six by Steve Waugh (in centre) brings in a big cheque of $140,000 in the Mercantile Mutual Cup match at Perth in October 1995. (Newsline /Tony McDonough)

Although Mercantile Mutual is currently the only sponsor offering prizes for six-hitting it is not the first to offer such incentives. Such inducements started on a small scale — mostly by well-off cricket-lovers. In 1945 an enthusiast in England offered an annual prize to a batsman who hit the most sixes in a season but nothing came of it. Probably, the conservative and war-ravaged Englishmen considered it as a cheap and unseemly effort to encourage fireworks. They had perhaps seen too many real fireworks during the war.

When the Australians toured England in 1953, a syndicate of firms offered a prize of £624 to anyone who could lift a ball across the river Thames, which runs past the East Molesey ground, and land it on Tagg's Island, a carry of 120 metres. This was a feat which had never been achieved before. Keith Miller, one of the greatest hitters in the history of the game, took up the challenge and came very close off the bowling of George Tribe, an expatriate Australian playing for Northamptonshire. Away went the ball in the air but influenced adversely by the chilly wind, it fell a few feet short of Tagg's Island.

In 1956, cases of Australian champagne were offered by a local enthusiast at Southerland, Essex, to anyone hitting a ball into a lake situated about 90 metres from the pitch. According to George Mell in *This Curious Game of Cricket*, the feat was achieved once by Gerry German, the Essex bowler. He celebrated his debut as no. 11 batsman by hitting the well-known Surrey and English off-spinner Jim Laker for six into the water.

The Melbourne Cricket Club offered $2000 to a batsman who could strike the pavilion clock at the Melbourne Cricket Ground during an Ashes Test in 1970–71. The *Daily Telegraph* (Sydney) offered a ten times higher award to anyone striking the Sydney Cricket Ground clock in the same Test series. Many batsmen had a go but none could strike the targets.

There could have been more such inducements for batsmen to jump out and hit a clock or a tower but the first corporate sponsoring of six-hitting was introduced in England as recently as 1986. Inspired perhaps by Ian Botham hitting headlines with 80 sixes in the 1985 English season (14 more than the previous record of English six symbol Arthur Wellard's 66 sixes in 1935), a computer equipment company, Basic-Six Ltd., based in the heart of England, backed a new inducement for bright cricket. It was called the Basic-Six 6-Hit Awards and was monitored by the prestigious English cricket magazine *Wisden Cricket Monthly* during the cricket season.

Prize money and a trophy were annually awarded on the following basis:

- For each six hit, from 20th onwards, a batsman received £10 (including for the previous 19 sixes; ie., no prize up to 19, but 20 brought him £200; 21 £210 and so on).

- The batsman with the highest total of sixes received a winner's bonus of £500 plus an elegant Basic Six-Hit Trophy at a gala presentation dinner at the end of the season in September. Based on the previous summer's statistics, Botham with his 80 sixes would have earned £1300 (£800 plus £500 bonus) and the trophy; Viv Richards £490 for his 49 sixes and Roger Harper £320 for his 32 sixes.

- If more than one batsman topped the table (as it happened in the inaugural year, 1986, when Botham and Richards hit 34 sixes each), the one with most sixes in an innings was the winner.

- Only sixes hit in the English County Championship, MCC, tourists' first-class and Test matches were considered for these awards.

Gerald Brodribb was the statistical coordinator.

Basic-Six sponsored these awards from 1986 to 1988 and from 1989 to 1991 it was sponsored by National Power, an electricity generating company. The list of winners in these six years are presented below:

YEAR	WINNER		RUNNER-UP	
	Name	No. of 6s	Name	No. of 6s
1986	Ian Botham (Somerset)	34	Vivian Richards (Somerset)	34
1987	Matthew Maynard (Glamorgan)	30	Ravi Shastri (Glamorgan)	22
1988	Graham Hick (Worcestershire)	40	Matthew Maynard (Glamorgan)	17
1989	Graham Hick (Worcestershire)	29	Ravi Shastri (Glamorgan)	24
1990	Vivian Richards (Glamorgan)	40	Neil Fairbrother (Lancashire)	30
1991	Carl Hooper (West Indies)	28	Matthew Maynard (Glamorgan)	27
			Tom Moody (Worcestershire)	27

Note: Although Botham and Richards — what a pair! — hit the same number of sixes, Botham's nine sixes in his whirlwind century against Lancashire gave him the edge, the £500 bonus and the trophy.

Hick was the only one to win the trophy twice, in 1988 and 1989 although the sponsorship had changed hands. In 1988 he hit 11 sixes in his astonishing innings of 405 not out against Somerset at Taunton.

Maynard's name appears three times in the honoured list, once as a champion and twice as a runner-up.

In 1988, the sponsors increased the bonus to £100,000 to anyone who hit 100 sixes in a season. And in 1989 the inducement for hitting 50 sixes in a season was a £10,000 bonus. But no-one approached this number. If only Botham had been a few years younger! Australia's Dean Jones seemed on his way during the tour of England in 1989 when he slammed 12 sixes in his majestic innings of 248 against Warwickshire. But he could manage only eight more sixes on the tour and finished third best after Hick and Shastri.

Unfortunately, the six-hitting sponsorship ceased in England at the start of the 1992 season. Had it continued, Queenslander Andrew Symonds, playing for Gloucestershire, would have been a run-away winner in 1995. He hit 48 sixes that English summer (including a world record 20 sixes in one match) which is the highest in a season since 1985.

In the six-year period of the awards, 4666 sixes were hit in county matches, reports Brodribb. The runs scored with sixes amounted to only 2.93 percent of the total number of runs scored — despite use of heavy bats and often shorter boundaries.

Oddly, not a single six record was created in the sponsorship period, Botham's record number of sixes, 80, preceded it by a year and Symond's six-sprees came four years after the awards ceased. Perhaps batsmen tried too hard and chanced their arm before their eye was in.

The history of Australia's domestic limited-overs competition is quite colourful, with different sponsors Gillette, McDonalds, FAI (an insurance company) and finally Mercantile Mutual — an insurance company on the rise. Mercantile Mutual took over from FAI in the 1992–93 season and has introduced many innovations, including wearing of shorts by the fielding team in 1994 and the presence of cheer squads, live bands, live commentary and the playing of a batsman's favourite song as he approached the middle in 1995. These were introduced to make the game brighter and more accessible to the public. It introduced the game to non-cricket lovers, which is to be applauded. Mercantile

Dean Jones hits out during a Mercantile Mutual Cup match for Victoria. (Mercantile Mutual)

Mutual launched the 1995–96 season with a six-hitting shoot out which was won by NSW batsman Richard Chee Quee.

The most popular innovation by Mercantile Mutual Cup has been the Hit The Sign competition introduced in their inaugural 1992–93 season. A cash reward of $10,000 which jackpotted by that amount as the tournament progressed until it reached $170,000 for the final was offered to a batsman who could drive a ball and hit on the full one of the four 6 by 4 foot (1.83 by 1.22 metre) signs. These signs were mounted atop the sightscreens (on left and right) at each end and prominently bore the sponsor's logo.

As hitting the signs became elusive, the sponsors increased their number from four to eight, the additional signs kept at mid-wicket regions at either end. 'Signs are strategically placed, consideration being given to spectators whose view should not be blocked by the signs,' explained Geoff Prenter, Mercantile Mutual's sponsorship manager.

Many batsmen came ooh so close, but the prize remained unclaimed for the first three seasons. Then on 22 October 1995, a batsman got lucky. 'Ice-Man' Steve Waugh thawed out the untouchability layer of the Mercantile Mutual sign and the commentators, spectators and media went berserk, with a colour pic of Waugh lifting his right hand in glee appearing on the front page of *The West Australian* and Sydney's *Daily Telegraph Mirror*.

'We are trying to introduce further incentives for players to hit more sixes and score faster,' Prenter said. 'We are proposing to the Australian Cricket Board to increase the value of six from six to ten runs if hit in the first 15 overs in our limited-overs competition. The idea originated from former South Australian and Test star David Hookes — a big hitter himself.'

Looking at my stunned expression, Prenter quipped, 'After all, when an umpire signals a six, he raises ten outstretched fingers above his head, not six!'

What a revolutionary idea! If introduced at first-class level, it may rock not only cricket foundations but the English language as well. What will happen to phrases like 'he hit me for a six'? And the title of this book may have to change from a provocatively quirky *Six Appeal* to a Cecil de Mille-ish *Ten Tall Commandments*!

Joke aside, revaluing the worth of a six from six to ten has some merit. A batsman today may well ask himself: Is it worth taking so much risk to sky a ball for a six (which is a glorified catch) and get only two more runs than a 'capital guaranteed' four? As the great West Indies batsman Everton Weekes advised a youthful Mushtaq Mohammad of Pakistan in 1960s: 'Two sixes or three fours give you the same number of runs, twelve, but a six can get you out much sooner'.

However, to get six more runs than a four may be worth the risk, as you get 150 percent higher yield than just the 50 percent you currently receive.

'We are also hoping to introduce a bonus point for a team that scores 90 runs in its first 15 overs,' Prenter added. 'This would encourage big hitting, probably more sixes and subsequently more excitement for the spectators live or on TV.'

Now for the innovation of the millennium. A single six (with laser-point accuracy) would make a batsman an instant millionaire. Prenter explained: 'For the year 2000, one of our signs will have a hole in the middle and a batsman putting the ball through that hole will receive a million dollars.'

Give me ten!

7

Calling all Sloggers

Batsmen come and batsmen go but those who linger in the memory are more likely to be those who spice elegant shot-making with occasional belts right out of the ground.

— Jack Pollard

Jack Pollard, the prolific Australian sports writer, must have meant batsmen like Victor Trumper, Frank Woolley, Wally Hammond, Vivian Richards, Brian Lara, Mark Waugh and Sachin Tendulkar. Not exactly six symbols, they could, when situation demanded it or mood prevailed, turn into elegant six-hitters.

One associates slogging with tail-enders whose one shot is jumping out, head held high, eyes closed, and swinging their bat in a mad round whirl. It is not always so. For sloggers to succeed even once in every five goes, they would require a keen eye, some sort of footwork and the confidence of a high-flyer. Both the technique and eye players have hit some enormous hits over the years.

It will never be possible to know for sure which single hit has sent a cricket ball the greatest distance. Readers are urged to peruse Gerald Brodribb's *Hit for Six* (1960) in which he has taken pains to confirm the authenticity of distance travelled by each six hit, to filter out 'legend' and approximations. He has details of some 15 measured hits of over 150 yards (137 metres) made before 1960.

By general consensus, the longest of these hits is still the one the Rev. Walter H. Fellows of Oxford XI hit when practising on the Christ Church Ground, Oxford, in 1856. It was measured as 175 yards (160 metres) from hit to pitch, although Brodbribb is not convinced about this distance.

England's mighty hitter Charles Thornton once approached it with a drive of over 168 yards (153 metres) at Hove, Sussex, a few years later.

The massive Somerset batsman W. H. Fowler made hits exceeding 150 yards (136 metres) twice within a month in important matches in 1882; a feat without parallel. One of them was off W. G. Grace and the other was clean out of the ground at Lord's.

One of the most famous hits at Lord's was Aussie-Anglo Albert Trott's immortal smite off Australia's 'Monty' Noble in 1899. It landed on the reverse slope of the roof protecting the topmost tier of the pavilion. It then bounced away to end up in the gardener's house situated behind the pavilion. Ironically, according to the rules before 1910, this was considered a four and not a six because it did not clear the roof.

Frank T. Mann, the burly and delightful Middlesex captain, approached this feat in a county match in 1921 when he clouted two consecutive balls onto the pavilion roof. Well-known and well-loved Test batsmen 'Patsy' Hendren of Middlesex and New Zealander Martin Donnelly, when representing Middlesex, were among others to have reached the roof.

Sponsors have used tall sixes to promote their own products. In the 1970–71 Ashes series prizes were offered to batsmen as an incentive to hit historic clocks. As mentioned previously the Melbourne Cricket Club offered $2000 to a batsman to hit the pavilion clock during a Test. To top this, Sydney's *Daily Telegraph* dangled a $20,000 carrot for a batsman to strike the pavilion clock at the Sydney Cricket Ground.

Till today these clocks remain untouched, challenging all-comers to come close — ticking along regardless. 'If only they could speak, they would scoff at reports that the Melbourne pavilion clock was broken by man-mountain George Bonnor in 1880 and by 21 stone [133 kilograms] Warwick Armstrong,' wrote Ray Robinson, the endearing Australian cricket author with a nice turn of the phrase.

Historians have discredited both the above hits as myths. The myth concerning Armstrong originated when two enormous drives by him off English spinner Len Braund flew in the direction of the clock in the old pavilion but did not reach it. Tom Goodman, a former cricket correspondent of the *Sydney Morning Herald*, humorously said that the SCG clock has certainly been hit once — but only by lightning during a storm!

A few old-timers in Sydney say that they remember the sound of breaking glass when the West Indies all-rounder Learie Constantine (later Lord Constantine) clobbered a ball onto the SCG clock in 1930. The truth, according to Pollard, is that the clock has never been covered by glass.

Are these historic clocks covered by insurance? Warren Saunders, former NSW captain and an insurance broker, informed Robinson: 'It is not the kind of thing Australian insurance companies have covered. I'll have to ask Lloyd's of London.'

If no batsman has hit these clocks yet, many have come close. Alan Davidson, the great Australian all-rounder, smacked a hip-high full toss from England's part-time spinner (and magnificent batsman) Colin Cowdrey for NSW v. MCC on the SCG in 1955. Pulled by Davidson, the ball soared high and higher when intercepted by the roof of the Brewongle Stand. An ecstatic Robinson borrowed a tape from curator Athol Watkins and measured the distance as 113 yards (103 metres) from the wicket and 40 feet (12 metres) above the outfield.

'Davo' remembers this famous six 41 years later with nostalgia. 'It was quite funny, Colin Cowdrey shouted "catch it!" to Tom Graveny fielding on the leg side boundary,' he told me. 'Tom just put his hands up in exasperation and laughed as the ball gained altitude on its way.'

Philip Derriman describes the Davo hit in 3-D effect in his book on SCG, *The Grand Old Ground*: 'It was the last over of the game ... Cowdrey sent down a full toss, which Davidson swung into and swung high over wide mid-on towards the old Brewongle Stand. For a few moments, after the ball reached its zenith and began to fall, it seemed as if it would clear the grandstand and land in the street outside. But it dropped quickly, hit the roof of the stand just below the ridge and dropped back on the concrete concourse below.'

Personally, Davidson does not consider this as his most satisfying six; hit as it was off a part-time bowler at the end of a 'dead' match. 'My most satisfying six was off David Allen, the English off-spinner in the fluctuating Manchester Test of 1961. When adding 98 runs for the last wicket with "Garth" McKenzie, I hit 20 runs (6, 0, 4, 0, 4, 6) in one over from David. The six off the last ball was the best shot I played in my career. Everything was perfect, my timing was spot-on, even if I say so myself. It sailed over the fence, over the spectators, over the stand and hit a wall. But for the wall, it would have ended in the railway yard.'

Before this onslaught Allen had bowled 37 overs, 25 of them maidens, and taken 4 for 38. Australia, trailing by 177 runs on the first innings went on to win the Test by 54 runs — an amazing turnabout brought about by Davidson's bold hitting and captain Richie Benaud's deadly leg-spin.

Memory of Davidson's mighty clout on the SCG was revived on 14 December 1964, when Pakistan's tall fast bowler Farooq Hamid gave his all, as a no. 11 batsman. His whole-hearted wallop landed on the roof of the two-deck Ladies' Stand. Derriman reckons that with little extra wind assistance it might have well carried over the top. Robinson wrote tongue-in-cheek that the clang startled some of the ladies knitting and nattering under the roof.

Goodman described the shot in the next day's paper as a 'ferocious swing' over mid-wicket. Oddly, Farooq hit this shot off left-arm wrist-spinner Johnny Martin, himself a master six-hitter. 'At first I thought it was going right over the stand. It was showing no sign of dropping when it smacked into the roof a few feet from the top,' reminisced Martin. He dismissed Farooq next ball, caught by Peter Philpott for 19.

According to Robinson's tape-measure, Farooq's lash travelled 10 metres less than Davidson's but struck another stand at a point about 14 feet (4.3 metres) higher; that is, a total of 16.3 metres above ground level. 'In the trigonometry of sixes, would Pythagoras hold that altitude counts as much or more than ground distance covered,' Robinson pondered.

Against the indignity suffered at Farooq's hands, Martin (nicknamed 'Fav' because he was everybody's favourite) hit nearly 300 sixes himself in all grades of cricket. His most spectacular was off Western Australia's change bowler John Rutherford to the roof of a single-deck stand against a wall that divided the Hill area (alas, no more) of the SCG from the Showground. It had a carry of 100 metres from midfield to a point about 9.5 metres above the outfield. 'Another three feet,' Martin added with relish, 'and it would have gone right over.'

There have been other classic six-hits on the SCG, starting from last century. Arthur Gregory who watched, played and reported major cricket matches since 1870s, wrote in 1890 that the biggest hit he ever saw at the SCG was by Charles Bannerman, the first batsman to score a Test century in the inaugural Melbourne Test of 1877. Batting from the Randwick end, Bannerman hit the ball over the Members' Pavilion, then a single-storey structure, onto the roof of the curator's cottage — an enormous distance.

Another hit which impressed historian Gregory was from an unknown batsman named Barnes who swiped the ball onto the roof of the Members' Pavilion in a match between the Criterion Theatre and Metropolitan Fire Brigade teams in 1899–1900.

The most celebrated Australian hitter of the late 1800s was George Bonnor (1.96 metres tall and weighing 108 kilograms). Nicknamed 'Bonnor the Basher' and 'Colonial Hercules', he was credited with hitting a ball from Victoria's Billy Midwinter right over the grandstand on the Melbourne Cricket Ground in 1880. Paradoxically, the highest hit Bonnor made at the SCG did not even reach the boundary. For NSW v. Victoria in 1886, Bonnor hit Fred 'Demon' Spofforth so high above mid-on that, according to one newspaper report, it seemed to go into the clouds.

Fielding at deep mid-on that day was Tom Horan who played 15 Tests for Australia and later became a renowned cricket writer. As the ball reached its pinnacle and slowly began to come down, Horan went round and round in circles to position himself under it. He failed miserably, the ball falling yards away from him and the crowd roared with laughter.

Six years earlier in The Oval Test of September 1880, Bonnor again lifted a ball sky-high. The hit was eventually caught by G. F. Grace (W. G.'s younger brother) about 105 metres away — a sure six on any modern ground. The batsmen in the meantime ran three. G. F. explained later: 'My heart stopped beating as I went on waiting'. This was G. F. Grace's only Test. He died the next month, aged 30.

Back to the SCG and the elusive clock batsmen love to have a crack at. Many have come close. Percy Chapman of England once hit a six that landed at the foot of the clock tower in 1920. According to Ginty Lush, two others have almost done it. One was E. T. Hall of Burwood who is said to have struck the rim of the clock-face during World War I. And the other was guess-who — the celebrated footballer Dally Messenger, who once hit the clock tower, says Lush.

According to the legendary wicket-keeper Bert Oldfield, the biggest six he saw at the SCG was hit by the marvellous English left-hander

Frank Woolley. 'It went into the Sheridan Stand still travelling on the same trajectory as when it flew over long-on,' Oldfield told Derriman.

Sir Donald Bradman seldom hit a six. Yet he is credited with hitting one of the loftiest sixes ever witnessed at the SCG. In a Sheffield Shield match for NSW v. Victoria in January 1934, Bradman hit four sixes off 'Chuck' Fleetwood-Smith in his innings of 128 in 90 minutes. One of the sixes landed on the top deck of the Ladies Pavilion. This has been verified by Sir Donald for Derriman's book *The Grand Old Ground*.

Few would argue that Keith 'Nugget' Miller is Australia's greatest six symbol since World War II. One of his biggest sixes at the SCG was a straight drive off Alec Bedser that sailed over the sightscreen at the Randwick end and landed near the base of the back wall between the Hill (which is part of history now) and the Sheridan Stand (also demolished). Miller used only a light bat (2 pounds 5 ounces, about 1.1 kilograms), but the power he generated was beyond belief.

'Keith [Miller] was the most magnificent hitter I ever saw,' says Davidson. 'He had great timing. Timing, in the final reckoning, is everything.' Miller was such an extraordinary character and hitter that the next chapter is devoted to his six-ploits.

Derriman also reports on a massive six on the SCG from a 17-year-old Jim Lenehan. Batting for a Combined Great Public School XI in 1955, he straight-drove a ball into the top deck on the M. A. Noble Stand. He is better remembered as a brilliant outside-centre and fullback for the Wallabies in rugby.

Brian Booth, a batsman in the classical mould, surprised the onlookers by hooking a bouncer from West Australian bowler Desmond Hoare onto the roof of the Ladies' Pavilion in November 1963 in a Sheffield Shield match. 'This is the farthest I have known a bumper to be hooked on any ground (not overlooking Richie Benaud's six off Fred Trueman into the Lord's grandstand in 1956),' Robinson commented.

No discussion on famous sixes at the SCG can be complete without mention of Garry Sobers in the exciting 1960–61 series. Sobers initially played forward to a slower ball from Ian Meckiff, changed his mind during the shot, went on the back foot and belted the ball over mid-off at the Randwick end. To hit a six over mid-off was a remarkable feat in itself, particularly off a quick bowler like Meckiff. To hit it off the back-foot bordered on the impossible.

Old-timers bracket it with the back foot six Bill Howell hit which landed on the roof of an MCG bar and scattered drinkers. Woolley's on-drive off Arthur Mailey was airborne for about 100 metres before bouncing into the Sheridan Stand. This held up the match for about seven minutes before Warren Bardsley could persuade the drinkers to return the ball.

Although no clocks have been struck on a major ground in Australia, there have been a few instances in England. At Bradford in 1914, Jack Hobbs hit eight sixes in a match, including one from bowler Drake of Yorkshire, which landed on the face of a clock on the football stand. This delighted Hobbs and he waved to his team mates in the pavilion. The time was 4 p.m. and the minute hand struggled on for 10 minutes and then fell with a flop to 4.30 p.m. and stayed like that until the clock was repaired after the war four years later. The exasperated bowler who was at the receiving end said that it was a pity the hands had not been knocked onto 6.30 'and then we'd have been finished with this mucking about for t'day.'

Ken Cranston of Lancashire made a soaring straight drive off Eric Hollies at Edgbaston in 1948 which shattered the pavilion clock. Cranston offered to pay the cost for the repairs but the Warwickshire Committee refused the offer, regarding his six as a remarkable one well worth the cost.

Although clocks are major targets for batsmen to aim at, it is not always so. In Hong Kong it was the plate glass window of the Communist Bank across the road from the cricket ground. NSW's attacking batsman Ray Flockton narrowly missed smashing it in the late 1950s.

Other targets have been artesian water swimming baths (as in Moree, NSW), rivers, lakes, ponds, or even roof tiles — a nominated roof tile to be precise.

England's classical batsman Archie MacLaren was told during his visit to Philadelphia, USA, that Australia's big-man Bonnor had landed a ball on a faraway roof marked by a blue tile to remind posterity of this hit. 'I'll break the one next to it,' MacLaren bragged half-jokingly. And he nearly did it too according to Jack Pollard. 'My eye was out,' MacLaren said. 'I missed it by several tiles.'

There are lusty sixes and there are thirsty sixes which prefer to land in the members' bar or in wine glasses. In 1885, S.W. Scott of Middlesex hit a ball from W. G. Grace right into the Tavern of Lord's, 'scaring the barmaid nearly out of her wits'. Having scared 'Miss Muffet' away, the ball bounced off the wall of the bar on to the grass. But that was not all.

A little later, Grace was again hit, this time by Timothy O'Brien, through the same door into the bar. The ball shattered a couple of claret glasses and the same barmaid's nerves. W. G. was not amused. But he could hand out punishment as well as receive it. He once drove a ball through the Committee Room window at Lord's. The same windows have been smashed by Jim Smith and Fred Trueman in the 1950s.

In their time Victor Trumper and Don Bradman broke many a window in minor grade cricket, which will be detailed in a later chapter. At Hastings one of Gilbert Jessop's longest hits landed in an upper-storey room and the old lady who lived there refused to return the ball until she was paid for the repairs. At Scarborough an old gentleman flatly refused to return a ball hit into his room. He assumed that it was a present for him.

At Swansea in Glamorgan a resident returned home to find one of her windows smashed. Assuming that a burglar had broken in, she rang for the police. After a prolonged search, they located the 'intruder' — a cricket ball — hiding under the sofa.

English fast bowlers of 1950s are also known for their ferocious hits. Frank 'Typhoon' Tyson of Northamptonshire (now settled in Melbourne) hit a tremendous six off Glamorgan's Allan Watkins in a festival match in Torquay. He hurtled the ball out of the ground, over a public road and into the garden of the Torquay station master.

His partner-in-pace Fred Trueman, when batting for Yorkshire, broke a plate-glass window in the pavilion door at Lord's with a powerful drive. A rare feat, it was achieved only once before by the Middlesex thunderbolt 'Big' Jim Smith to win a bet.

Kent's left-handed batsman J. L. Bryan drove a ball through the pavilion window at Cardiff in Glamorgan and smashed a picture. The ball had so many glass fragments embedded in it that it had to be replaced by a new one.

The versatile genius of Wally Hammond could make him switch from a classical musician to a rock star of six-hitting without apparent change of gears. A punishing off-drive from him disturbed the calm of press box adjoining the pavilion by going straight through the window and spreading a shower of glass splinters. Then at Lord's in 1945 he sent a ball straight through the open doorway of the Long Room. It struck the glass front of one of the display cases without causing any damage.

In the February 1971 Kingston Test against West Indies, India's Dilip Sardesai hooked a six off leg-spinner Arthur Barrett which gate-crashed the glass-screened press box and scattered splinters everywhere.

It is not only the Test cricketers who give scorers a hard time. Schoolboy Anderson once hit a ball clear over the big scoreboard, over Father Time and into the secretary's garden on the other side. The occupants of the scoreboard perched high above the ground had the unusual experience of seeing the ball approaching them and still rising as it went over their heads.

Somerset's big hitter Guy F. Earle dunked a ball into the nearby Taunton River three times in half an hour against Kent in late 1920s.

Thus rivers are as tempting a target as clocks for six-obsessed batsmen. At the turn of the century, Albert Trott drove two consecutive balls into the Taunton River. Noted English cricket statistician Irving Rosenwater speculated that the river must hold a good collection of cricket balls.

Keith Miller sunk three balls into ponds or river (in India in 1945–46 and in South Africa in 1949–50). They are described by Miller himself in the next chapter.

Test batsman Arthur Milton of Gloucestershire celebrated his century by splashing a six into the Taunton River. Another ground where a river provokes a six response from a batsman is the Ebbw Vale. In the first match ever played there, a Worcestershire batsman hit the ball into it three times. Such watery adventures have proved economic disasters because balls cost money and retrieval of them is extremely difficult. Rosenwater narrates the following amusing salvage operation stories.

At Hinckley in England, a pull by Worcestershire batsman Wolton (year not specified) ended up in a nearby stream. The game was held up as one of the fielders was lowered into the ditch by his colleagues to retrieve the ball.

Another rescue mission was in operation when 'Bomber' Wells in the mid-1950s made a huge pull which sent the ball into the rain gutter of the Cheltenham College Gymnasium. Bill Knightley-Smith, a Cambridge Blue, climbed over the rails of the players' pavilion and crawled along the sloping roof to recover the ball.

There have also been a few unsuccessful attempts. When Surrey batsman B. Constable smacked a ball over a tall wire fence and out of the ground at Guildford, Surrey, two Oxford University players went through a hedge to look for it. They were away so long that their captain had to send a search party to locate them. The fielders were found but not the ball. Another lost ball at Cardiff in Glamorgan brought a batsman's flourishing innings to a sudden end. Rather than waste time searching for the ball, the captain declared the innings closed. One hopes the batsman was not in his nervous nineties then.

Doug Walters, the hero of the Hillites in Sydney, remembers his huge six at the old SCG No. 2 ground with pride and joy. Walters was only 16 at the time, batting for NSW v. Queensland in a Colts match in November 1962. He hammered a wrong 'un from a leg-spinner with perfect timing and the ball sailed over a brick wall and vanished into the Kippax Lake, quite some distance from the wall. The ball was wet when it was retrieved but Walters suspects it did not fall straight in

The popular Aussie Test trio of Bob Simpson, Doug Walters and Alan Davidson. Davidson's big sixes on the SCG and Old Trafford are still remembered with awe. (Sydney Morning Herald)

the lake but had 'a couple of favourable bounces off Driver Avenue to finish in the lake', he told me. 'As that ground has now disappeared (to become the Sydney Football Stadium), nobody will ever hit a bigger six there.'

Walters has hit many other more famous sixes (at Perth in 1974 off English speedster Bob Willis, for example) but according to him, the SCG No. 2 six is the biggest of his career.

Another target a batsman aims at but with little success is the sightscreen. In 1956, Barricks of Northamptonshire hit a mighty six which pierced a canvas sightscreen. After the match he was presented the torn fragments as a memento.

Of late, the Gabba ground in Brisbane seems to have become a heaven for big hitters. The tall Tom Moody clouted four big sixes for Australia against Pakistan in the 1989–90 World Series match. One landed in Stanley Street while another one ended on the roof of the press box. There was a delay while one of the journalists had to climb on the roof to fetch the ball.

In a Sheffield Shield match the same season between Queensland and Tasmania, also at the Gabba, Scott Hookey from Tasmania hit a six over the Clem Jones Stand which landed in Stanley Street. In the 1990–91 Sheffield Shield match against South Australia, Queensland batsman Peter Cantrell belted Test spinner Peter Sleep onto the roof of the press box and the ball ended up in a car park at the far side of Vulture Street. A season earlier Mark Waugh, the elegant Australian batsman, had hit Peter Sleep onto the roof of Members Stand adjacent to the clock tower.

In 1993–94 Mercantile Mutual Cup match against Tasmania at the Gabba, Queensland's stroke-player Jimmy Maher skied a six which shattered the glass of one of the windows in the press box.

To end this chapter on a greasy note, what better than to narrate the 'Fried Calamari Stopped Play' story? *Wisden 1996* reports on a Castle Cup match in Paarl, South Africa, between Border and Boland in February 1995. Test batsman Daryll Cullinan hit a six off R. Telemachus which landed in a hot frying pan. It was about 10 minutes before the ball was cool enough for the umpires to remove the grease. Even then bowler Telemachus was unable to grip the ball and it had to be replaced.

8

Nugget's Towering Sixers and 'Ponders'

Lot of bull has been written on six-hitting... Not even Jack Nicklaus could hit the ball from SCG into Kippax Lake.

— Keith Miller

Ask any knowledgeable cricket follower to name 10 greatest all-rounders, 15 fastest bowlers, 10 most awe-inspiring hitters, five handsomest cricketers and 10 most interesting characters of the game and only one name will be there in all these lists. It would be Keith Ross Miller, universally adored, respected and nicknamed 'Nugget'.

He was Australia's most adventurous batsman since World War II and only England's dynamic all-rounder Ian Botham in recent years could challenge him in consistent high hitting. Tall and handsome, dashing and debonair with a mane of dark hair, Miller exuded sex and six appeal. Yet he was not just a slogger. Had he not been asked to concentrate more on bowling fast (he formed a menacing pace-like-fire combination with Ray Lindwall), he would have been recognised as a batsman of class. According to his biographer Mihir Bose, 'the pedigree of his stroke play rivalled Hammond's'.

Miller is more than a six symbol, being a living legend before words like 'legend' and 'icons' became commonplace with the advent of computers and inferior writers. He scored 2958 runs at 36.97 in 55 Tests, making seven centuries and 13 fifties, and 14,183 runs at 48.90 in 326 first-class matches (with 42 centuries, highest being 281 not out against Leicestershire in 1956 when he was 36). He also took 497 wickets at 22.26 in first-class matches including 170 at 22.97 in Test matches.

After his brilliant batting during the 1945 tour of England with the Services team, C. B. Fry — a contemporary of Ranjitsinhji and later a noted critic — said over BBC: 'In our eyes Miller is Australia's star turn. We know we have been watching a batsman already great who is likely, later on, to challenge the feats of Australia's champions of the past. Apart from his technical excellence, Keith Miller has something of the dash and generous abandon that were part of Victor Trumper's charms.'

Famous English cricket-writer R. C. Robertson-Glasgow described Miller's stroke play as 'dignity with the brakes off'. Gerald Brodribb in 1960 ranked Miller as the most dominating all-round cricketer of the post WW II period.

The only Australian to rival Miller as the numero uno in big six hitting was man-mountain George Bonnor whose six-hitting feats became legendary in the 1880s. However, Bonnor was a savage hitter of the ball and Miller a classical batsman who hit savage sixes.

From Miller's first appearance on English fields in 1945 it was obvious that an extraordinary batsman had arrived. The first of these high-flying innings was his 185 for the Dominions against England at Lord's. He ended the day with a colossal six off Eric Hollies (the man who bowled Don Bradman for a duck in his final Test innings in 1948) high up into the top tier of the pavilion.

Keith Miller, both a six and a sex symbol, with his stylish hitting, good looks and dashing personality. (Jack Pollard Collection)

The next morning he added 124 runs in 90 minutes, including six more sixes. No one had ever hit so many sixes in an innings at Lord's and *The Times* correspondent wrote, 'One began to wonder whether Lord's was a big enough ground for such terrific hitting.' One of his sixes is remembered with awe. He slammed an on-drive off Hollies that pitched on the south tower of the pavilion just above the commentator's box over the dressing room. Former English captain Arthur Gilligan who was then commentating later said, 'The hit came up over mid-on rising all the time as it came. On hitting the pavilion it fell into a hole that had been made in the roof of the commentary box by a shrapnel and the ball had to be poked up by a stick.'

This hit nearly equalled Albert Trott's famous hit over the Lord's pavilion in 1899 off the bowling of 'Monty' Noble. Experts believe that had the match been played on a more traditional pitch Miller might have equalled the record. His sixes in this memorable innings included straight drives over the bowler's head, towards mid-on and over long-on; a full gamut of power cricket.

When touring England in 1948 with Bradman's invincibles, Miller scored a quick 163 against MCC, bombarding the Tavern with huge hits. He smote the deadly English off-spinner Jim Laker (who eight years later captured 19 Australian scalps in the famous Manchester Test) for three sixes. This included 'one great blow square from the shoulder to the upper and non-alcoholic regions of the Tavern', to quote Neville Cardus. In 1953, Miller continued his onslaught at Lord's, slamming a full toss from left-arm spinner John Young of Middlesex over the sightscreen — a rare achievement.

When I recently talked with Miller, 76-years-old and recovering from a mild stroke, I found him friendly and forthright in his opinions. He cut out all red-tape and started with a 'six': 'Lot of bull has been written on six-hitting. They say Doug Walters, when about 16, had hit a ball from SCG No. 2 ground right into the Kippax Lake, a huge distance away. No one saw the ball fall directly into the lake, still so-called sports writers rave about it. Obviously, it landed on the road and then bounced into the lake. Not even Jack Nicklaus at his peak could put a golf ball from SCG No. 2 into the Kippax Lake!'

With preliminaries and pleasantries over, he said, 'Ask me any questions on horse-racing and classical music, but please not on my cricket statistics! I am not a figures man.'

Yet within half an hour he could recall some of his six-hitting sprees in 3-D effect with appropriate quotes and dramatic pauses, as well as sensational sixes hit in recent times by Kim Hughes and Ian Greig.

'I am not very good on dates, even years, but the one six I remember most vividly was against England at the SCG. I straight drove Alec Bedser over his head. It went a long, long way and landed near the concrete stand.

'A straight hit for six is the real thing. A hook shot or a hoick to mid-on does not mean that much to me because the batting pitch in use could be near the boundary line and even a gentle push could end up as a six. So you cannot judge a batsman as a hitter only by the number of sixes he hits.'

Then he recalled his famous sixes for the Dominions at Lord's in 1945, which is already detailed in this chapter. 'I hit a ball straight over the stand and it landed far away. It reminded some writers of Albert Trott's six many decades ago.'

Six is a matter of timing, according to Miller, and the use of heavier bats does not help much. He only used a bat weighing the standard 2 pounds, 5 ounces.

'I enjoyed Kim Hughes' splendid six in the Lord's Centenary Test of 1980. It was a straight hit, a beautiful six.'

Now Miller was getting into top gear, reminiscing as if to an old mate. 'I'll tell you a funny story way back from the 1945 tour of England. I hit a straight six in the direction of BBC room. Rex Alston, the famous English commentator, was on air then and I was told his description went like this: "Miller has hit the ball in the air, I think it is coming this way. It *is* coming this way" and then crash, kaboom as the ball shattered the BBC room's glass pane!

'When I toured England in 1953, an English newspaper offered a cash award of about £600 — not a bad sum of money then — to anyone hitting a ball across river Thames and into an island named Tagg's Island, a carry of around 130 yards. It was a friendly warm-up game. I gave the ball a mighty heave-ho and it sailed across. There were "oohs" and "aahs" among spectators craning their necks to see whether the ball had reached Tagg's Island. I waited and waited but the crowd's

Keith Miller looking at one that got away — a lull before the storm. (Jack Pollard Collection)

disappointed chorus of "oh, no!" indicated that I had missed the target by a few feet.'

By now 'Nugget' was in mid-season form. 'I'll tell you an incredible story, but believe me, it's true. I was there. It was in the early 1990s and I was invited for lunch in the Committee Room for a match between Surrey and Sussex at The Oval. Tables were stylishly set for the invitees — crockery and cutlery and wine glasses and wine bottles (red and white) — and the door was open. The batsman at the crease was Ian Greig of Sussex, who is the younger brother of Tony Greig. He hit the ball hard and high, it entered the Committee Room through the open door, touched a wall and ricocheted back without breaking a single item of glass. So amazing, it did not touch a thing! I've not read this story anywhere, have you?'

It is typical of Miller that he remembered the hits by others and not some of his own. These are summarised below:

During his 153 for Victoria against NSW in a Sheffield Shield match at Melbourne in 1946–47, Miller hit Ernie Toshack, a medium-paced left-arm bowler, high over the fence in his first over, as soon as he arrived at the crease. He hit Toshack for two more and Ray Robinson considered these sixes as the most powerful shots he had seen. One of these shots was truly amazing, it was a one-handed six!

In Swansea, Glamorgan, in 1948, Miller enlivened a dull, damp day with five sixes in his score of 84. During this innings he swung another left-arm medium-pacer, Allan Watkins, high in the sky and into the crowd at fine-leg using only his left hand. Jack Fingleton, a former Australian Test cricketer turned respected political and cricket correspondent, described this shot as 'positively an unbelievable stroke ... the most amazing batting feat I've seen'.

In the Leeds Test on the same tour, Miller's 58 included an off-drive from Laker which was the tallest shot Fingleton had seen. Another of his sixes soared up and came down among trees at Kirstall end — a carry of 115 metres.

During the 1948 tour, Miller hit 26 sixes in 22 matches — some of them coming at the most critical moment in Test matches. For example, in the Lord's Test he came to the crease with Norman Yardley on a hat-trick. He was very nearly dismissed first ball, but having survived, hit a huge six behind square-leg soon after. And it landed halfway up the grandstand. In a county game against Hampshire in Southampton he hit off-spinner C. J. Knott for three sixes in a row.

Not that Miller's high-hitting was restricted only to England. In Australia, India and South Africa, his name is synonymous with excitement and glamour. At Brisbane on the Gabba ground in the first Test of the 1946–47 series against England he scored a hurricane 79 which included a six over long-on to the roof of the members' citadel which was considered the longest hit ever hit on the ground.

In the Adelaide Test of the same series, he hit a six off the first ball he received, a no-ball from Douglas Wright. It landed at the foot of the viceregal box. He went on to play one of his best Test innings of 141 not out.

Against Sheffield Shield debutants Western Australia at Sydney in 1947–48, Miller smacked three colossal sixes. One went right up the back wall of an alley between the pavilion and the Noble Stand and another 'gate-crashed' on the top-deck of the Ladies' Stand.

Apart from the towering sixes, Miller also specialised in 'ponders' — dispatching balls into ponds and rivers. At Eden Gardens, Calcutta, in an unofficial test match against India in 1945–46, he borrowed a bat from team-mate R. S. Whitington as they crossed on the way to the crease. Knowing Miller's penchant for smash-hits, Whitington requested him to be careful with the bat. Miller nodded and promptly drove India's celebrated left-arm spinner Vinoo Mankad over the sightscreen for four sixes in two overs. To Whitington's relief Miller was soon stumped. The four sixes landed in a pond outside the ground. After retirement, both turned journalists and co-authored the popular books *Cricket Caravan*, *Straight Hit*, *Bumper* and *Gods or Flannelled Fools*, among others.

Miller sent two more sixes into their watery grave while touring South Africa in 1949–50. At Port Elizabeth against Eastern Province he hit six sixes in his breezy 131. On jogging his memory on this century, Miller said, 'Oh yes. I remember reaching my ton with a six, one of the nicest and longest sixes I ever hit. It cleared the grandstand and landed in a pond in the park outside the ground. It was one of the shots that clicked.'

On the same tour, Miller hit a huge six in his brief innings of 24, against North Eastern Transvaal at Pretoria. It cleared the trees and landed in the Aapies River. A local reporter was so carried away by this fantastic hit that he got the name of the river wrong and named one 18 miles away. Not even golfer Jack Nicklaus could hit a ball that far. Not even six-sultan Keith Miller!

Gerald Brodribb who has put all six-hitters until 1960 under his microscope and viewed their sixes through a telescope in his *Hit for Six*, paid Miller this accolade: 'No batsman since Jessop has been so acclaimed by the crowd as he came in to bat. Spectators saw in Miller the fine, Tarzan-like physique they would all like to possess, the devil-may-care attitude to bowlers (and to statistics) they would all like to adopt, and the daring and powerful style of play they would all like to call their own.'

9

Vintage Six Symbols

Hitting a six compares with flattening the town bully in one dramatic blow, a brave triumph against odds, and nothing damages a bowler's morale as much as being hit for a six.

— Jack Pollard

A bowler would disagree with the above sentiment. To him a regular big six-hitter is the town bully who ruins his bowling analysis and shatters his morale. Instead of sensibly blocking the ball or obligingly snicking it to the wicket-keeper, the so-and-so show-off has the nerve, the hide, the gall and the audacity to jump out and hit him for a six time and again!

By my definition a six symbol is a batsman who has made it a habit of hitting big sixes season after season till his name is synonymous with tall-hitting. In the history of first-class cricket there have been so many big hitters — especially before World War II — that it would be impossible to include all of them. Only twelve six-hitters of my choice are featured in this chapter and, just as no two critics will select the same World XI, I do not expect readers to acclaim my choice.

Tall-hitters before WW II are featured in this chapter. The top-class batsmen Victor Trumper, Frank Woolley and Wally Hammond who have hit some colossal sixes are not included here — they are too elegant to mingle with my 'tonkers' and 'town bullies' although some of them, like Gilbert Jessop, had a pleasing style and solid technique.

Post-WW II hitters have been highlighted in the next chapter. The multi-talented and many-splendoured Keith Miller and the extraordinary Ted Alletson have been featured in separate chapters. Below are profiled pre-WW I and II six-hitters in more or less chronological order.

The daddy of all six-symbols was:

CHARLES INGLIS THORNTON

Nicknamed 'Buns', Thornton played for Kent and Middlesex. 'Like many of his day, Thornton always regarded cricket more as a game than as serious business,' wrote *Wisden 1930*. 'He was one of the biggest — if not the mightiest — of hitters.' He stood 6 foot, had sloping shoulders and was admirably proportioned for hitting balls high and wide. He had small forearms and biceps but his enormous power came from the strength of his hips and loins; from the tremendous swing of the bat and the impetus of his jump down the wicket. He seldom donned pads and wore gloves only late in his career.

All those who saw him bat were unanimous that he hit a ball harder, higher and further than any of his contemporaries and perhaps even those who came later. For the risks he took, he scored fairly consistently, at times opened the innings, and was not just a slogger. Surprisingly, there are more measured hits for Thornton than for other batsmen although his career ended almost 100 years ago (in 1897). He seldom scored 50 runs without hitting a ball a distance of 125 metres.

Born in 1850, he made a first-class debut in 1869 and died in 1929, aged 79. Fenner in Kent was his favourite ground and in 1871 he hit 20 runs (6, 4, 4, 6) from David Buchanan's one four-ball over — the two sixes vanishing over the distant confines of the huge ground. (As mentioned before, only hits clearing the ground counted for six before 1910 in England.) His 111 at Canterbury for Kent v. Surrey in 1871 came in 93 minutes, with 18 fours, many of which cleared the boundary line and were the equivalent of sixes. 'I hit Southerton 12 times into one tree on the on-side; there was a bit of cross wind,' recalled Thornton.

His many big hits made W. G. Grace comment: 'Thornton stands quite alone as the hitter of my time and will never be excelled, even if he is equalled.' One of Thornton's favourite matches was for the Gentlemen of South v. the Players of South in 1871. Needing 249 to win, Thornton came in to bat at 5 for 53. He attacked after an over or two and belted 61 runs in 53 minutes but still his team lost by 3 runs.

At Hove in Sussex, he made his longest hit on 25 August 1876, the distance measured by cricket historian Jim Pycroft at 154 metres. At Scarborough Thornton scored 107 not out for Gentlemen v. I Zingari in 1886. Trailing by 209 runs, Gentlemen lost 5 for 133 and seemed destined for annihilation, but 'Buns' had other ideas. He hammered

107 runs out 133 in only 70 minutes, opening his account with a six. In all he hit eight sixes and 12 fours. Two of those sixes became famous; a drive through a second storey window at the back of a house in Trafalgar Square near Scarborough, and the other clean over the top of the same house into the square beyond. The distance was measured as 126 metres, and it flew spectacularly high. Only one other batsman, Australia's C. G. Pepper, was able to equal this feat in 1945.

Thornton's top score was 124 (for Kent v. Sussex at Common ground in Tunbridge Wells in 1869) when he was only a teenager. He smote nine sixes but so huge were these hits that a Sussex fielder said, 'Had the hits been run, they would probably be worth eight runs each'.

GEORGE JOHN BONNOR

Bonnor, the Australian giant, was a contemporary of Thornton and a regular six-thumper. He was tall (6 foot 6 inches), broad, bearded and powerful. His modus operandi for six-hitting was different from Thornton's. Because of his huge frame, Bonnor could sweep the ball with a heavy lunge and in belting a long-hop far, far away, he was superior to Thornton. But he did not have the latter's finesse. To quote W. J. Ford, himself a six-smiter, 'huge as his drives were, they were dull and heavy as compared to the Englishman's — lacking that beautiful crack and the whip of the wrist which made Thornton's hitting so memorable'.

All the same, Bonnor was a crowd favourite in both England (where he was born) and Australia (where he settled). He was also an agile fielder with an arrow-like throw from the fence. There were times he became defence-oriented to show that he was not a slogger. To prove his point, he would go in his shell and play what he called a 'sweetly pretty' game which infuriated both his team-mates and the crowd. On his dual personality wrote W. G. Grace: 'He was a born slogger but somehow got the notion that he could bat with scientific patience. It was rubbish ... his genial temperament was against patient batting while his enormous reach and tremendous strength designed him for hitting.'

W. G.'s younger brother, G. F. Grace, sampled one of Bonnor's gigantic hits. In The Oval Test of 1880 against England, Bonnor gave the ball bowled by Alfred Shaw a tremendous clout. Up it went, up and up and as the batsmen crossed three times, the ball slowly came down in G. F.

Grace's direction. He stood motionless waiting for what seemed an eternity. 'My heart stopped beating as I went on waiting', he admitted later. But he took the catch, a six on any other ground because it was 95 metres away.

Like Albert Trott, Bonnor enjoyed hitting targets at some distant horizon. To see him hit out 'was a sight for the Gods', wrote George Giffen, Australia's captain. One of Bonnor's favourite memories was reaching his century with a colossal six off Fred 'Demon' Spofforth, normally his team-mate. It was in a Smokers v. Non-Smokers match made up at random from English and Australian cricketers in 1884. Playing for Non-Smokers, he had an opportunity to face Demon's bowling, and as per his boast, hit him for a six which sailed over the wall behind the pavilion. A little later, he smote Spofforth for another six to the roof of the pavilion. It was his fifth century and the most satisfying.

Another of his memorable innings was his 74 in 80 minutes against the Gentlemen of England in 1882. This included a hit which went through the window of the secretary's room. 'I was just going to unlock a door when a ball, hit by Bonnor off R.C.Ramsay came into the room,' narrated Surrey Secretary C.W.Alcock. 'After striking against the cornice in front of the window, it knocked the keys out of my hand and smashed the old picture of a Kent v. Sussex match. You can see the mark on the engraving now [in 1913]. I was never so startled in my life.'

One of his most powerful shots resulted in his dismissal. In the Lord's Test of July 1884, he hit a half-volley from George Ulyett — himself a big hitter — off the middle of the bat. Ulyett put a hand out in a reflex action, and while everyone was looking to the boundary to see where the ball had landed, a sad Bonnor was returning to the pavilion; caught and bowled by Ulyett. The high velocity shot had stuck to Ulyett's palm and wouldn't let go! Had the Bonnor missile hit his arm or wrist, it would have snapped his limb as if it were a stick. *Punch* magazine suggested that Ulyett should be sent to war to catch enemy cannonballs!

JOHN (JACK) JAMES LYONS

Australia's Jack Lyons was a terrific hitter who was overshadowed by Bonnor. Lyons had weakness against spinners but on a hard, true pitch he was a dangerous batsman who could demoralise the best of bowlers. His most scintillating innings was for the touring Australians against the MCC at Lord's in May 1893. The tourists were 181 runs behind in the first innings when the contrasting pair of Lyons and the ultra-defensive Alex Bannerman opened the innings. They knocked off the deficit in only 95 minutes, Lyons scoring 149 of them. He reached his 100 out of 124 in an hour, then a record at Lord's. The shots to remember in this innings were a pull to the awning above the seats in the grandstand, a drive into the pavilion enclosure and a huge hit to leg towards the entrance gate between the Tavern and the old tennis court.

Even his shorter innings included hefty shots. His 31 runs in 20 minutes in The Oval Test of 1893 included a drive to the roof of the pavilion. The ball bounced over and finished on the road for one of the biggest hits ever seen on the ground. The next ball landed on the tin roof of the members' enclosure and only just missed going over the pavilion and out of the ground. The bowler to suffer these indignities was Bill Lockwood, one of the best fast bowlers the game has seen.

His other dazzling innings were his 99 out of 117 in 75 minutes for the Australians v. MCC at Lord's in 1890 and his 134 out of 175 in 165

Two six-smiters are present in this group photo of South Australians in 1894; Jack Lyons (third from left, back row) and Joe Darling (right in centre row). (Jack Pollard Collection)

Jack Lyons was one of the most spectacular hitters among Australian cricketers. (Jack Pollard Collection)

minutes in the Sydney Test of 1891–92 against England. He hit many legendary hits in Sheffield Shield matches and is reputed to have bashed a ball into the river which flows past his home ground in Adelaide.

GILBERT LAIRD JESSOP

Jessop was the most famous and prodigious of six-hitters in the history of the game. According to *Wisden 1956*: 'There have been batsmen who hit the ball even harder than Jessop, notably C. I. Thornton and the two Australians George Bonnor and Jack Lyons, but no one who did so more often or who, in match after match, scored as rapidly. Where Jessop surpassed all other hitters was in the all-round nature of his scoring.'

Jessop could make runs from any ball, however well-pitched. Although only 5 feet 7 inches (170 cm) in height, he bent low as he got ready to bat, hence earning the sobriquet 'The Croucher'. Bright-eyed, with a determined square chin, he was extraordinarily quick on his feet. He could convert a good-length ball into a half-volley with a dainty shuffle as no one else could. He was fearless and danced down the pitch to even the fastest bowlers like Tom Richardson and Arthur Mold.

He announced his arrival in first-class cricket (for Gloucestershire v. Yorkshire in 1894) by hitting 63 out of 65 in under 30 minutes and till his retirement in 1914 was a scourge of bowlers, their nightmare. Brodribb estimates that Jessop scored at a rate of 80 runs an hour, year after year from 1894 to 1914. As a comparison, well-known stroke-players, Victor Trumper and Frank Woolley scored at 55 runs an hour, Charlie Macartney, Ranjitsinhji and Duleepsinhji at 50 per hour and Don Bradman, Everton Weekes and Denis Compton between 45 to 50 runs and hour.

Jessop was a quality batsman who made 53 centuries. In 12 of these innings, he reached his 100 within an hour, the fastest being his 101 in 40 minutes at Harrogate in 1897. For Gentlemen of South v. Players of South at Hastings in 1907, he slammed 191 in 90 minutes. His greatness was emphasised in the fact that he attacked the deadliest of bowlers with rare abandon; the stronger the attack, the harder he hit.

Once C. B. Fry was moved to write in the *Daily Telegraph*: 'It is not an overstatement to characterise Jessop's manner of batsmanship as altogether unique. His stance was such, so was his footwork, so was his swing.'

On his home ground in Gloucestershire, Jessop hit several balls to the top of the pavilion but failed to clear it like another big-hitter V. F. S. (Frank) Crawford did at Bristol. It was at Bristol that Jessop inspired the Notts veteran John Gunn to write: 'I think the biggest hit I ever saw was when Mr Gilbert Jessop hit Jimmy Iremonger out of the Bristol ground and the ball went right across the football ground as well before dropping. I think that was the biggest hit I ever saw.'

'Croucher' Jessop's only century in 18 Tests came at The Oval in 1902. Set 273 to win on a difficult pitch, England lost 5 for 48. The desperate situation brought the best out of him and he mauled the Australian attack to score 104 out of 139 in 75 minutes and England won the thriller by one wicket.

Apart from touring Australia in 1901–02, he visited USA in 1897 and 1899. An American was so delighted with 'Croucher's' fireworks that he wrote a verse about:

... the human catapult
who wrecks the roofs of distant towns
when set in his assault.

Among many tributes paid at his death on 11 May 1955 aged 80, the best was from Sir Jack Hobbs: 'He was undoubtedly the most consistent fast scorer I have seen. He was a big hitter too, and it was difficult to bowl a ball from which he could not score. He made me glad that I was not a bowler. Gilbert Jessop certainly drew the crowds, too, even more than Bradman I should say.'

What loftier tribute can you pay to any cricketer than this?

ALBERT TROTT

The Albert Trott story is a tearjerker. An all-rounder with unlimited talent, he could hit the ball with a vengeance. But luck was always against him and he shot himself when only 42. Born in Melbourne in 1873, his Test debut at Adelaide against England in 1895 was sensational, scoring 38 not out, 72 not out and taking 0 for 9 and 8 for 43. In the next Test at Sydney he hit an unbeaten 85 and did not bowl. He failed in the final Test in Melbourne but still had totalled 205 runs at 102.50 and captured 9 for 192 at 21.33 in his maiden Test series. His selection for the tour of England in 1896 was as certain as taxation and death but for some obscure reason he was dropped.

Devastated and disgusted, he came to England on his own and subsequently qualified to play for Middlesex and represented England in two Tests. He was soon to become a crowd favourite with his hefty hitting and effective bowling and is especially remembered for two feats. He remains the *only* one to ever hit a ball over the Lord's pavilion, which was in 1899 and the *only* one to take four wickets in four balls and then a hat-trick in the same innings during his benefit match in 1907. As this double hat-trick ended the game abruptly, he lost the next day's gate money. His sad comment on realising this was that he played himself into penury.

Trott is remembered for his other big hits, amongst them hitting the great spinner Wilfred Rhodes right out of the ground at Scarborough in a festival match. A little later, he blasted 50 runs in 22 minutes out of a stand of 52 runs with Gregor MacGregor who scored the other two. Then it was all the way down for the tragic Trott.

According to some, that famous hit over the Lord's pavilion in 1899 marked the beginning of the end. Trott became a compulsive 'tonker', going for the bowling before his eye was in. Although he did succeed at times, he failed far too often and it was not so much lack of technique as lack of judgment. His Middlesex captain MacGregor once told him: 'If you had a head instead of a turnip, Alberto, you'd be the best bowler in the world'. The same applied to his batting. Albert thought little and swung a lot till he completely lost form and confidence.

He had practically no money and was ill for a long time, with little hope of recovering. Finding the monotony of life in hospital intolerable, he thought a pistol shot the best way out. Albert Trott deserved better, his hurricane hitting enlivened many lives but his own.

GUY FIFE EARLE

Playing for Surrey and Somerset, Earle attacked bowlers immediately on arrival, striking the bowling with contempt as if he hated the bowler. He was a Dennis Lillee in reverse. Earle was a whole-hearted hitter, a big man both in stature and spirit with forearms so strong that he could smack a ball 70 metres one-handed when giving fielding practice.

He reserved his best for Kent, especially its Test leg-spinner A. P. 'Tich' Freeman. Earle's memorable encounter against Kent was at Taunton (Somerset) in 1927. He hit the first ball he received from Freeman for four and later hit him out of the ground and into a river. Next over, he hit Frank Woolley into the new pavilion and the second ball was despatched over the roof of the stand. He then smote Freeman for a four and a terrific six over the trees to the far bank of the river. Freeman was replaced by spinner 'Wally' Hardinge, whose first ball was also hit into the river. Earle scored 51 (included five sixes and two fours) in 26 minutes off 22 balls.

In first-class matches, he hit only two centuries; 111 v. Gloucestershire at Bristol in 1923 and 130 for the MCC v. Hindus at Bombay in 1926–27. His chanceless 111 included five sixes (four of them were massive hits off slow left-arm bowler Charlie Parker over the track) and reached his 100 in exactly an hour.

His 130 v. Hindus at the Bombay Gymkhana ground came in 90 minutes and included eight sixes and 11 fours. With another big hitter Maurice Tate, he put on 154 runs in 67 minutes. Earle remembered one of his sixes which went over the road and into a tree which 'seated' a few free spectators on its branches. His penchant for sixes earned him the title of 'over-boundary player' from the Indian journalists.

Earle was a member of the English team to visit New Zealand in 1929–30 and his highest score on the tour was 98 in 40 minutes with three sixes and 11 fours. On the way to New Zealand, he punished the great Australian spinner Clarrie Grimmett for 22 (6, 4, 6, 6) when the MCC met South Australia at the Adelaide Oval — a large ground with long straight hit boundaries.

His 43 in 35 minutes (two sixes, five fours) out of Somerset's paltry total of 74 against Lancashire at Old Trafford in 1925 inspired Neville Cardus to write: 'Earle's ideas about batsmanship are, I imagine, unambiguous; he seems, indeed, a batsman with a "fixed idea" — sixers. He wasted no time; straightaway he smote two boundaries and a six in one over from Perkin — not to mention a hit for three over the wicket-keeper's head. His first sixer cleared the Ladies' pavilion — one of the biggest hits ever known at Old Trafford since Jessop rode the whirlwind here.'

COLONEL C.K. NAYUDU

He was India's answer to Guy Earle and the greatest consistent tall-hitter from Asia. In the same match that Earle hit the Hindu attack for eight soaring sixes, C. K. Nayudu countered by slamming 11 sixes the very next day, 1 December 1926 — watched by around 25,000 highly excited and delighted Bombayites.

In reply to MCC's 363, Hindus were 3 for 84 when Nayudu went in to bat. And before you could say 'Cottari Kankaiya' — his first two names — he had lifted G. S. Boyes onto the pavilion roof. Nayudu enjoyed this and clumped Boyes to the tents twice before lifting him over the Gymkhana in the same over. 'The umpires were observed clapping this stroke,' wrote *The Times of India* correspondent.

Wickets fell at the other end but Nayudu continued with the onslaught. Quality bowlers like Maurice Tate, J. Mercer, G. Geary and W. E. Astill were hit mercilessly by the Indian. He reached his century in 65 minutes and 153 in 116 minutes, in all hitting 11 big sixes and 14 fours. His 11 sixes created a world record which has been broken many times in the last 70 years.

A cartoon appeared in the next day's local paper depicting a group of spectators sheltering from the six-bombardment pleading: 'Don't hit us, C. K., we are not playing.'

Famous Indian commentator Berry Sarbhadhikary described the inning as full of strokes 'which terrified the fieldsmen, dazzled everybody's eyesight, broke all rules of batting, science and logic, and stirred the crowd to wonder and delight'.

C. K. Nayudu, India's first Test captain in 1932 was, to quote C. B. Fry, 'one of the finest living cricketers, an artist and a great performer'. His debut in first-class cricket was an eye-opener. In a Quadrangular match between Hindus and Europeans in 1916, the former were in strife at 7 for 79, Australia's Frank Tarrant causing the havoc. Coming in at no. 9, the 21-year-old played the first three balls of the dreaded Tarrant defensively before hitting the next one for a six.

When touring England in 1932, he hit 32 sixes (one source wrongly says he hit 36). One particular high-flying shot at Lord's was described by an English writer as 'the ball last seen sailing in an Easterly direction'. Another notable innings on that tour was his 162 v. Worcestershire at Edgbaston, Birmingham. India was in trouble at 7 for 91 in the second innings and staring at defeat when he was joined by N. D. Marshall. The two hit 217 exhilarating runs in 140 minutes to save the game. Nayudu hit six sixes and 13 fours. A six off googly bowler Harold Jarrett is still talked about. Nayudu hooked a ball which cleared the River Rea and, as the river formed the boundary between Warwickshire and Worcestershire, this hit may be regarded as a real example of hitting the ball into the next county.

On that tour he also became the first Indian to score a century on debut at Lord's (v. Middlesex). Some English journalists called him the Indian Bradman but Neville Cardus disagreed: 'He shows no resemblance to Australia's great, flawless and rather steely master. Nayudu is lithe, wristy and volatile ... for each of his shots you get the impression of a new-born energy, of a sudden improvisation of superb technique. ... unlike Bradman his skill is his servant, not his master.' After scoring 1618 runs at 40.45 and taking 65 wickets at 25.53, he was honoured as one of *Wisden's* Five Cricketers of the Year.

Nayudu was also wrongly called an Indian Jessop. Although both were mighty hitters, Jessop was more consistently so. Also, Jessop crouched when batting, but C. K. stood tall and stately — like a Shehanshah or an emperor. Both were, however, loose in all their actions and hit with a beautiful swing of the bat.

According to his biographer Vasant Raiji, the biggest hit by Nayudu measured about 150 yards (136 metres) in 1921. Writes Raiji in his book *C. K. Nayudu* (1995), 'His first century included a hit which cleared the boundary wall on the southern end of the Madras Cricket Club compound and landed near a coconut tree fifty yards beyond the ground'. A hit of 136 metres is perhaps the longest hit by any player on the Chepauk ground in Madras.

When paying tribute to him in his centenary year, 1995, Raiji wrote in *Wisden Cricket Monthly*: 'Nayudu is the only Indian cricketer for whom the word "majestic" can be used without the fear of being accused of hero-worship or exaggeration. His walk to the wicket was like Hammond's; regal, poetry in motion.'

Wally Hammond saw in Nayudu the grace of George Headley. Douglas Jardine described him as a right-handed Frank Woolley, adding 'Both remain masters of execution of every shot that the game knows'.

SIR LEARIE (LATER LORD) CONSTANTINE

Neville Cardus described Learie Constantine of the West Indies as a genius. He was a great all-rounder, a superb hitter, an exciting fast bowler and an acrobatic fielder.

His obsession was to attack every ball, parading every range of strokes, orthodox or ad lib. A unique slant of his bat despatched balls to places a ball had never travelled before. His hits at Lord's were remarkable. For the West Indies against Middlesex in 1928, he hammered 86 out of 107 and 103 out of 133 in the same match; taking under an hour for each innings. He also captured 6 for 11 and contributed richly to the Windies' narrow victory. Two of his strokes impressed Sir Pelham Warner so much that he exclaimed that he would remember them till his dying day. One of them was a deflection over extra-cover's head and far up into the grandstand below the scoreboard.

'It wasn't a cut and it wasn't a drive; it was just Constantine,' remarked Brodribb.

Against MCC at Lord's in 1933, he scored 51 out of 66 in 27 minutes. One shot off Maurice J. C. Allom was extraordinary. He hit a 'head' ball

Cricket legends 'Gubby' Allen, Sir Learie Constantine, Alec Bedser, Keith Miller and Sir Len Hutton. Constantine and Miller were magnificent attacking all-rounders. (*Sydney Morning Herald*)

over the wicket-keeper's outstretched hands, cleared the press box and was never recovered. On his previous tour to England in 1928 he hit at least 37 sixes; the most fascinating ones were off 'Tich' Freeman to the roof of the pavilion and off C. Wright clean over the top of a tree.

Constantine toured Australia in 1930 - 31 and although he failed in Test matches, he scored 100 v. Tasmania in 52 minutes and 59 v. NSW at Sydney in 35 minutes. He later said this Sydney innings was one of the best he ever played.

ARTHUR WILLIAM WELLARD

For the number of sixes hit, season after season, Somerset's Arthur Wellard was peerless. He was tall (6 feet 2 inches), possessed strong hands and used a heavy bat (2 pounds 11 ounces) and was not obsessed with hitting the ball out of the ground. Just six runs will do nicely thank you, appeared to be his philosophy. From 1929 to 1949, he scored 12,575 runs in first-class matches with the help of 561 sixes, which works out at over 25 percent — an amazing statistic. In four of the six seasons from 1933 to 1938, he exceeded 50 sixes every season; a feat without parallel. His sequence:

51 in 1933,
66 in 1935 (not 72 as previously believed),
57 in 1936,
57 in 1938.

His 66 sixes in 1935 remained a record till surpassed by Ian Botham in 1985 when he clobbered 80. No other batsman has hit 50 sixes in an English season, Vivian Richards coming closest with 49 in 1985, and A. W. Carr, John Edrich and Andrew Symmonds with 48 each in 1925, 1965 and 1995 respectively. It may be prudent to point out that the number of matches played in an English county season has reduced since Wellard's time, with more limited-overs non-first-class competitions sprouting up.

Wellard is also the only one to hit five sixes in a six-ball over *twice*. His two 30-plus runs per over feats are worth detailing. The first time was against slow left-armer T. R. Armstrong of Derbyshire at Wells in 1936. He started off with 17 runs off an Armstrong over (0, 4, 6, 6, 1, 0) and the bowler was changed. When reintroduced, Wellard blasted him for 30 (0, 6, 6, 6, 6, 6) straight away. He had already taken nine wickets in the match and his 86 in 62 minutes brought his side a one-wicket win.

Again at Wells, a small ground, against Kent in 1938, he clouted Frank Woolley for five sixes in an over (6, 6, 6, 6, 6, 1); four of them right out of the ground of which three were lost. He attempted another six off the last ball of the over but skied it near the sightscreen. The fielder got a hand to it but dropped it and the batsman took a single. Wellard later said that if the fielder had not touched it the ball would have carried over the line for another six.

Wellard scored 57 runs with seven sixes and went on to score 37 with four sixes in the second innings, which gave him 11 sixes in the match in which his match aggregate was 94. Thus 70.21 percent of his runs had come in sixes, a staggering statistic. He also took 13 for 115 in the match and was the man behind Somerset's victory.

Next year he belted Test spinner Douglas Wright of Kent for three sixes in three balls and ten years later in 1949, gave another Test bowler Eric Hollies of Warwickshire a similar treatment.

Wellard scored only two first-class centuries and both were studded with sixes. His first ton v. Surrey at The Oval in 1934, included a six which sent a ball on to the roof of East Stand. His second century, v.

Lancashire at Old Trafford the following year, included five sixes — four of them out of the ground. Although not a hitter of huge sixes à la Thornton or Bonnor, at least one of his sixes could be termed colossal. It happened in an unofficial test match at Brabourne Stadium, Bombay, during Lord Tennyson's tour of India in 1937–38. To quote famous Test cricketer and team mate Bill Edrich from his book, *Cricket Heritage*:

> Wellard straight drove Amar Singh [one of India's top bowlers] sky high over the sightscreens, over the top of the stand behind it, and out of sight. I was sitting at the other end of the ground, and I said, "Good heavens, that one's gone right over the top!" Lord Tennyson said, "Don't be a damn fool; no one could do it." This was interesting because Tennyson himself was a tremendous hitter. I confirmed my statement and Tennyson said, "I'll lay you a pound you're wrong." I took his bet and his money. It was 97 yards when we measured the distance from the wicket to the edge of the turf where the sightscreen stood; then there was a cinder track, then a series of terraces, then the stand, over 60 foot high. The ball had skied over the whole lot into the blue Indian distance.

'It was obviously one of the greatest hits in the history of the game', concludes Brodribb.

South Africa produced two big hitters before WW II, James H. Sinclair and H. B. 'Jock' Cameron.

JAMES H. SINCLAIR

A genuine all-rounder, Sinclair was called the W. G. Grace of South African cricket. He was the first great cricketer in his country's history. In the Cape Town Test of April 1899 against England he top-scored with 106 out of 177, hitting the bowling of Albert Trott and Schofield Haigh hard and high — including a hit off Trott over the ropes and into a pond. He also captured 6 for 26 and 3 for 63 in the Test but South Africa lost convincingly. Later he clobbered big sixes over the gum trees in Johannesburg which impressed Sir Pelham Warner.

During his tour of England he smote Wilfred Rhodes so hard out of the Harrogate ground that a taxi-driver was knocked out of his cab.

His dismissal for a first-ball duck in the Cape Town Test of 1902–03 by Australian spinner Bill Howell so angered Sinclair that he played with vengeance in the second innings. After smacking Howell's first delivery for a six, he turned his attention on medium-pacer Bert Hopkins. The six went like a bullet and fielder Clem Hill remarked: 'I suppose that was about the biggest whack I ever saw.'

Sinclair scored 34 runs off eight consecutive balls bowled to him (one six, five fours) and reached 100 in 80 minutes, the fourth quickest century in Test history.

'JOCK' CAMERON

A world-class wicket-keeper, Cameron's sixes provoked one of the best-known one-liners in cricket literature. When touring England in 1935 he smashed seven sixes (five of these in his second inning of 103 not out) against Yorkshire. Off Hedley Verity's over, he got 30 runs (4, 4, 4, 6, 6, 6). At the end of the over the jovial Yorkshire wicket-keeper Arthur Wood consoled Verity: 'Go on, Hedley, you've got him in two minds. He doesn't know whether to hit you for four or six!'

Yorkshire's bespectacled fast bowler Bill Bowes said that Wood's droll sally turned the over into a comic interlude but 'it never occurred to Hedley that he was bowling badly, or using wrong tactics.' In later years Verity described the assault by Cameron as 'champion hitting'.

This bit of 'champion hitting' which led to a victory over Yorkshire shot up South Africa's morale sky high. A few days later, Cameron scored a quickfire 90 with three sixes. 'We have seldom, if ever, seen a batsman who hits the ball so hard and so far with so little effort,' wrote *The Cricketer* correspondent.

Then came his magnificent 160 out of 230 in 140 minutes against Leverson-Gower XI at Scarborough. J. M. Kilburn was moved to write: 'Cameron showed no emotion whatever and his batting had an air of absent-mindedness and nonchalance'.

But tragedy was to strike this nonchalant punisher of balls a few weeks after his Scarborough magic. A charming and strong personality, he died of enteric fever on his return to his homeland. He was only 30.

Although this chapter has covered most pre-WW I and II six symbols, the list is not exhaustive. I wish I could have included a few more: George Ulyett, Percy Fender, Frank T. Mann, and Harold Gimblett who had made a fairytale debut for Somerset against Essex in 1935 when, as a 20-year-old 'nobody', he scored a century in 63 minutes and went on to hit 265 sixes in a brief career. But then what about W. H. Fowler, Frank and Jack Crawford, K. G. MacLeod, Freddie Brown, Amar Singh, A. C. Watson, Fred Barnett, Errol Holmes?

But the book is on the *appeal* of sixes and *not* a definitive study of all six-hitters. However, no book on six appeal could dare exclude 'Big Jim' Smith, alias Village Blacksmith.

CEDRIC IVAN JAMES SMITH

Jim Smith was a big man, 6 feet 4 inches tall, weighed 101 kilograms and was nicknamed 'Village Blacksmith'. He bowled fast and hit the ball faster. A slogger in the true sense of the word, Middlesex character Jim Smith had only one stroke — a devastating swing hit in the same direction. He was an eye-player *in excelsis* with no technique whatsoever, having played five Tests as a pace bowler.

The Hon. Terrence Prittie described Smith's windmill six thus: 'as sudden and violent as the first crash of the big drum in a Wagner opera'. He continued: 'Smith hits the ball with the same flat trajectory as the golf drive, rising steadily in its flight, only attaining its maximum some 60 to 80 yards from the wicket and dying quickly away.'

True, Jim Smith missed more than he hit yet his misses grabbed attention. Even some of his snicks went over the fence. Once after he was dismissed for 27 in 10 minutes, a member leaned over the pavilion and said, 'That was a good six', to which he replied quite honestly and without a trace of arrogance: 'Ah, but if only I had got hold of it!'

He must have got hold of one pretty much in the middle of the bat when he skied it vertically. Even Bonnor could not have hit it so high and so straight — up and up above the stumps. Wicket-keeper 'Hopper' Lever of Kent got ready to catch it. He revolved round and round in circles about five times, missed his 'orbit', forgot where the stumps were and crashed into them while the ball landed triumphantly nearby. It was sheer Laurel and Hardy stuff.

'It was one of the most spectacular misses it has been my lot to see,' wrote Ian Peebles in *Talking of Cricket*. 'It took time to restore order. Someone then callously suggested that if "Hopper" hadn't interfered, the ball would have descended on top of the middle stump and the batsman would have been out "played on".'

Big hitting made Big Jim Smith popular wherever he played. Against Kent at Maidstone, he reached his 50 in 14 minutes scoring 66 in 18 minutes in 1935, and hit his 50 in just 11 minutes v. Gloucestershire at Bristol in 1938. His only century, 101 not out v. Kent at Canterbury in 1939, took 81 minutes (slow by his standard!) when he added 116 runs for the last wicket with Ian Peebles, Smith's contribution being 98.

10

Modern Six Smiters

When Ian Botham walks out to bat you can close your eyes and touch the atmosphere. There is a sense of expectancy, a chance of history.

— Brian Bearshaw

The immediate post–World War II period was lit up by Keith Miller's tall and majestic hitting, which is already detailed in Chapter 8. He passed on the baton of enterprising ball–bashing to three fellow Australian all–rounders, Alan Davidson (featured among others in Chapter 7), Richie Benaud and Johnny Martin.

RICHIE BENAUD

In my opinion Benaud was the most versatile of cricket personalities. He was a world–class leg–spinner, an exciting hitter, a fielder with cat-like agility, among the shrewdest captains ever, one of the pioneers of limited–overs cricket as we know of now (being a key adviser to those who set up Kerry Packer's World Series Cricket), a smooth and convincing broadcaster on radio and television, and a man who not only thought deeply on the game but influenced the thinking of two generations. Also, with Frank Worrell, he revived Test Cricket in 1960s by playing aggressively and captured the imagination of cricket–lovers all over the world.

Although only a middle to lower order batsman, some of his batting displays were memorable. His drives powerfully projected with a full follow–through were often lofted. For Australians at Scarborough in 1953, he hit 11 sixes and nine fours in his 135 against T. N. Pearce's XI. It was a taunt by Len Hutton that brought out the fierce batting dynamo which was dormant within him. Benaud had been defending for an hour in this festival but first-class match when Hutton teasingly remarked: 'What's the matter, laad? Art [are thou] playing for average?' Benaud's response was a six-spree, mostly drives off left-hander Johnny Wardle and off-spinner Roy Tattersall and a hook off Alec Bedser — Test players all. In the middle of this onslaught, fielder Bill Edrich jokingly went past the boundary line and stood much further back at the Trafalgar Square end. He entered the field before the next ball, only to see it land where he had playfully stood. Eleven sixes by Benaud equalled a record that has since been broken many times.

When 24, Benaud scored the third fastest century in Test cricket. It was in the Kingston Test against the West Indies in 1954–55 when his hundred came in 78 minutes, the fastest Test ton by time taken since WW II. When he smote fast bowler Frank King for 20 runs in an over, a Jamaican barracker shouted: 'Do it to England, mahn; not to us'.

He did it to England in 1956 by scoring 97 off 113 balls in the Lord's Test — Australia's lone victory in the Laker-dominated Test series. A highlight of that innings was a violent six off a Fred Trueman bouncer right into the grandstand.

Benaud and Davidson were once involved in a six give-away strategy. For the NSW v. West Indies match preceding the first Test in 1960, skipper Benaud advised Davidson to bowl easy balls to the Windies fast scorer but less reliable opener Cammie Smith. The strategy was that if Smith impressed the selectors with a good score, he would be included in the team at the expense of the steady Joe Solomon. Smith hit a couple of boundaries in the first over and midway through Davidson's second over hooked a tall six in the crowd. Satisfied, Benaud told Davidson, 'You can stop pulling punches. He's all yours, bowl normally now.' To which Davidson countered: 'What do you mean? I *was* trying in this over.'

JOHNNY WESLEY MARTIN

Small, jaunty and unceasingly chirpy, Martin was everybody's favourite which explains his nickname 'Fav' or 'Little Fav'. An unorthodox slow left-arm bowler and an aggressive batsman, he was — to quote David Frith from *Wisden Cricket Monthly* —'as great an entertainment package as almost any cricketer to come out of NSW'. He hit over 160 sixes for his grade club, Petersham, alone. For a man of his size he gave the ball a tremendous clout.

His Test debut at Melbourne in the exciting 1960–61 series against the West Indies was remarkable. He went in at no. 10, scored 55 fast runs including a six off Frank Worrell, and added 97 runs in 72 minutes with Ken Mackay. Then with his chinamen (left-arm googlies), he dismissed master batsmen Rohan Kanhai, Garry Sobers and Worrell in four balls. He did nothing of note in his next seven Tests although he left his mark in Sheffield Shield and grade matches as an entertaining all-rounder and a jovial person.

Apart from being a six symbol, he was a six counter as well: he counted every six he hit and remembered the background behind each. Recalls Barry D. McDonald in a letter to me: 'I was fortunate to be a club mate of Johnny Martin when he came down from Burrell Creek in NSW to play in Sydney grade cricket with the Petersham-Marrickville Club. Forever modest about his own ability, he nonetheless

Small, jaunty and forever chirpy, Johnny Martin enjoyed hitting sixes. (Sydney Morning Herald)

maintained a mental record of every six he had hit in his career — including the trajectory of the hit and its landing point — and could tell you at any time, how many he had hit. Whenever he smote one, he would tell his batting partner and fielders "that's number 75" (or whatever). He once hit a massive six over the Members Stand roof on the Sydney Cricket Ground.'

Another big hit was a pull shot off John Rutherford, a change bowler for Western Australia, in 1957–58. Batting at Randwick end, Martin struck the ball over mid-wicket and onto the roof of the Bob Stand. Although this was his biggest six at the SCG, he hit even bigger ones on other grounds, including the oval at Marrickville.

The West Indies became and remained world beaters from 1960s to early 1990s, mainly because of their express bowling and magnificent batsmen who could hit with wild abandon. Batsmen like Garry Sobers, Rohan Kanhai, Clive Lloyd, Vivian Richards, Roy Fredericks, Gordon Greenidge, Desmond Haynes, Richie Richardson, Roger Harper, Carl Hooper and Brian Lara could fill a stadium with their dynamic stroke-play. None of them was a six-symbol — only Richards came close — but they held spectators spellbound by their sparkling batting.

SIR GARFIELD ST AUBURN SOBERS

When Sir Learie Constantine was in Australia in early 1950s, Sir Donald Bradman asked him his views on the up-and-coming left-handed youngster Garry Sobers. Constantine replied that Sobers was the hardest hitter of a ball he had ever seen.

After seeing Sobers (later Sir Garfield) perform in Australia, Bradman agreed with Constantine's assessment — a cricketing knight listening to another knight about a future knight.

'With his long grip of the bat, his high backlift and free swing, ... Garry Sobers consistently hits the ball harder than anyone I can remember,' wrote Bradman in *Cricket Advance*. 'This makes him such an exciting batsman to watch because the emphasis is on power and aggression rather than on technique — the latter being his servant, not the master. The uncoiling of those strong steely wrists, as he flicks the ball wide of mid-on is a real joy to watch because it is unique and superbly controlled, whilst the full-blooded square-cut is tremendous.'

On figures alone (8032 runs at 57.78 including 26 centuries, 235 wickets at 34.03 and 109 catches in 93 Tests) Sobers can be called the most complete cricketer of all time, just as Bradman has the title of being the most successful batsman. As mentioned in an earlier chapter, Sobers hit one of the most extraordinary and talked-about sixes in history. In the famous 1960–61 Test series against Australia, he initially went on the front foot when facing fast bowler Ian Meckiff. Changing his mind at the last moment, he went on the back foot and slammed the ball for a six over mid-off at the Randwick end. It was a freak shot befitting a genius.

In 1968 he climbed the so far unscaled Himalayan peak of six-hitting. For Nottinghamshire against Glamorgan at Swansea, he hit Malcolm Nash for six sixes in a six ball over — a perfect score. Many in the past had come close in a first-class match but Sobers was the first — Edmond Hillary and Tenzing Norgay rolled into one. So far, this feat by Sobers has been equalled only once by India's Ravi Shastri — normally known for his defensive batting at Test and one-day levels; for Bombay v. Baroda at Bombay in 1984–85. Details on these six-sprees are given in Chapter 14.

Ravi Shastri, only the second man after Sir Garry Sobers to hit six sixes in an over, in traditional headwear. (Khel Halchal, India)

Blessed with every necessary attribute for greatness as a cricketer, Sobers had rare natural genius, determination, stamina and the capacity to produce high quality performances year after year.

CLIVE HUBERT LLOYD

Lloyd, alias 'Super Cat', was another West Indies left-hander whose very presence filled stadia. 'Nobody dozes, drinks, knits, pours the wine, attacks the crossword, when Lloyd bats,' wrote Brian Bearshaw in *The Big Hitters*.

Whether it be the sombre atmosphere of Test cricket, greyish evening in a county match or the slog overs during a one-dayer, Lloyd played the type of cricket crowds approved of. He was tall and bespectacled, with a rather clumsy walk to the middle, as if he were an absent-minded professor who had lost his way. But once at the crease he was full of feline grace with the speed of a cheetah and the majesty of a Maharajah. He hit often and he hit hard, and seemed to do it all instinctively. When asked about the secret of his power-packed elegance, he replied: 'If ah can see the ball, ah can hit it'.

My favourite Lloyd innings was his century in the inaugural World (Prudential) Cup final on 21 June 1975 at Lord's. Even a black and white TV set could not diminish the magnificence of his innings against the bowling of Aussie quickies Dennis Lillee, Jeff Thomson, Gary Gilmour and Max Walker. The Windies were struggling at 3 for 50 when in came skipper Lloyd and showed his mastery. He hooked Lillee square for a six and put Walker off the back foot past cover with ease.

He hit two sixes and 12 fours in his scintillating 102 off 82 balls. Batsmen have hit more sixes in an innings, even in an over, and have scored faster but this was something out of the ordinary, an innings to convert a non-believer into an addict. Cheered on by bongo drums and calypso songs by the London-based West Indians, Lloyd's men won the fabulous final by 17 runs.

Lloyd played many other memorable innings, his 163 for Lancashire against Kent in 1970 included seven sixes, mostly off Derek Underwood who had boasted that he could contain Lloyd. That year Lloyd hit 44 sixes for Lancashire, 25 of them in first-class matches.

His unbeaten 242 in the Bombay Test of 1974 prompted India's record-breaker Sunil Gavaskar to comment, 'He flogged the bowling about and twice hit Bishan Bedi deep into the Garware stand'.

During the West Indies tour of England in 1976, Lloyd hit a ball into the railway station near Torquay and another into a duck pond when hammering 145 against the Minor Counties. On the same tour against Glamorgan at Swansea, he smacked seven sixes and 28 fours in his double century; the second hundred took him only 40 minutes. One of Lloyd's sixes in 1975 for Lancashire v. Surrey, measured 140 yards (127 metres), which Lloyd himself considers as his biggest hit.

ISAAC VIVIAN ALEXANDER RICHARDS

Viv Richards, better known as 'Master Blaster', will go down in cricket history as one of the greatest batsmen of all time. It is difficult to single out any of Richards' innings, as almost all were finely chiselled and exquisite. However, for absolute domination, one innings stands out.

It came in the fifth Test against England in April 1986 at St John's, Antigua, his home ground. A few days before, his father had suffered a mild stroke and he was determined to play a brilliant innings in his honour. To his dismay he was caught off Botham for 26 in the first innings. In the second knock, Viv came in to bat at 1 for 100, amid loud cheering from his home crowd. Soon he started hitting sixes off

Vivian Richards, the 'Master Blaster', hooks Derek Pringle during his blistering 189 against England in the Texaco Trophy match at Manchester in 1984. (Patrick Eagar)

'King' Vivian Richards — looking every inch an Indian Maharajah. (*Sportsweek,* India)

Richard Ellison and John Emburey to post 28 runs in 15 minutes before tea. After tea he accelerated, reaching 50 off 35 balls with three sixes, 'saluting the landmark with a devastating six over long off from Emburey, a shot which landed far outside the ground', wrote Peter Roebuck in *Great Innings*. Later Jack Bannister measured the distance and it was 110 metres.

Every run, every four, every six was greeted with a cacophony of noise as Richards continued the carnage and a barracker chanted: 'Captain, the ship is sinking'. To top it all, Richards hit a one-handed six off Emburey. Even Botham was not spared; one of his good length balls was hit so straight it almost parted Botham's hair and missed the umpire's head by inches.

He reached his 103 in 56 balls, easily scoring the fastest Test century by the number of balls faced. Previously the record was held by Australia's

Jack Gregory against South Africa in the Johannesburg Test of 1921 - 22, when his 100 had come off 67 balls in 70 minutes. However, Richards' hundred had come in 81 minutes, fifth fastest by time, after Gregory's in 70 minutes, Gilbert Jessop's in 75, Richie Benaud's in 78 and James Sinclair's in 80 minutes.

Richards' 110 in 58 balls included seven sixes and seven fours. Only Wally Hammond (10 sixes in 1932–33), Chris Cairns (nine in 1995–96) and Navjot Sidhu (eight in 1993–94) have hit more sixes in a Test innings. English writer John Thickeness described the Richards innings as 'unimaginable, stupendous, awesome, magical'.

Richards' most prolific year for six-hitting was 1977 when he hit 44 sixes in first-class matches for Glamorgan and 73 in all matches. Against Lancashire at Southport that summer he was a menace as much to householders as to the bowlers when scoring a firepower 189 out of 308. He bombarded the houses with nine sixes, reaching his 50, 100 and 150 with sixes.

In 1985 he hit 49 sixes in first-class matches for Somerset compared to Botham's 80, a bonanza for Somerset spectators. The next season both smote 34 sixes each. David Frith best summed up Richards the man in *Wisden Cricket Monthly*: 'He walks with a swagger, he chews menacingly; he thumps that cricket ball as if it contained all the evils of a millennium of mankind'.

CUTHBERT GORDON GREENIDGE

With Roy Fredericks, Barry Richards and Desmond Haynes, Gordon Greenidge formed opening partnerships which would rival any other in quick, adventurous scoring.

One of the shortest West Indian cricketers, Fredericks is remembered for a 'six-and-out' and for a six off the edge — both off Dennis Lillee. In the inaugural World (Prudential) Cup final at Lord's on 21 June 1975, Fredericks hooked a bouncer from Lillee high over fine leg for six only to lose his balance and tread on his wicket.

Fredericks' best knock was in the Perth Test of 1975. He began by edging Lillee's second ball of his first over for a six. He played a brilliant innings, his 100 coming in 116 minutes off 71 balls. His 169 is still talked about with awe and the Windies won by an innings. Seldom had high quality fast bowling been treated with such contempt.

Greenidge played many fabulous and fast innings for West Indies and for Hampshire. He is the only batsman to hit 13 sixes in a first-class innings *twice*. The first time he smote 13 sixes was for D. H. Robbins' XI against the touring Pakistanis at Eastbourne in 1974 in his unbeaten 273. He repeated the feat the next year for Hampshire v. Sussex at Southampton in his 259.

There is an interesting story behind Greenidge's 13 sixes against Pakistan as revealed to me by Dr Peter Handford from Western Australia.

'I was the scorer in that match. When Greenidge had hit 12 sixes, I delved into my bag and found a copy of *Wisden* and confirmed that the record then was 15 sixes in an innings by John Reid. After a quick consultation between all scorers, we decided that Derrick Robbins should be informed about the record before he declared the innings closed.

'For this mission, we sent Jack Funnell, the scoreboard operator aged 70 and not the fastest of men, to inform the captain about Greenidge being near a record. But before he could reach the Dressing Room, John Murray, the captain, declared with Greenidge on 13 sixes and he was thus "robbed" of a record. Robbins was quite keen on statistics and at the interval gave me a mock-serious telling-off for not making him aware of the position earlier!

'Greenidge was in the swimming pool when Robbins entered to tell him that he had just missed breaking a record. Greenidge asked whether it was a first-class match. When informed that it was, he did a backward somersault in the pool in exasperation.'

On his unbeaten 214 against England in the 1984 Lord's Test, Peter Roebuck wrote: 'Seldom has any attack been so brutally torn to pieces, seldom has any team had its hopes so conclusively crushed. Broken, England slumped to heavy defeats in all three remaining Test matches.'

COLIN MILBURN

Now on to the English six-clouters Colin Milburn and Ian Botham. For a happy-go-lucky man who enjoyed batting with the enthusiasm of a schoolboy, Colin Milburn had more snakes than ladders in his short career. Weighing 114 kilograms, he loved to thump the ball and was thrilled to see it flying in the sky. But tragedy struck him when on 25 May 1969 he was involved in a car accident which left him with sight in only his left eye. He tried a comeback in 1973 but without success and died in 1990, aged 48. However, his many huge sixes in England, Australia and Pakistan are remembered by all those lucky enough to see him bat.

Nicknamed 'Ollie' after Oliver Hardy, he was a scientific hitter and a box-office draw. When only 17 he scored an impressive century for Durham against the touring Indians in 1959, and on joining Northamptonshire became an attacking opening batsman. He was a fearless hooker, savage when square-cutting and drove uppishly or on-the-ground with vigour. In 1966 he scored a century before lunch three times and made his Test debut against West Indies at Old Trafford scoring 0 and 94. He attempted a big six off Lance Gibbs to get his 100 but was bowled. He did score a century in his next Test at Lord's which remained his favourite innings.

To show their appreciation, several English spectators ran from the Tavern bar and tried to lift their hero. But Milburn proved much too heavy for them. 'They failed miserably,' he said proudly.

The same season against Essex, he scored 203 which included four sixes and 22 fours. Earlier in 1964, during an MCC tour of East Africa he hit five successive sixes off a leg-spinner in a non first-class match and was caught off the last ball of an eventful over.

When left out of the England team, he decided to play for Western Australia in 1966 – 67. His explosive batting is still recalled in Australia whenever the topic turns to six-hitting. Of his 129 against South Australia, wrote Les Favell, himself a fast scorer: 'Milburn became a combination of heavy bomber and an artillery piece as he bludgeoned my bowlers into a daze with his tremendous hitting from the crease'.

Two year later he played another Sheffield Shield classic, hammering 242 off 226 balls in 230 minutes against Queensland in Brisbane on a hot, hot day. All the bowlers were mauled by him and he took 21 in one over from P. J. Allan's tenth over, smacking 6, 4, 4, 6, 1.

Of this dazzling innings, Milburn recalled: 'Everything was right that day. Every shot went between fielders and it was as if I just couldn't do anything wrong.'

In 1969 he played only one championship match for Northamptonshire. He hit five sixes in his 158 at Northampton against a Leicestershire side that included Test bowlers Graham McKenzie, Barry Knight and Ray Illingworth. This was followed by the car accident and we were left contemplating the many might-have-beens for the dynamic 27-year-old.

IAN TERRENCE BOTHAM

Botham, nicknamed 'Beefy' and 'Guy the Gorilla', was among the most dynamic all-rounders in the history of the game. He possessed a super-abundance of all the qualities required for success; immense natural talent, the strength of a bull, determination to succeed, confidence with arrogance, courage, pluck and common sense. He was both a technique and an eye-player and among the two great six symbols of WW II era — the other being Keith Miller.

Just marvel at his Test record, 5200 runs at 33.54 with 14 centuries (highest score 208), 383 wickets at 28.40 (five wickets in an innings 27 times) and 120 catches in 102 Tests. Apart from the statistics, he was a match-winner with his never-say-die attitude which Australians will remember — especially in 1981 when he almost single-handedly converted a lost series into a triumph. John Arlott described him as 'an instinctive and exultant winner of cricket matches'.

Six symbol Ian Botham hits Allan Border for a six in the Leeds Test of 1985.
(Patrick Eagar)

Botham showed his courage and winning attitude when only 18. For Somerset against Hampshire in a Benson & Hedges quarterfinal at Taunton on 12 June 1974, he came in at 8 for 113, Somerset needing 183 to win. He was hit full in the mouth off an Andy Roberts' bouncer. West Indian Roberts was then the fastest bowler in the world. Botham declined to leave the field despite bleeding profusely and spitting out two teeth — he was to lose two more that evening — and continued batting. He hit two marvellous sixes while making an unbeaten 45, his team won and he received a Gold Award. The crowd ran in to salute the new hero who made headlines on every sports page in England.

He started the 1976 season with zest, scoring 97 against Sussex with two sixes (one off Tony Greig) and made his first century, 167 not out, with six sixes and 20 fours, against Nottinghamshire. The folk hero had arrived with a bang.

His finest, most dramatic and topsy-turvy season was 1981 when under his captaincy England lost the first Test to Australia and drew the second at Lord's, where his contribution was 0 and 0. He resigned as captain before he was sacked. In the bewilderingly fluctuating third Test at Headingley, Leeds, England under Mike Brearley was forced to follow-on 227 runs behind. They were 7 down for 135, still 92 runs behind, when a rejuvenated Botham added 117 runs in 80 minutes for the eighth wicket with John Lever. 'Beefy' Botham remained unbeaten with a magnificent 149 (one six and 27 fours) and England won the Test, Bob Willis taking 8 for 43. The flop and 'has-been' Botham had taken 6-96 and 1-14 and scored 50 and 149 runs to snatch victory out of thin air.

Botham was also the hero in the next Test at Birmingham, taking 5 for 11 in 14 overs in the second innings, and England won. Then he hit 118 with six sixes and 13 fours at Manchester and England led the Test series 2-1. Wrote Mike Brearley, the captain, 'He [Botham] played even better than at Headingley. An innings of classical power and splendour, of off-drives, hooks and cuts.'

His 118 had come in 123 minutes, his century in 104 minutes and reminded old-timers of 'Croucher' Jessop. When 'Both' was on 28, Dennis Lillee took the new ball and in his first over was hit for 22 runs. It included two majestic hooked sixes. Botham went from 28 to 100 in 37 minutes.

Botham's century in the 1986–87 series against Australia at Brisbane is remembered with awe. He hit four huge sixes and 14 fours in 138 off 174 balls, taking 22 runs off one over from Merv Hughes (2, 2, 4, 6, 4, 4). One of his sixes went within centimetres of smashing the office window of the Queensland Cricket Association secretary Grantley Evans. Another one spiralled into a tin roof in front of a press contingent in retreat!

'Botham's daredevil display was simply awesome, given the importance of the occasion, the start of a new Ashes series', recalled Ken Piesse, currently the editor of *Australian Cricket*.

One could write a book on Botham's six exploits and still leave gaps. After his Manchester masterpiece of 1981, he scored a sensational century in 61 minutes in a John Player league match for Somerset v. Hampshire at Taunton, belting seven sixes and nine fours. His second 50 took only nine minutes and he outpaced Vivian Richards in an amazing display. There have been many other six-sprees by Botham, too many to enumerate. But we cannot ignore his 80 sixes in the 1985 first-class season; a record which still stands.

'One of the great pleasures for Somerset followers in recent years has been the sight of Botham and Richards batting together. Cricket can have few more splendid prospects,' wrote Brian Bearshaw in *The Big Hitters*. 'When Botham walks out to bat you can close your eyes and touch the atmosphere. There is a sense of expectancy, a chance of history.'

MIKE JOHN PROCTER

There have been quite a few brilliant stroke-players from South Africa — Graeme Pollock, Barry Richards and Mike Procter. Of them, Procter lifted the ball more often and is considered as among the most eye-catching all-rounders. He is the only cricketer to score a century before lunch and take a hat-trick in the same match. This was for Gloucestershire v. Leicestershire at Bristol in 1979.

A dynamic personality, he was a match-winner by bowling extremely fast and batting with rare gusto. Yet he was consistent enough to hit six first-class centuries in succession in 1970 - 71, a feat accomplished in the past by only two: C. B. Fry in 1901 and Don Bradman in 1938–39.

When batting for Gloucestershire at Lord's in 1971, he scored the fastest century of the season in 79 minutes, clouting six sixes. Against Glamorgan in 1973, he made 152 in 140 minutes with six sixes and 17 fours. His double century against Essex in 1978 was described by *Wisden* as being 'generally regarded as the best innings seen on the ground since Hammond's heyday'.

He clobbered the Surrey attack at Guildford for eight enormous sixes and 18 fours in his 154 made in less than two hours in 1978. He hit 32 sixes the next year, including the season's fastest century in 57 minutes. Then at Taunton against Somerset on a wet pitch he smashed 93 in 46 minutes including six sixes in successive balls off two overs from Dennis Breakwell. He also hit Australia's off-spinner Ashley Mallett for five successive sixes for Western Province at Cape Town in 1970.

Team-mate Brian Brain wrote: 'The amazing thing is that he [Procter] will play with any bat he picks up; he never seems to worry about the weight, balance or pick-up of the bat; he just goes out there and hammers it. He is a natural.'

The same could be said about Keith Miller. What a pity that due to his country's politics, the super-talented Procter played only seven Tests and not one when he was at his peak.

JOHN REID

New Zealand produced quite a few big hitters in the post WW II period. Reid's record of 15 sixes in an innings of 296 for Wellington v. Northern Districts at Wellington on 15 January 1963 stood as a record for 32 years till eclipsed by Anglo-Aussie Andrew Symonds in August 1995. Reid scored 174 runs before lunch, reaching his 50 in 67 minutes, 100 in 99 (with six sixes and 15 fours), 150 in 134, 200 in 167 and 250 in 195. His last 46 came in 25 minutes and included five sixes.

Four of his 15 sixes were hit off T. E. Shaw, three each off P. H. Barton, D. B. Clarke and G. D. Alabaster and two off N. Puna. Reid also hit 35 fours. Thus, 230 of his 296 (78%) were from boundary hits.

A strong, sturdily built aggressive batsman, he later captained New Zealand in 34 Tests and scored 3428 runs at 33.28 (10 centuries) in 58 Tests.

The six-hitting sprees of Kiwi hitter Lance Cairns and his son Chris are mentioned in Chapter 5. All-rounders both, they remain cricket's most hard-hitting father-son combination.

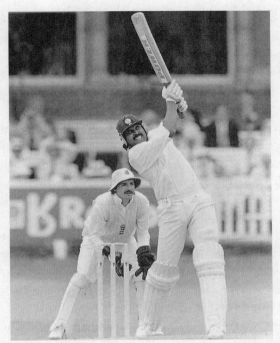

Kapil Dev smites the second of his four successive sixes off Eddie Hemmings to save India a follow-on in the 1990 Lord's Test. (Patrick Eagar)

KAPIL DEV NIKHANJ

India's Kapil Dev, the 'Hariyana Hurricane', was a flamboyant and cavalier all-rounder. Although an accomplished pace bowler, 'in fullness of time, he may be remembered more for his care-free, hawkeyed batting,' opined Mike Selvey in *Wisden*. His rate of scoring was phenomenal in match after match. In the 1982 Lord's Test he smashed three sixes and 13 fours in his 89 off 55 balls.

One of his moments to savour came in the 1990 Lord's Test remembered for Graham Gooch's 333 and 123. India needed 24 runs to avoid a follow-on but Kapil had only no. 11 batsman Narendra Hirwani left. So Kapil went the whole hog, slamming four successive sixes off Eddie Hemmings. Just as well, for Hirwani, blinking nervously at the other end, got out to the first ball he faced.

The proudest hour for the tall, handsome Kapil Dev was leading India to a totally unexpected victory in the final of the 1987 World Cup at Lord's. But for Kapil's magical batting a week earlier, India would not have qualified for the semi-finals. The Indians were in strife, four of their best batsmen dismissed by the least fancied Zimbabwe for just nine runs when Kapil went in to bat.

'I felt like I was in a trance. I had no time to think what I had to do. I simply decided to bat as if it were a five day game,' said Kapil, his eye asparkle.

Another wicket fell and India were 5 for 17. It was a hopeless situation, but Kapil was the only person not convinced. He felt relaxed, confident, ten feet tall. He took the score to 7 for 78; and then to 8 for 140. With Syed Kirmani joining him, Kapil realised that he had defended enough and it was time to use the long handle. In 18 balls, he struck three sixes and three fours.

He continued with the onslaught and India recovered from a depressing 5 for 17 to a healthy 9 for 266, Kapil scoring an unbeaten and uninhibited 175, including six sixes and 16 fours. It was an innings of a lifetime — especially as India not only won this match but also went on to lift the cup.

Kapil was a six symbol at 20, hitting a hurricane hundred in 33 minutes (with 10 sixes and eight fours) in a benefit match in Bangalore in 1979. When touring Australia in 1980–81, he struck a spectacular six in the Benson & Hedges World Series Cup match at Brisbane. It was off New Zealander Jeremy Coney and it sailed over the Clem Hill Stand and into Stanley Street. This enormous shot made Coney wave his white handkerchief as if in surrender.

One of Kapil's best Test innings was against England at Kanpur in 1982 when he scored a century (including two sixes and 16 fours) in 83 minutes.

He also played many dazzling innings representing Northamptonshire in county cricket. In 1981 he made a 79 v. Worcestershire which was studded with six sixes and six fours. August 1982 was a month of incredible hitting for Kapil, starting with 103 (three towering sixes and 11 fours) on a dusty, wearing pitch against Sussex at Eastbourne. In the next match he hammered an unbeaten 65 (four sixes, four fours) and 100 not out in 98 minutes (one six, 11 fours). In between these innings he played in the limited-overs John Player League and scored 75 runs off 48 balls with four sixes and 11 fours. Thus in seven days he had amassed 343 runs at 171.50 with two tons, 12 sixes and 37 fours.

When touring England the same summer, he scored 89 (three sixes, thirteen fours) out of 117 in 77 minutes off only 55 balls in the Lord's Test. He hit Botham into the grandstand to reach 50 and belted two sixes off Phil Edmonds.

In the final Test at The Oval, he hit 97 runs in 102 minutes. He had clouted two sixes into the Vauxhall Stand, one of them off Botham. Then in 1986, he led India to her first ever win over England at Lord's. And it was a six from Kapil that brought India the victory.

On figures Kapil was among the most prolific all-rounders; 5248 runs at 31.05 (with eight centuries) and taking 434 wickets — a Test record — at 29.64 and 64 catches in 131 Tests. Apart from the statistics, Kapil will be remembered for his sparkling eyes, toothy smile and fearless big hitting — especially in a crisis.

DAVID WILLIAM HOOKES

Back to Australia and the occasional hitters Sam Loxton, Rod Marsh, David Hookes, Simon O'Donnell, Dean Jones and Michael Slater. I have a vivid memory of Rod Marsh hitting New Zealand fast-medium

Carl Hooper smashes one into the crowd during the Lord's Test of 1995. (Patrick Eagar)

All eyes towards the sky as Rod Marsh clouts Andy Roberts for a six. (Ken Piesse Collection)

Rod Marsh smites a delivery from Tony Greig for six on the opening day of the first Test between Australia and England at Birmingham in 1975. (Sydney Morning Herald)

Simon O'Donnell hits Bill Athey for a six for Victoria against England on the MCG in 1986. (Ken Piesse Collection)

David Hookes strikes a hard blow for South Australia v. Victoria on the MCG. (Ken Piesse Collection)

Michael Slater in full flow. An elegant stroke-player he smote five sixes — a record for a Test in Australia — in his 219 v. Sri Lanka at Perth in December 1995. (Sydney Morning Herald)

Merv Hughes can hit with the bat too. (Ken Piesse Collection)

bowler Lance Cairns for three sixes and two fours in an over in the Benson & Hedges World Series Cup match in Adelaide in 1980–81. Also I remember Slater smacking five sixes in his 219 against Sri Lanka at Perth in December 1995 which is a record number of sixes in a Test in Australia. Another Australian to hit five sixes in a Test innings was Sam Loxton, in the Leeds Test against England in July 1948 when scoring 93. It remains as a record for an Australian in a Test in England. However, none of the above could be called a six symbol — except perhaps David Hookes, a delightful left-hander from South Australia.

His first century in 1977, when he was 21, included spectacular hitting. He had come in at 5 for 100 but went out in glory after scoring 163. He belted Victorian leg-spinner Colin Thwaites for 29 runs in an eight-ball over (four sixes and one four). In the next match against Queensland at Adelaide, he played aggressively to score 135 and 156 and was selected in the Centenary Test against England at Melbourne in March 1977. He made his debut memorable by scoring a quick 56 which included five consecutive fours in an over off Tony Greig.

Hookes played club, Sheffield Shield and Test cricket with equal gusto. In a club match in June 1975, Hookes had made headlines belting six sixes off an over from Bexley's Geoff Burton at Dulwich, South Australia. Seven years later he played two scintillating innings.

Against Queensland in January 1982, he hit leg-spinner Dennis Lillie (*not* the great Lillee) for four sixes in an over. 'I hit the first four balls for six and blocked the fifth, on the middle and leg, and I'll always regret it …But I was the captain then and playing responsibly. If I had not been the captain, I would have gone for it', said Hooksey. He did hit a four off the last ball to score 28 runs in an over.

In October 1982, against Victoria at Adelaide, he scored the fastest century by an Australian in first-class cricket. It came in 43 minutes off 34 balls and is the quickest century by number of balls faced. Annoyed at rival captain Graham Yallop's late declaration — setting South Australia a run–chase of 272 in about 30 overs — he opened the batting. He savaged the Victorian attack with such vigour that his 50 came in 17 minutes and 107 in 55 minutes with 17 fours and three sixes. One of the sixes was a gigantic hit onto the roof of the Members' Grandstand. Hookes himself considers this as his biggest hit.

ANDREW SYMONDS

Two world records for six-hitting were established in one match in August 1995 by a Birmingham-born, Queensland-raised 20-year-old cricketer with West Indian blood playing for Gloucestershire. During a championship match against Glamorgan at Abergavenny, Glamorgan, Andrew Symonds hit 16 sixes in the first inning to eclipse John Reid's record of 15 sixes set in 1962 – 63. Symonds then smote four more sixes in the second innings to get past Jim Stewart's record of 17 sixes (10 in the first innings) for Warwickshire v. Lancashire at Blackpool in 1959.

Coming in at 4 for 79 in reply to Glamorgan's 334 on 24 August 1995, Symonds lost his captain Mark Alleyne soon and the score was a depressing 5 for 79. Undaunted, he proceeded to add 213 with Reggie Williams. At stumps Symonds had raced to 197 not out with 13 sixes. The next morning he hit two sixes off successive balls from Test medium-pacer Steve Watkin to put him level with Reid. Then another six from Watkin brought up the new record. The sixteenth six sailed over the outfield, a hawthorn bush, a patch of bindweed and on to a nearby tennis court. He ended with an unbeaten 254 and passed 1000 runs for the season.

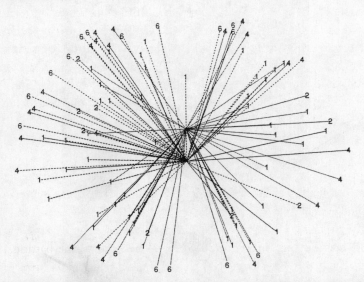

Andrew Symonds created a world record in August 1995 when he smacked 16 sixes in his unbeaten 254 for Gloucestershire v. Glamorgan at Abergavenny (Run chart, courtesy *Wisden Cricket Monthly*)

In the second innings his 76 included four more sixes for a match total of 20 sixes — his second record in two days. The bowlers to suffer at Symonds' hands were Watkin and Robert Croft (six sixes each), Neil Kendrick (five) and Darren Thomas (three). Interviewed after the six-spree, Symonds modestly said that he was not overwhelmed by the records; what mattered was playing the best for his team.

In the Sunday League game that followed he hit seven sixes in his breathtaking and match-winning 69 off 35 balls against Glamorgan at Ebbw Vale. Performances like these led to his being elected as the Young Cricketer of the Year, the Young Player of the Year and selection in the England 'A' team to tour Pakistan in 1995–96. After a lot of deliberation, he declined the offer and opted to play for Queensland (whenever selected) in Sheffield Shield and Mercantile Mutual Cup.

The latest six symbol Andrew Symonds is the holder of two first-class records; 16 sixes in an innings and 20 sixes in a match. (Australian Picture Library / Allsport)

Hitting sixes is nothing new for Symonds. When touring India with the Under-19 Australians a year earlier he plundered 10 sixes and 20 fours to score 163 on a powdery spinner's pitch. Soon comparisons were made with Mark Waugh for his effortless and elegant strokeplay. However, his idols are Viv Richards and Richie Richardson. Talk of triple nationality!

SANATH JAYASURIYA

The year 1996 was dominated by Sri Lanka's six-smiter Jayasuriya, the Player of World Cup 1996. The 27-year-old balding Sri Lankan created quite a few records in six-hitting in Limited-Overs cricket in Singapore in the Singer Cup in April 1996.

In the first match against a strong Pakistani attack, he lifted 11 sixes in his blistering knock of 134 in 104 minutes off 65 balls. His 11 sixes set up a record, surpassing Gordon Greenidge's eight against India at St John's, West Indies, in 1988–89. Jayasuriya's first 50 came in 32 balls and second 50 in 16 balls. Thus his 100 came in just 48 deliveries (with nine sixes) which put in the shade Indian captain Mohammad Azharuddin's century off 62 balls against New Zealand at Baroda in 1988–89. Jayasuriya scoring 29 runs (plus one wide) in one over off Pakistan skipper Aamir Sohail (including four successive sixes) is also a record in limited-overs cricket. The overall match aggregate of 664 runs (Sri Lanka 349, Pakistan 315) also surpassed the 652 scored by Sri Lanka and Kenya in the 1996 World Cup match in Kandy, Sri Lanka.

Jayasuriya was at it again next week. On 7 April 1996, on the same small Pedang ground in Singapore, he established another record in limited-overs cricket. His 50 off 17 balls was the fastest, bettering the previous record by Australia's Simon O'Donnell who had taken 18 balls to reach his 50 against India at Sharjah in 1988–89. Jayasuriya raced to 76 runs in 28 balls with five sixes and eight fours. He added 70 runs for the first wicket with Romesh Kaluwitharana of which Jayasuriya scored 66, sundries were four and the normally aggressive Kaluwitharana zero. The ball-by-ball sequence of Jayasuriya's 50 in 17 deliveries is as follows: 2, 4, 2, 4, 0, 1, 1, 6, 0, 6, 0, 4, 6, 6, 4, 1, 6.

Despite Jayasuriya's brilliance and belligerence the Sri Lankans lost to Pakistan by 43 runs.

Sanath Jayasuriya holds most records in limited-overs internationals; quickest century (in 65 balls), quickest 50 (in 17 balls), 11 sixes in an innings and 29 runs in an over. (Australian Picture Library / Allsport)

The Pedang ground is very small with the boundary line barely 55 metres from the batting pitch. This, one may argue, gives the batsman an unfair advantage and in a way devalues a six. In the 1996 World Cup 150 sixes were hit in 35 matches, Sri Lanka leading the way with 30 in six matches, New Zealand and Australia 16 in six and seven matches, respectively, and India 15 in seven.

In the Sri Lanka v. Kenya match at Kandy on 6 March 1996, as many as 21 sixes were belted, Sri Lanka contributing 14 of them. (Arvinda de Silva smacked five, Jayasuriya and Asanka Gurusinha three each). Gurusinha hit the most number of sixes in the Cup, 11, followed by Jayasuriya and Salim Raza of United Arab Emirates (eight each) and India's Sachin Tendulkar (seven). Gurusinha hit six sixes in one match against Zimbabwe at Colombo, Salim Raza also six sixes v. Holland at Lahore, Tendulkar five sixes v. Sri Lanka at Delhi and de Silva also five against Kenya at Kandy.

Such proliferation of sixes could be more due to shorter boundary lines and batsmen-friendly pitches than the hitting-power of batsmen. But then such statistics point to the evolution of cricket. The boundary lines have been shrinking gradually and six-hitting is easier now than ever before. Prior to 1910 in England, as stated before in Chapter 2, one had to clear the ground to get a six.

Such changes would make it a mockery to assess and compare six-hitters from different eras. Suffice it to say that all the six-hitters from Thornton, Bonnor and Jessop, via Wellard, Earle and Miller to Milburn, Botham and Kapil brought the joy and thrill of cricket to spectators whether they were 120, 100, 80 or 60 metres away.

They risked their averages and their place in the team by jumping out to smite the ball up and away — a blurring miracle of spring and willow annihilating leather, cork and twine.

11

Hurricane Comets

O, but it's glorious, swinging the bat.

— E.V. Lucas

In case you wonder what hurricane comets are, they are six symbols which do not last long. They arrive on the scene from nowhere, razzle and dazzle spectators with an incandescent innings and after a few good knocks fade away without fulfilling the expectations aroused by *that* innings.

Not many readers may have heard of Edwin (Ted) B. Alletson and Dady R. Havewala. Alletson was a right-handed attacking lower-order batsman who played for Nottinghamshire before World War I. Havewala was a left-handed Parsee from Bombay who represented India in two unofficial test matches against England before World War II. Both were useful bowlers and hurricane hitters who became instant celebrities for just one magnificently scintillating innings played 22 years apart.

Alletson's 189 out of 227 in 90 minutes (with eight spectacular sixes and 23 fours) against Sussex at Hove in 1911 converted a certain defeat into a near victory and inspired John Arlott to write an entertaining monograph titled *Alletson's Innings*, reconstructing the innings ball-by-ball and stroke-by-stroke some 40 years after the event — with the help of statistician Roy Webber. Havewala's 515 in the final of a non–first-class but major tournament in Bombay in 1933 included 32 sixes (29 in a day) and 55 fours. Sir Jack Hobbs, then in India as a journalist to cover the 1933–34 English tour, sighted the 'Havewala comet' in full flow. At one stage he was so concerned by Havewala's savage sixes coming his way that, according to a report, he jokingly opened his umbrella to protect his head.

First to Hove, Sussex, on 20 May 1911 where a single innings made Alletson, a strapping 27-year-old six-footer, an immortal. Till that day he was in and out of the Notts team — more often out — during his five years as a professional. He went in to bat in a crisis, in Notts' second innings, at no. 9. They were nine runs ahead with only three wickets in hand. As 50 minutes remained before the lunch break on the final day, Sussex were confident of winning before the break. In the first innings, the last three Notts batsman had made 13 runs, Alletson scoring seven.

The son of a wheelwright on the Duke of Portland estate in Nottinghamshire Dukeries, Alletson was more of a bowler than a batsman and was selected in this match mainly because Tom Wass, their front-line bowler, was injured. Alletson himself was recovering from a sprained wrist and barely passed the fitness test. Fate works in mysterious ways!

With Notts trailing Sussex by 176 runs in the first innings, and the score 7 for 185 in the second, Alletson joined G. M. Lee. The former kept the innings going until lunch, the scoreboard reading a hopeless 9 for 260, only 84 runs on. He was 47 at lunch scored in 50 minutes, hitting five fours, two threes, four twos and 13 singles. Nothing extraordinary, but he was still there, thanks to two chances put down when he was 25 and 42.

With nothing to lose — a defeat was inevitable in any case — Alletson asked his captain whether he could attack after lunch. The captain gave him the go-ahead and the famous Notts character George Gunn, who had made 90 and 66 in this match, urged him to 'give the bastards a bit of stick'.

What happened after lunch was incredible. In just 40 minutes from 2.10 to 2.50 p.m., Alletson added 142 runs to his total before being wrongly given out, caught by Charles L. A. Smith (whose feet were over the boundary line) off George Cox for a spellbinding 189. Technically he was not out and it should have been his ninth six, which would have taken him to 195. Despite protests from the spectators (to whom Alletson was the opposition) and the fielders, the Hero of Hove left amid almost hysterical applause.

Everyone lucky enough to watch this innings said that they had never seen anything to approach such power and timing. After lunch his innings was devoid of a single mishit. Brodribb wrote: 'big hitting that surpassed the wildest dreams of the lustiest, legendary blacksmith

... one innings which included the most powerful hitting in the whole history of the game'.

Here is a blow-by-blow description of the famous innings. His 47 before lunch came in 50 minutes and after reaching 50 in 60 minutes, he went berserk — doubling his score in 15 minutes and adding another 89 in 15 exhilarating minutes. From seven overs he made 115 out of 120 and in all hit eight sixes, 23 fours, four threes, 10 twos and only 17 singles. He faced 51 balls after lunch, and according to Arlott and Webber's research his run sequence was: 0, 4, 4, 1, 2, 4, 2, 0, 1, 6, 0, 4, 2, 4, 6, 4, 0, 6, 3, 4, 4, 0, 2, 1, 4, 6, 0, 4, 3, 4, 6, 6, 0, 4, 4, 4, 6, 0, 0, 0, 0, 4, 4, 2, 2, 6, 1, 4, 4, 0, W.

Only twelve of the 51 deliveries were dot (no run) balls. The most amazing spell came in the middle of the 40 minute period after lunch. In the course of five overs, three by slow left-hander Ernest Killick and two by G. Leech, Notts picked up 100 runs, 97 to Alletson and only three to W. Riley. One over from Killick — including two no-balls — went for 34 runs (4, 6, 6, 0, 4, 4, 4, 6) — a record for an over until West Indies great Garry Sobers hit Malcolm Nash for 36 runs (six sixes at Swansea) in 1968 and later India's Ravi Shastri gave Tilak Raj the same treatment at Bombay in 1984–85.

All of Alletson's eight sixes were huge hits and Brodribb doubts whether anyone — except Charles Thornton — had hit such towering shots in one and the same innings. *Wisden 1912* refers to Alletson 'driving with a power that has perhaps *never* been surpassed'.

From a hopeless 7 for 185, Notts reached 412, setting an exhausted Sussex 237 to win. They finished 24 runs short with two wickets remaining. It was a remarkable match kindled by an extraordinary individual effort.

Five days after this epic, Alletson was at it again on a miniature scale and scored 60 out of 80 in 30 minutes, reaching 53 in 23 minutes. He hit four sixes, three were huge on-drives and a straight drive that came close to smashing the clock on the top of the Bristol pavilion in Gloucestershire.

Perhaps too much was expected from Alletson after these two mighty efforts which yielded 249 runs in two hours. He achieved little afterwards, hitting only four more fifties in his career, and that memorable 189 remained his only century in first-class cricket. 'No man could have played two innings like that and lived,' commented Bob Relf, the bowler he hit for one of his eight sixes on 20 May 1911.

When runs dried up it was believed Alletson became defence-oriented, which did not help. There were occasional flashes of brilliance, though, when he on-drove the great Wilfred Rhodes for three sixes off three consecutive balls in his 35 for Notts v. Yorkshire at Dewsbury in 1913.

Later he scored 88 (four sixes and seven fours) out of 109 in exactly one hour against Derbyshire at Trent Bridge. When he hit slow left-handed Bracey for 6, 4, 6, 6, 1 in two consecutive overs, two of the sixes were gigantic hits. One landed on a house in Radcliffe Road, a hit of about 140 metres. Alletson said that it was the biggest hit he ever made.

His career ended three years later, having made 3217 runs at a modest average of 18.59. During World War I he served in the Royal Garrison Artillery and later worked at Manton Colliery. He died on 5 July 1963 aged 79 and will be remembered for his magnum opus at Hove.

The name Alletson is still revered in Nottinghamshire. There is a pub in Worksop called *The Innings*. As you enter you see perched on a 12-foot pole the figure of Ted Alletson in action on one knee, informs Brian Bearshaw in *The Big Hitters*. This statue is to commemorate Alletson's magical innings of 189 in 90 minutes. Inside the front door is a plaque describing that innings. Alletson Bar is the games room and hanging on the wall is the bat that hit all those fours and sixes.

Dady Havewala was only two when Alletson played his famous innings in 1911. The six-blaster from Bombay grew up to play a memorable innings.

Phenomenal scoring was witnessed at the Islam Gymkhana, Bombay, on 4 and 5 December 1933. Playing for B B & C I Railway against St Xavier's College in the final of *The Times of India Shield* (a major tournament with quality players participating but not granted first-class status), Havewala, 25, electrified spectators by scoring 515 runs.

In reply to St Xavier's total of 446, B B & C I Railway amassed 7 for 650 on 4 December, with Havewala unbeaten on 453 (29 sixes and 45 fours). This was a record in India in any class of cricket and would have broken Don Bradman's world record of 452 not out at Sydney in 1929–30 if the match had been given first-class status.

The next morning B B & C I Railway lost their last three wickets for 71 runs of which Havewala contributed 62 (three sixes and 10 fours). Thus 58 of his 62 had come in boundaries that day. He was the last man out when he mistimed a ball from Shete and was caught by Lalji and his team totalled 721.

Out of Havewala's 515, as many as 412 (80%) were scored in boundaries: 32 sixes and 55 fours. He had equalled the world record for hitting most sixes in an innings in any grade of cricket. In England in 1902, W. Hyman (359 runs) had hit 32 sixes for Bath Association v. Thornbury. Hyman had hit Dr E. M. Grace for 32 runs and 30 runs in successive overs. In 1939–40, D. Hope (253) broke the record when hitting 36 sixes for Standard Bank v. Levers of Durban, South Africa. And in 1989 Kevin Hutchinson, a 17-year-old schoolboy, blasted 39 sixes in his unbeaten 311 for Trinity College v. St Paul's College in Adelaide.

Ten years earlier, in 1923, Havewala, 15, had taken all 10 wickets in an innings (10 for 23) for Petit Orphanage School v. St Xavier's School. It is possible that he is the only cricketer to do the 'double' of 500 runs and all 10 wickets in separate matches.

After his 32 six-blitz in 1933, there were exaggerated expectations from the dashing Dady and a buzz of excitement followed his walk to the wicket. His quickfire 71 in 58 minutes with six sixes and six fours against Jack Ryder's Australian team of 1935–36 at the Bombay Gymkhana impelled the great Charlie Macartney to comment: 'I can truly say that I have seldom seen finer hitting than that by Havewala'.

In a club match on the Parsee Gymkhana, Havewala once hit Clarrie Grimmett (in India on a coaching assignment) for a couple of sixes.

Another notable effort was his 106 in 93 minutes for the Maharajah of Patiala's team v. Lord Tennyson's Englishmen at Patiala in 1937–38. This innings earned him a place in the Indian team for the fourth and fifth unofficial tests at Madras and Bombay. In the Madras 'test' which India won by an innings, he made 44, the second highest score for the side.

He also played for Bombay in Ranji Trophy from 1934–35 to 1941–42, his highest score being 103 against Western India in 1935–36. These were all good performances but nothing out of the ordinary. He would have been a forgotten man when he died on

21 July 1992, aged 73, but for the single mammoth, six-studded innings he played in 1933.

There have been quite a few other hurricane hitters who have come, smashed sixes and phased out of orbit, but none played an innings as sensationally as Ted Alletson did in 1911 and Dady Havewala in 1933.

12

Hits and Myths

Tall shots often mean tall tales in minor cricket.

Like the size of a fish, the distance and height of a particular six-hit keeps escalating in minor/junior/club cricket. Unless a writer is careful he could be perpetuating myths.

There are many stories of Joe Blow smashing the dial of a clock at Woof Woof park, witnessed by the story-teller's mother-in-law's uncle. The most common con is about A. Person hitting the ball high and wide till it lands in a moving train/truck/bus and is recovered the following week at the next railway station or beyond.

'Every ground which has a railway passing by has some such legend,' wrote Brodribb. 'It has been difficult to discover how much, if any, truth lies in these stories.'

One such train story appears genuine. The groundsman of Old Trafford in Manchester with its Warwick Road station assured Brodribb that Eddie Paynter did put a ball into a moving goods wagon which took it to Chester. There may be other tall but true tales. A reliable eye-witness saw Errol R. T. Holmes of Surrey hit a ball out of the Guildford ground into an open charabanc which drove serenely on.

But the story which reveals that C. B. Fry hit the first ball he received from K. S. Ranjitsinhji into a train with such pinpoint accuracy that after a few bounces on a boiler it went down the funnel appears suspect.

George Mell in *This Curious Game of Cricket* and Christopher Martin-Jenkins, who edited *The Cricketer Book of Cricket Disasters and Bizarre Records*, give many stranger-than-fiction accounts. A selection appears below — believe them or not!

Many years ago, a big hit from a Kendall Club batsman landed in the engine cab of a passing train. The considerate driver stopped the train, threw back the ball and the match continued. On another occasion, a big hit from the same ground landed on a passenger train and was carried to Windermere.

Now to the most outrageous claims when umpires refused to call an unreachable but visible ball a 'lost ball' and the batsmen kept running — once as many as 286 times. Let us start with the most bizarre of them all.

At Bonbury in Western Australia in December 1893 or January 1894, the local team played host to a Victorian club team. The Victorians batted first and the opening ball was slammed into a three-pronged branch of a tall jarrah tree within the boundary line. The home team appealed for 'lost ball' but the umpire said it was not lost because it could still be seen. They looked for an axe to cut down the tree but failed to find one. All this time the Victorian batsmen kept running and running between wickets. Someone eventually brought a rifle and the best shot in the home team was assigned the job to knock down the ball. After several misses, the ball came down but nobody thought of catching it. The Victorians claimed and got 286 runs for that one hit and declared. The target was too much for the local side. Just as well they did not turn the rifle on each other or to the exhausted visiting openers who had run approximately 5.8 kilometres that day non-stop, turning their direction 285 times.

A similar but slightly more plausible incident is said to have occurred in South London on 26 May 1894. Camberwell Albion team totalled 129 runs, leaving Peckham Pushers only 55 minutes to get the runs. J. H. Brown hit the first ball of the innings into a tree growing inside the boundary. The ball was visible and was lodged in a rook's nest. As the fielders endeavoured to extract the ball, Brown and his partner A. Archer ran 93. Encouraged by this unexpected start, the Pushers won by four wickets.

At Thorpe Perrow in Yorkshire's North Riding in 1885, a single hit yielded 31 runs. And a few years later at Ingleby Cross in Cleveland Hills in England, the ball was driven down a steep slope and the batsmen took 34 runs while relays of fielders recovered the ball.

Gerald Howat, the meticulous author of *Learie Constantine* and *Walter Hammond*, mentions one such story in *Village Cricket*. A single hit on Beacon Hill ground near Rottingdean, Sussex, (year not specified) produced 67 runs. The ball rolled down to the nearby village and was retrieved by a relay of fielders. At the final stage, a fielder got over-enthusiastic (or frustrated beyond belief) and threw the ball over the wicket-keeper's head and it rolled down the other side of the hill. Meanwhile the batsmen on the summit tore triumphantly back and forth 67 times.

Can you take any more? A team in 1880 at Chatham Lines, Kent, needing 47 runs for a win, got them in one ball. (And we got excited when Sri Lankan Jayasuriya scored his 50 in 17 balls in mid-1996.) The ball rolled down a steep hill called Brook and several fielders went after it, throwing the ball to each other. Unfortunately, some 'catches' were dropped and the ball rolled back some distance. Not concerned by this 'ball goes up, ball comes down' Homer Simpson antic, the batsmen ran 47 times and claimed victory.

To score a century is always memorable but this century was extra special. D. H. R. Martin of Oriel Orphans completed his only century with a hit for 14. Against Radley 2nd XI at Radley in about 1928 when several games were in progress side by side on the same ground, Martin, on 87, hit the ball into a neighbouring game. The fielder of the different match picked up the ball and for reasons not quite understood, flung it in the opposite direction. A grateful Martin ran 14 to get his freaky ton.

The November 1924 issue of the *Australian Cricket* magazine describes a hit for 101:

The following letter appearing in an English paper is vouched for, and the stroke referred to must have been one of the most productive the game has known.

'A friend of mine, who died about five years ago, once told me that he was batting for a small Devonshire Club against the local lunatic asylum. Either my friend or his partner hit the ball to mid-wicket. The lunatic [intellectually handicapped, in today's language] fielding there stopped the ball, examined it closely, threw it high in the air, caught it, looked at it again, and then ran off with it.

'The rest of the fielders set off after him, and when they returned with the ball they found the batsmen completely exhausted, for it was a very hot day, and lying on the ground, having run 101.'

Such crazy things happened — if they happened at all — because of lack of boundary lines.

Now to a story which sounds distinctly 'fishy'. In a match played in the Solomon Islands, the ball was hit into the sea. For some reason it was regarded by the umpire as in play, so the batsmen kept running. As killer fish patrolled the waters, said the narrator, no fielder was keen to wet his creams. By general consensus the fielder nearest to the point of entry was nominated and the square-leg fielder was pushed in. By the time he salvaged the ball, the batsmen had run 56.

The only explanation I find for umpires not calling such balls as 'lost balls' could be the fact that in minor matches, umpires are usually from the batting side. Or some of the stories could be exaggerated if not entirely fabricated.

Jonathan Rice narrates a more plausible story in *Curiosities of Cricket*. Playing for Bradford Gymkhana Cricket Club on 12 July 1986, Tony Nasser scored 107 in 23 minutes; 104 of them coming in boundaries (12 sixes and eight fours). The reason for this swashbuckling innings was that he was in a hurry to meet his sister at the Manchester airport that afternoon. He should have played faster or got himself out earlier because he was still half an hour late for her flight.

For once W. G. Grace and Freddie Trueman do not figure in an apocryphal story. But Australia's character and opening batsman of 1940s and 1950s, Sid Barnes, does.

Barry D. McDonald from Petersham-Marrickville Cricket Club and now living in Epping, Sydney, sent me an interesting story. 'Local legend has it that on one occasion at Petersham Oval in Sydney, as Sid went out to bat, a spectator offered him a £5 wager if he could hit a six into an open 44-gallon drum which the groundsman used to house grass cuttings. Looking around Sid saw two drums side by side outside the boundary near the dressing rooms so he turned to the spectator and said, "If you double the wager, you can nominate which of the two drums you want me to hit it in".'

McDonald does not remember the outcome, but is sure — given Barnes' penchant for such off-field activities — that such a conversation and wager did take place.

Now for the ultimate, the mysterious healing power of a six. On one occasion in late 1980s the story goes, a six from the celebrated hitter Charles Thornton smashed through the bedroom window of an elderly invalid who had been bedridden for 15 years. So scared was she of the red-hot round object flying in, that she fled downstairs and led an active life after then.

13

Minor Skyscrapers

In the trigonometry of sixes, would Pythagoras hold that altitude counts as much or more than ground distance covered?

— Ray Robinson

The sky is the limit for minor grade records — especially for six hits. But these come more in the realms of reality than the unbelievable 286 off one ball, a shark swallowing a ball or a train carrying a ball to Turramurra.

Let us start with the deeds of two of the greatest batsmen in the world — Victor Trumper and Don Bradman.

When batting for Paddington against Glebe at the Redfern Oval, Sydney, in 1902–03, Trumper and Dan Gee put on 423 runs for the opening wicket. Trumper scored 335 (22 fives and 39 fours), Gee 172 (10 fives and 24 fours) as Paddington amassed 9 for 618 in about 225 minutes — watched by a crowd of over 10,000. What makes their feat even more awe-inspiring is that before 1906 in Australia, a hit above the boundary line counted five and not six and the batsman lost the strike.

'Yabba' (real name S. H. Gascoigne), the famous Sydney barracker, saw Trumper play the above innings. 'In one over — a six ball over in those days — Vic and Dan Gee got three fives each. It was a case of one hit and one walk down the wicket. The uninitiated would have thought they were walking a single.

'I shall never forget the hit that landed on the boot factory,' he was quoted in Sydney's *Sun-Herald*. 'Another went right out of the southern end of the park into the balcony of a two-storey terrace of houses. Another landed right out and nearly went into the Australian XI Hotel (since demolished) bar in Elizabeth Street. All traffic was held up. The stroke which gave Trumper his 300 was also a "lost ball". It went into a carrying yard.'

Trumper then retired but an official, Mr Ironsides, forced him to return to make 350. The fielding side did everything to dislodge the super bats, trying underarm, chucking, keeping nine fielders near the fence but without success. Then in desperation the wicket-keeper removed his gloves and pads and started bowling. Vic, on 335 in 165 minutes, ran 10 metres down the pitch to hit a pitched-up delivery, fell and got tangled up with his bat and was out. He was plain exhausted.

If there were sixes those days, imagination boggles as to how many runs he would have scored, as he would have retained the strike. Said 'Herbie' Collins, later an Australian captain, 'So many of Trumper's strokes landed the ball on the adjacent bowling green that bowls play was suspended while the players lined the bank to watch Trumper.'

There is a bit of history behind the Trumper 'fiver' that smashed a window on the second floor of John Hunter & Sons shoe factory in Chalmers Street. Rather than being asked to pay for the broken window, Trumper was entertained lavishly by the shoe company directors and taken on a tour of the factory.

The broken window was preserved as a memorial to the great Australian legend but in 1963 the South Sydney Leagues Club bought the factory and demolished it for extensions. 'It was later decided to mount the window in a place of honour in the club,' wrote Sydney's *Sun-Herald* in 1963. However, according to an article by Ian Heads in the *Sun-Herald* of 14 April 1996, the mounted window has not been seen for years and South's club historian Tom Brock fears the worst — that it has ended up on the tip. But according to Peter Sharpham, the biographer of Victor Trumper, the smashed window was never mounted by the South Sydney Leagues Club.

Trumper played many memorable innings at the highest level and is considered as an immortal. His last tour was an unofficial one to New Zealand in 1913–14 which was organised through the enterprise of New Zealand millionaire Sir Arthur Sims. Two batsmen shone out on that tour; one was Trumper and the other Jack N. Crawford, a big hitter from England who also played in Sheffield Shield cricket for South Australia. Against a local side at Tenuka, Crawford scored 354 (14 sixes and 45 fours) and added 298 runs in 69 minutes with Trumper.

Trumper also hit up 293 glorious runs (three sixes, 44 fours) in 190 minutes against Canterbury at Christchurch in on that tour. Sadly, it was to be his last big innings; he died the following year aged 37, mourned by cricket-lovers all over the world.

Sir Donald Bradman, despite his near century average and run-a-minute strike rate, was not a big six-hitter. No doubt, he could have blasted sixes if he had wanted to, but in his scheme of things, of batting without risk, sixes did not fit in. He hit 45 sixes in 338 first-class innings and only six in 80 Test innings; five against England and one against India.

However, when he was younger, and not quite a run-machine, he did let himself go. As a 17-year-old, Bradman hit 234 in a day in a non first-class match, the last 50 included four sixes and six fours. This was for Bowral against Wingello at Bowral (now named Bradman Oval) in 1925 and the opposition included Bill O'Reilly, the greatest bowler in his era according to Bradman.

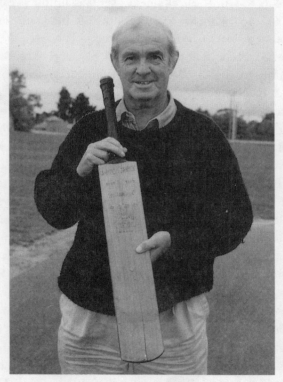

The bat with which Sir Donald Bradman scored 100 runs in three overs at Blackheath in November 1931. (Pic by Peter Allen supplied by Fred Calcraft)

Perhaps no hitter will approach Bradman's assault of bowlers in an exhibition match at Blackheath in the Blue Mountains outside Sydney on 3 November 1931. He was playing for the Blue Mountains team against the Lithgow Pottery Club in a match staged to mark the official opening of their new ground and to test a malthoid pitch being used for the first time in that area.

Bradman went in at no. 3 and raced to 256 with 14 sixes and 29 fours. In the midst of this onslaught he hammered 100 out of 102 in just three overs (off 22 balls) —belting 10 sixes, nine fours, one two and two singles.

Annoyed that the off-break bowler Bill Black was boasting about dismissing him in an earlier match cheaply, Bradman took revenge by hitting him for 6, 6, 4, 2, 4, 4, 6, 1 (33 runs) in his first over and retained the strike. Off the next over from Horrie Baker, Bradman scored 40 with 6, 4, 4, 6, 6, 4, 6, 4. Black's next over was almost as expensive, 29 runs (1, 6, 6, 1, 1, 4, 4, 6); the first and fifth balls being hit for singles by his considerate partner Owen Wendell Bill.

A chastised Black 'had to plead with his captain to be taken off, nursing an analysis of 2-0-62-0', wrote Irving Rosenwater in *Sir Donald Bradman: A Biography.*

Now to some other well documented records in minor cricket. According to a report in the *Sydney Morning Herald* of 19 June 1993, the record for most sixes off successive balls went to West Somerset League cricketer Rob Kelly, aged 24. He hit 11 sixes in 11 balls and remained unbeaten with 111; the power of one!

Before Kelly, the record (nine sixes in nine consecutive balls) was shared by three six-smiters. The first to achieve this was C. I. J. 'Jim' Smith, alias 'Village Blacksmith', of Wiltshire, Middlesex and England. A gigantic hitter even at first-class level (refer to his exploits in Chapter 9), he clobbered nine sixes in nine deliveries while batting for Middlesex XI v. Harrow & Districts at Rayner's Lane, Harrow in 1935. A renowned big-hitter, he frequently peppered the area between Old Tavern and Q Stand at Lord's, including blows that reached St Wood Road.

Smith's feat was equalled in Cairo, Egypt, by A. D. (Dudley) Nourse, the prolific Test batsman and captain of South Africa. He hit nine consecutive sixes — including six sixes in a six-ball over — for a South

African XI against the Military Police in 1942–43. Nourse went on to hit 11 sixes in 12 balls.

Another batsman to strike nine sixes in nine balls was Tim Nilsson for Northern Districts against Chermside Pastimes at Brisbane in 1961–62. It happened in a Queensland Cricket Association Warehouse Division A3 grade match. Nilsson scored 250 out of 370, with 21 sixes and 17 fours, according to a letter in *Playfair Cricket Monthly* of February 1962.

Graham Clayton of Blacktown, NSW, informs me that J. Steel hit eight sixes off successive balls for Wedderburn v. Gisborne at Bendigo, Victoria, in 1985 and R. Cooper seven successive sixes for Murrurindi v. Glenbawn at Blandfield, NSW, in 1967.

The world record for most runs in an over in minor cricket is 62. In a Queensland country match in 1968–69, H. Morley struck nine sixes — not off successive balls — and two fours off an eight-ball over which included four no-balls.

S. K. ('Shunter') Goen of South Africa (with two Test appearances) scored 50 runs in seven minutes for Gezira v. the RAF in 1942 when he was 40. He did not have to run even once, his 50 came in boundaries, one six and 11 fours.

The fastest double century came off only 58 balls. Playing for Alderney v. Sun Alliance, Dav Whatmore of Victoria, Australia and later a successful coach of Sri Lanka in their 1996 World Cup campaign, scored 210 runs off 61 balls with 25 sixes and 12 fours on 19 June 1983. His first century came off 33 balls, his second off only 25.

The record for most sixes hit in an innings in minor cricket goes to Kevin Hutchinson, aged 17, in 1989. In South Australian school cricket, he blasted 39 sixes and 14 fours in his unbeaten 311 in three hours. He was batting for Trinity College v. St Paul's College at Adelaide, according to a report in *Cricketer* (Australia) of February 1990.

The following batsmen have hit 30 or more sixes in an innings in minor matches.

6s	Score	Batsman	For	Against	At	Season
39	311*	K. Hutchinson	Trinity College	St Paul's College	Adelaide	1989–90
36	253*	D. Hope	Standard Bank	Lever Brothers	Durban	1902
34	415*	R. Butterworth	Dover	Raminea	Hobart	1933–34
32	359*	W. Hyman	Bath Association	Thornbury	Alveston	1902
32	515	D. R. Havewala	BB & CI Railway	St Xavier's College	Bombay	1933–34

* = not out. This list may not be complete

Among other well-known Test cricketers to hit over 20 sixes in a minor match were:

- Basil L. D'Oliveira who slammed 28 sixes in his 225 for Croxley v. Mariedah, South Africa, in 1953. In one eight-ball over, he hit 46 runs
- Wally Hammond smote 24 sixes in his unbeaten 365 for Borders v. Jeriner, a house match for his grammar school, Cirencester, England, in 1920.

According to renowned cricket statistician Irving Rosenwater, hitting of six sixes in an over is fairly common in minor cricket. However, the following feat deserves a mention.

Former Australian Test bowler Neil Hawke, 32, shone as a batsman in a centenary match in England. He slammed each ball of a six-ball over for six when batting for Whitbread Wanderers at Thornbury in Gloucestershire in a Lancashire League match in 1971. Four of his sixes cleared the roof of a nearby hotel as he hammered 79 in 36 minutes. The bowler to suffer this onslaught was Derek Hawkins, the former Gloucestershire all-rounder.

Randwick and NSW Sheffield Shield batsman Martin Haywood smashed his way into the Sydney grade record books with six sixes in an over off former NSW off-spinner Wayne Mulherin at Petersham Oval on 5 February 1994. Haywood went from 167 to 203 in the over and hit all the sixes in the arc between long-on and long-off. His first hundred took 224 minutes and the second only 82. He batted for 306 minutes, hitting 10 sixes and 21 fours to be 204 not out when Randwick declared at 2 for 365.

A week earlier, on 29 January 1994, Sean Pope of Bankstown hit the headlines in Sydney press by hammering five sixes and 29 fours in his 275 off 225 balls in 307 minutes. The innings was remarkable because it was a big ground.

L. Barrett of Foresters hit six sixes against Manly Methodist in Manly-Warringah C grade competition in November 1947. He dominated a tenth wicket partnership of 71 by scoring 69.

Paul Pittioni, 13, of Carlingford, Sydney, hit a century in 16 minutes on 14 March 1982. He retired after scoring 146 in a total of 8 for 465 for St Patrick Marist Brothers High School, Dundas against Epping

YMCA on Boronia Park, a small ground. His first 100 included eight sixes and 11 fours. Off his first four overs he hit 20, 29, 18 and 22.

Andrew Symonds became a six symbol after his two world records (16 sixes in an innings and 20 in a match) in England in August 1995. He had shown promise as a 17-year-old. In December 1992, he had shared in an opening stand of 446 — a record for limited overs cricket — with Matthew Mott in a 50-overs match for Gold Coast Dolphins against Souths at Wynnum, Brisbane. Symonds' 220 came from 99 balls and included 14 sixes and 27 fours. Mott's 208 came from 117 balls and he hit 14 sixes and 20 fours.

Philip Coorey, 17, from Strathfield, NSW, also hit 14 sixes (and 17 fours) when scoring an unbeaten 162 in 13 overs for Trinity Grammar v. Barker College in December 1975. His century came in seven overs. The scorers could not time his innings, said a report in Sydney's *Daily Telegraph*, because he lost two balls and several minutes were spent searching for them. They estimated that his 100 came in 35 minutes.

Coorey went in to bat with his team in strife at 5 for 48 chasing 181 runs in a 22-over game. The Barker boys thought that Philip would be an easy picking as he came in wearing shorts, one glove and one pad. He struggled with the first ball but struck the second ball for a six. He got his 50 in four overs, the next 50 in three and the final 62 in six.

On 2 January 1963, schoolboy Garry 'Chaka' Watson scored a whirlwind 204 before lunch. In a Johannesburg Under-18 competition he reached his first hundred in 45 minutes and the second in 48. In all, he hit 10 sixes and 27 fours.

Rob Langer who later played six Tests for Australia, once slammed 134 runs (13 sixes and seven fours) in 75 minutes in Western Australia's win over Illawarra in a one-day match at Wollongong on 10 November 1976. Mainly due to Langer's blitz, the WA team amassed 297 runs before lunch.

K. Sullivan's pleasure to be selected for NSW Country XI against the strong South African team at Parkes in 1963–64 turned sour when he bowled to the majestic Graeme Pollock. After Trevor Goddard had taken a run, Pollock finished the eight-ball over with 4, 6, 6, 4, 2, 6, 6; a total of 35 runs. As compensation, Sullivan hit the first ball he received for a six which smashed the windscreen of a parked car.

New Zealand all-rounder Lance Cairns played many dashing innings at higher levels but his 174 for Bishop Auckland in Durham, England v. Glostrup, a Danish team touring England, was remarkable. His innings lasted 64 balls and he hit 15 sixes and 16 fours.

Indian Test cricketers at times became six-hitters in minor cricket. As many as 33 sixes were hit in a festival match at Shivaji Park, Bombay, in April 1970. Witnessed by over 20,000 fans, 813 runs were plundered in 320 minutes. The usually sedate former Test captain Ajit Wadekar hit nine sixes (four of them in one over), Chandu Borde and Eknath Solkar three each, and Gundappa Viswanath and Polly Umrigar two each. Umrigar was called 'Palm Tree Hitter' in the West Indies, after his tall-hitting in 1953 and 1962.

When playing for Tata Sports Club in 'A' Division of the *Times of India Shield* in 1979, the elegant Sandeep Patil smashed 21 sixes and 20 fours in his swashbuckling 284 in 214 balls. In the next match he scored 209 v. Mafatlal Sports and 205 v. Tata Electrics. In one month he had aggregated 1249 runs, hitting three double tons and 63 sixes.

During the inauguration of Dadoji Kondev Stadium at Thane, Bombay, in 1981, Bombay Cricket Association amassed 339 runs in a 40-over match of which Patil scored 227 with 19 sixes and 23 fours.

This was not unexpected from a player who, as an 18-year-old in 1974–75, had scored 210 runs with 10 sixes in an inter-university match. When Patil bats, sixes are not far behind — in club or first-class cricket. In an important Ranji Trophy match for Bombay v. Saurashtra on 9 January 1980 in Bombay, he struck 243 off 205 balls which included seven sixes and 19 fours. His last six was hit so high and hard that it sailed clear over the roof of the long-on stand and landed on the adjoining Bombay Hockey Association ground. It was the longest hit ever made at the Wankhede Stadium.

Even at Test level he was a crowd-pleaser. In the Manchester Test of June 1982, he created a Test record by hitting English captain Bob Willis — bowling with a new ball — for six fours in an over (which included a no ball). The fifth of the fours took him to his only century in England.

Another Indian Test great, Dilip Vengsarkar, played a scintillating innings of 126 in 84 minutes for Dadar Union XI against New Hind

Sports Club in the A Division of Kanga League match in 1988. He belted 14 sixes.

When leading India in Australia in 1967–68, Nawab of Pataudi (Jr) scored 44 runs v. Western Australian Country XI. He hit three sixes, one of which struck a TV technician aboard a truck.

Steven Downes, 14, hit an unbeaten 108 for Cheshire League Club Styal in an Under-15 competition at Holmer Chapel, England, in June 1977. His last 50 came in 10 balls producing 4, 6, 4, 6, 4, 6, 6, 6, 4, 4.

A six-hit over Pentridge gaol wall ranks as one of the most sensational ever seen in a cricket match in Australia. This mighty stroke was one of seven sixes by Gordon Robinson, a member of a well-known sporting family.

Playing for Brighton Cricket club in 1920 against Coburg whose ground was then alongside Pentridge gaol, Victoria, Gordon (whose nephew Ray Robinson later became a world-renowned cricket writer) played a spectacular innings one Saturday afternoon, including his hit into Pentridge — 'a hard place to get out of but harder still to hit a cricket ball in to', quipped the *Melbourne Herald*. One of the fielders, Jack Huntington, recalled the gaol-bound hit. 'This immense six was a straight drive over the head of the bowler, Rupert Robinson, no relation. I measured the distance ... and it was approximately 130 yards [120 metres]. It is certainly the best and longest six I ever saw in 20 years as a player and a spectator ... The ball was never returned which shows the kind of people there were in Pentridge in those days.'

Five of the other six sixes Robinson, 32, hit, went so far out of the ground that the balls were lost; some of them over pine trees at the south and furthest from the goal. By now the teams had run out of balls — they lost five — and the curator hunted out an old, battered, soft and greenish ball. It achieved the 'impossible', dismissing Robinson for 70.

This knock is remembered in certain circles as a 'striptease' innings. He was unbeaten at the end of the first Saturday. The next Saturday, he was working and was late to resume his innings. Just as his captain F. Francis gave up all hopes of his turning up, and the opposition captain Charles Stranks claimed his wicket as 'absent, out', Robinson rushed in — panting.

His Brighton colleagues hurriedly strapped pads on his legs and he came out to bat in his street clothes — except for his coat. At the end of the first over, his team-mates ran out with his cricket boots. The next over, they removed his tie and shirt and made him put on his cricket shirt. This continued till he was in his regular cricket gear — trousers, socks and all.

Angered by the opposition captain's attitude, Gordon Robinson tore into the bowling with a vengeance and hit all those huge sixes, making gaol an unsafe place to live in.

Such six-hitting stories are just the tip of an iceberg; there would be many such high-altitude dramas. But none as memorable as Vic Trumper's 'five' which smashed the window of a shoe-factory, Don Bradman stroking 100 runs in three overs, Rob Kelly hitting 11 sixes in 11 balls and Gordon Robinson clouting one over Pentridge gaol wall soon after an on-field striptease.

14

Sixomania

It has to be an instinctive thing. The best shots are rarely premeditated.

— Alan Davidson

This chapter predominently includes stories by readers of the *Sydney Morning Herald*, *Australian Cricket* and *Wisden Cricket Monthly* (England), their own and of others, at times accompanied by clippings and score-sheets to prove their authenticity.

Six in the Zoo

Bill Howell was a mighty six-hitter from NSW. A correspondent who called himself 'Another Old Bill' narrated this story in *The Argus* of 27 November 1954. When representing NSW against MCC on the Sydney Cricket Ground in 1897–98, he gave a splendid display in his score of 95 in 66 minutes. 'We could not see where one of his sixes landed but suddenly there was a blood-curdling roar and one of our group sitting on the hill quietly remarked: "By cripes, Old Bill has hit a lion in the zoo". The zoo was then located at Moore Park.'

Taking it on the Chin

Another correspondent, E. B., tells about the mightiest of all hitters. E.B. was one in a capacity crowd on the Hill at the SCG in 1920s, enjoying hurricane hitting by Jack Gregory for NSW v. MCC. When Frank Woolley replaced Johnny W. H. T. Douglas at the bowling end, E. B. shouted: 'Lift him out of the ground, Jack'.

'It then happened,' remembered E. B. 'It landed on the point of my chin and up there I was soaring which must have been very much higher than the clock in the grandstand. I almost passed out with pain.

'I did not wait to ask his name but that Englishman sitting next to me (whom I had offended by barracking his hero Woolley) will always remain in my memory as the mightiest of all hitters.'

Showboat Sideshow

The musical comedy *Showboat* was a hit with Sydneysiders at Her Majesty's Theatre in 1929. For a change, a picnic match was arranged at Woollahra Oval, Rose Bay between the Showboat XI and a strong Australian XI captained by Alan Kippax and including emerging stars Archie Jackson and Don Bradman. Kippax and Jackson hit so many sixes that quite a few extras were hired to retrieve the balls.

Charles Covell of Kingsford, NSW, who did some beyond-the-boundary-line fielding, remembers a classic catch taken by an actor for the Showboat XI. 'Running around the outfield he held the ball low down with an outstretched left-hand. I had to wait for over 40 years to witness a similar catch. That was taken by Jeff Thomson who streaked around the SCG fence covering an impossible distance to make a remarkable catch with an outstretched left hand.'

Hendren — a Ladies' Man

Percy Chapman's MCC team amassed a grand total of 7 declared for 734 v. NSW on the SCG on 10 November 1928; Wally Hammond 225 (one six, 30 fours) and Patsy Hendren 167 (three sixes, 19 fours) adding 333 for the fourth wicket. In desperation, Don Bradman, playing his first international, was brought in to bowl. Hendren greeted him by hoicking him for a couple of sixes into the Ladies' Stand. But when he tried to repeat it, the shot, he was caught in the deep by J. N. Campbell.

'Ironically, Bradman, by figures the greatest batsman of all and hardly recognised as a bowler, had taken an English wicket before he had scored a run against them,' remembers Charles Covell, an engrossed eye-witness. Incidentally, Bradman went on to score 87 and 132 not out in this match. On Hendren hitting Bradman in the Ladies Stand, an English friend quipped to Covell, 'It seemed as if Patsy was trying to impress the ladies'.

Spectacular Catches and Misses

South Africa's Paul Winslow, 6 feet 3 inches, was coached by Patsy Hendren and enjoyed hitting big sixes. When touring England in 1955, he scored 40 runs off eight balls (30 in an over from Jack Ikin) against Lancashire. In the third Test in Manchester, he came in to bat in a crisis and made 108 in 190 minutes, reaching his century with a hit over the sightscreen. He off-drove the ball to the topmost scaffolding set up for TV cameras and then into the car park. This remained his only Test century. On the tour he hit 27 sixes.

Back at home in a Currie Cup match, he hit famous off-spinner Hugh Tayfield for two consecutive sixes and was 'caught' by the same spectator.

Ian Foxall of Lindfield, NSW, wrote to me about an Arthur Mailey story which may be known to some of you. Following Victoria's 1107 v. NSW at Melbourne in 1926–27 when Mailey had the unflattering figures of 4 for 362, he wrote in his newspaper column the following day that his bowling figures would have been much improved had all the catches been taken from his bowling. 'The first dropped catch was by a man in a grey suit sitting by the scoreboard.'

Initiation Blues

In a letter published in *Wisden Cricket Monthly*, Ross R. Smith of Innermay, Tasmania, wrote that in the Perth Test of 1992–93, West Indies opener Desmond Haynes hooked Australian fast bowler Jo Angel for a six in the bowler's first over in Test cricket.

In the exciting Manchester Test of 1995, debutant Englishman Mike Watkinson was hit for a six by West Indian Keith Arthurton in his first over. But after that nervous full toss, Watkinson recovered to take five wickets in the match.

Dial 'M' For Murder

Foxall narrated another six-story of an Aussie Legend. In the early 1930s, Charlie Macartney played a brilliant innings in a first grade match at Chatswood Oval, Sydney. He stroked 94 delightful runs in 32 minutes with nine sixes — one of which hit the scoreboard, dislodging the letter 'M' from his name.

Simon Says

Victoria's Simon O'Donnell, who played six Tests for Australia, was a crowd favourite. He remembers his biggest six with pride. 'It was hitting Greg Matthews into the Great Southern grandstand one day on the Melbourne Cricket Ground. He bowled it, I hit it and without even bothering to look at the ball, he said, "It's a big one, isn't it?". I just smiled and nodded. It went straight back over his head into the second tier.'

No Colour Bar

In a match to forget for Australian off-spinner Ashley Mallett (Australians v. Western Province at Cape Town in 1969–70), he was belted for 31 runs in an over. After M. H. Bowditch scored a single off his first ball, Mike Procter hit five successive sixes with a couple ending up in the adjacent brewery and railway yards. A replacement ball had to be used which was thrown on the ground and was picked up by Doug Walters. As Mallett was walking away after the over, Walters quipped: 'Well, Ashley, that finishes up the reds, now we start on the colours'.

What A Way To Go!

Graham Clayton of Blacktown, NSW, has supplied quite a few potpourries for this book. When batting for Queensland v. NSW at the Gabba in a Sheffield Shield match in October 1975, Greg Chappell hit a six which split his bat in two pieces. Set to score 165 runs to win in 18 overs, Chappell opened with Sam Trimble and attacked Gary Gilmour, Len Pascoe and David Colley with power. Doug Walters was brought in to slow down the run rate. Instead, Chappell hit him for a soaring six over mid-wicket which cleared the greyhound track and broke the bat. 'What a way for a bat to go,' was Greg's sad comment. But it was a happy match for him, scoring an unbeaten 105 and 86 in Queensland's victory.

Freeman's Free Hit

In his Test debut (v. India at Brisbane in 1967–68), Australia's Eric Freeman started with a six from the bowling of the legendary off-spinner E.A.S. Prasanna. It was Freeman's first scoring shot, perhaps the first such occurrence at Test level. West Indies batsman Carlisle Best later joined Freeman in this exclusive club when he made his Test debut against England in the Kingston Test of 1985–86. He opened his Test account with a hook off Ian Botham's third ball which went for a six.

A Jolly Good Six

India's respected cricket statistician and historian Anandji Dossa was a capable batsman at club level. For Jolly Cricketers v. Fort Vijay in Kanga League A division in Bombay on 29 August 1954, the former needed seven runs to win with two balls and one wicket remaining. Normally a defensive bat, Anandji lifted pace bowler G. R. Sunderam (who later played two Tests for India) over the tent for a six. With wicket-keeper Bhatia standing well back, Anandji and last man in V.P. Shah stole a single —a bye — to win the match off the very last ball.

Intercepted Six

Ken Longley of Hornsby Heights, NSW, reports on a similar nail-biting finish of a first-grade match between Sydney University and Northern District at Waitara Oval in the early 1960s.

Sydney University needed six runs for a win off the last ball and Northern District one wicket as Mike Pawley faced leg-spinner John Phillips. In desperation, Pawley jumped out to hit the final delivery. The ball was going over the fence when long-on fielder John Blazey leapt in AFL fashion to intercept the ball just before it flew over the boundary line and Northern District won by five runs.

Some well-known cricketers played in this cliff-hanger, amongst them Jim Burke, Neil and Lyn Marks and Alan Crompton, the former chairman of Australian Cricket Board who kept wickets for Sydney University.

Head In the Crowd

During a cricket tour of North Yorkshire in 1938 with a Scottish team called The Fireflies, Frank Taylor was fielding on the boundary line directly behind the fast bowler. Remembers Frank after 58 years, 'The opposing captain hit a mighty six that whistled over my head. I leapt up but could not catch it. I turned to a man in the crowd and sighed, "Oh, I wish I could have caught that," and he replied "Ee lad, never mind. It would've taken thee head with it." '

Six Both Ways — 1

John Collier of Cronulla, NSW, remembers a six a fifth-former at James Ruse Agricultural High School, Carlingford, hit during net practice in

1963. The ball was lifted so far over long on that it broke a window high up in a classroom block about 40 metres beyond the boundary. 'It was a magnificent hit and would have been a six on the SCG,' recalls Collier. 'But far from congratulating him, the administration's response was to haul him up and cane him for breaking the window. He got "six" both ways.'

Six Both Ways — 2

Keith Ross of West Ryde, NSW, knows how it feels to hit a six and to be hit for a six. When representing Waverley Blues in the B grade Centennial Park competition (now defunct) in 1948, he clouted a straight six to give his team an outright win. 'It was double joy for me as apart from being a winning hit, it was the only one I ever hit.'

In another B grade match for Denistone East at the Boronia Park, Epping, in the mid-1960s, his leg-spin delivery was mishit by a batsman. 'The ball went up towards point and should have been caught by him. Instead, he let it go over the boundary for a six.'

Wides Galore

In a match between the cricketers and hockey players of Lisbon Sports Club at Carcavelos, R. P. Rankine with the help of wides, scored the 48 runs needed for victory off the final 15-ball over: wide, 6, wide, 6, wide, 4, wide, 6, 6, wide, wide, 6, wide, 6, wide.

Jack Brown, the scorer-statistician from Wallsend Cricket Club in NSW, sent another wide-and-tall story. For Belmont v. Waratahs in a 15-overs competition in 1985, Chris Williams hit 98 (12 sixes and only two fours). One over from Geoff Alms yielded 34 runs: 6, wide, 6, 6, wide, 6, 2, 6.

To Hit a Six (in Verse)

To hit a six! Memory holds a glow of glory; I did it only once. The ground was very small, but who cares now, for it was a joy for me, a stingy scraper after runs, who poked and pushed the ball past point or into the desert waste from square to fine.

But on that day (dear God, although it is a life away the heat and dust remain upon my lips as salt tonight) a lunatic desire had conquered caution as the ball was bowled and I swung the bat at it, the stumps behind mere monuments.

It hit the best part of the wood and mounted into sky, a ball become a bird. All of us stood and watched it fly. Each was astounded, filled with wonder — nobody moved — that a prim prodder should have found a sword.

It flew across the cycle track that was our boundary, the umpire's hands clutching at clouds in proud salute, and bounded and bounced into the shimmering pepper trees. I was embarrassed by attention, so settled on my bat again and next ball, sedate as ever, pushed it carefully to cover point, deciding that adventure should belong to other men.

— Patrick Coady

Sixes in Women's Cricket

In 1963, Hazel Buck, a member of the touring Australian team, hit three sixes from consecutive balls by S. Sahl of Middlesex. The last ball of her second over and the third and fourth balls of her third over were dispatched over the fence, with Miriam Knee taking a four and a single from the first two balls of the third over. Sahl finished with 0 for 31 from 3 overs.

In 1975, Australia's Lynn Denholm hit two sixes in one innings against Otago, one from the bowling of F. Broad, and one from J. Hall.

In 1993, Australia's Denise Annetts hit two sixes in an innings against the North of England's N. Holt. In the same innings Belinda Clark hit one from K. Leng, and Julie Calvert one from M. Reynard.

In 1987, Chris Matthews and Karen Brown each hit one six from consecutive balls from Barbara Daniels, representing the England President's XI. Matthews hit hers from the last ball of the over, and Brown from the first ball of the following over.

(Supplied by eminent cricket statistician Erica Sainsbury.)

He Hit a Huge Six but Scored 0 Not Out

No, it's not a misprint. I know, it does not make sense but it did happen, informs Paul Upham of Riverwood, NSW, in the Municipal and Shires competition A grade between Bexley and Lane Cove in December 1993. He described the amazing background and details for the Bexley Cricket Club Newsletter and the report is reproduced in full below:

> Bexley A grader and fast bowling legend David 'Freddie' Rosa can no longer claim batting bunny status after one of the greatest "0" not outs ever seen in Shires cricket.
>
> Those of you who have played at Lane Cove's home ground, Longueville, will be aware of the unusual fence that surrounds the Western side of the ground. Legend has it that after years of having cricket balls land on his house, the local Mayor had this major structure erected on one side of the ground, the fence standing approximately 30 metres in height.
>
> Our 'Freddie' was suitably impressed with the fence, claiming it gave him a great target to hit over when he batted. He was then shocked to learn that a hit straight over the fence was a dead ball and no runs! For the rest of the day all you could hear from him was, 'I can't believe you can hit the ball that far and get no bloody runs'.
>
> Finally, 'Freddie', batting at his usual no. 11 spot, strode to the wicket. First ball was allowed to go to the keeper, second ball saw a cover drive to a ball down the leg side. Third ball the bowler dropped it short and 'Freddie' rocked onto the back foot and played a cracking pull shot, the ball not just scraping over the fence, but clearing it by 20 metres, landing two houses back across the street. Paul 'Coota' Bristow then obliged by getting out first ball next over. Bexley all out, D. Rosa 0 not out.

Hourn's Top Score

David Hourn of NSW was an effective spinner but a batting bunny. And that is why team-mates, opponents and spectators looked aghast when he hit a six off the first ball he received during a Sheffield Shield match against South Australia in 1970–71. Soon after he was stumped by Rex Blundell off Terry Jenner for six. This remained his highest score for five years — till 1975–76!

Greig's Huge Sh-Hit

On 31 May 1975 Tony Greig, making use of all his 79½ inches, hit a fast 226 for Sussex v. Warwickshire at Hastings. He went down in a blaze of glory after clouting the fist four deliveries from Peter Lewington for sixes. He skied the fifth one and was caught by Dennis Amiss.

Greig was also 'caught out' when commentating on Channel 9 during a limited-overs match between Australia A and West Indies on the SCG on 10 January 1996. Dr Thais Miles from Merewether Heights, NSW, informed me about a Greig faux pas. 'One of the batsmen hit the ball beautifully, a glorious shot high in the air. Tony Greig got very excited and yelled out, "That's a HUGE six!" However, the ball was hit so high that as it descended it looked as if it would land just inside the boundary, so Greig changed his mind to yell, "That's a HUGE hit!" What actually came out of his mouth was "That's a HUGE shit!"'

Cricket's McEnroe

Tantrums — what's new? Cricketers threw tantrums before John McEnroe was born. Hampshire's George Brown was extremely upset when he was dropped down the order in a local match in 1922. He came in to bat, fuming with anger, and smashed a ball for six over the wicket-keeper's head. The bat was split, so he tore it in two with bare hands, passed on half of the blade to the umpire and batted comfortably with the other half. Muscular and fearless, Brown used to pride himself in batting against fast bowlers without gloves.

Underarm Six

Ron Hynd achieved in 1965 what was considered impossible in 1981. Batting for Dee Why United v. Norfolk in the Manly-Warringah B1 grade match at Balgowlah Oval, Hynd hit 114 in 32 minutes — smacking 13 sixes and four fours. The bowler to cop maximum punishment was Ashley Simmons.

'I don't know how many sixes he hit off my bowling, but I do remember one particular ball,' writes Ashley. 'Hynd had just hit two consecutive sixes off me and I had a phobia that the next ball would go for another six. So I told the umpire that I had enough and I will bowl underarm. The umpire gave due notice to Hynd and I bowled a mullygrubber along the pitch. But incredibly the ball hit something and bounced up about six inches. That was enough for Ron Hynd to launch into it and away it went over square-leg for another six.

'I have always thought that the Trevor Chappell underarm incident in 1981 attracted an over reaction. Brian McKechnie — the New Zealander batsman who threw away his bat in disgust that day in Melbourne — should have at least tried to hit the Trevor Chappell grubber; he made no effort.'

Eighth Wonder of the World

The Grand Slam of six sixes in an over (6, 6, 6, 6, 6, 6) by Sir Garry Sobers and Ravi Shastri has already been mentioned. Here are the details of their 'double tri-fecta'. *Sobers for Nottingham v. Glamorgan on Saturday 31 August 1968 at St Helen's, Swansea.*

Left-arm spinner Malcolm Nash's six deliveries were hit for sixes as follows:

1st ball   to long on
2nd ball   to long on
3rd ball   to long off
4th ball   to mid-wicket
5th ball   to long off which was 'caught' by Roger Davis and Sobers started walking back to the pavilion. But the impact forced Davis to fall back over the boundary line. The crowd chanted 'six, six' and eventually umpire John Langridge signalled a six.
6th ball   Tremendous excitement as a unique feat was about to be performed. Glamorgan captain Tony Lewis put all his fielders around the boundary. The ball soared over the wall and into a road outside and was not recovered that night. On Monday morning a small boy arrived at the ground and handed the ball over. Later it was identified as genuine, mounted and sent to the Trent Bridge museum.

     Glamorgan's Peter Walker at first slip summed up the final blow: 'It wasn't a six. It was a twelve!'

Shastri for Bombay v. Baroda, Bombay on 10 January 1985
In all Shastri hit 13 sixes and 13 fours in his 200 not out scored in 113 minutes off 123 balls to record the fastest double century in first-class cricket — outpacing six symbols Gilbert Jessop (in 120 minutes at Hove in 1903) and Clive Lloyd (also in 120 minutes at Swansea in 1976).

Here is how Shastri hit Tilak Raj, a fastish spinner, for sixes:

1st ball   straight six
2nd ball   to long on
3rd ball   to long on
4th ball   to square leg
5th ball   to long on
6th ball   was bowled wide of the off-stump, but Shastri got quickly
      in position and the ball flew over the sightscreen.

'Only after hitting the fourth six did I think of emulating Sobers' feat,' Shastri later revealed.

Paradoxically, only a week earlier Shastri had scored a painstakingly slow century against England in the Calcutta Test. The crowd was so exaperated by this seven-hour marathon that they threw oranges at him when he fielded near the boundary. When asked how his barrackers reacted to his six-bonanza in Bombay the following week, he smiled and said, 'They thought it was the Eighth Wonder of the World'.

'Gunner's Six Spree

On its way to England for the 1961 Ashes tour, Richie Benaud's Australians played a match against Ceylon (now Sri Lanka). Their captain C. I. Gunasekara hammered 27 runs (three sixes, two fours) in an over from left-arm acrobatic off-spin and googly bowler Lindsay Kline.

Senaka Weeraratna of Clayton, Victoria, sent me an abstract of a book *First Love* by Lucien de Zoysa in which this hitting spree was described by Jack Fingleton, a guest commentator. Unfortunately, Fingleton had as many problems pronouncing Gunasekara's name as Kline had bowling to him. so Fingleton simplified it to Gunner-as-kara, and later just as Gunner. Well, after that over, Kline did feel a bit gunned down.

All-Run 'Sixes' to Reach Tons

There have been very few instances of all-run 'sixes' in first-class cricket. I could locate only two instances when batsmen reached their century with such 'ground-level sixes'.

The first time was in the Surrey v. Warwickshire match at The Oval in 1914. Surrey amassed 541, Percy Fender (who later scored the fastest century in first-class cricket, in 35 minutes in 1920) top-scored with 140. He moved from 94 to 100 with an all-run six, according to Andrew Martin in *The Cricket Statistician* of 1988.

The second such instance happened on 10 August 1933. In reply to Warwickshire's total of 7 declared for 367, the touring West Indians made 474 (George Headley 182 and C.A. Merry 146). When on 94, Merry cut George Paine and the ball sped away to the boundary. Or so it seemed, and the cover point did not bother to even chase it. However, the ball stopped inches within the boundary line and the spectators drew the attention of the fielders. By the time the wicket-keeper retrieved the ball and threw it back, Merry and Headly ran six and a very merry Merry reached his ton with this bonus.

Aerial Bombardment

In the semi-final of Grade A Churches Cricket competition in Victoria, Highfield Road Methodists were dismissed for 85 on 2 March 1946. The Mont Albert Methodist team, made up of former RAAF aircrew men, declared at 1 for 238 in 18 overs — that is at 13.2 runs per over. Stanton Greenwood opened with John Dew and put on 96 runs in 45 minutes of which the former scored 70 with five sixes and six fours. Then Frank Rush contributed a whirlwind 108 not out with 10 sixes, 11 fours and only four singles. Dew, who sent me the story and the scorecard, was the sheet anchor with an unbeaten, unspectacular and six-less 46. He must have felt like a sleeping partner as he saw 15 sixes hit from the other end.

The worst-treated bowler was one Mr Wicks; his only over was bombarded for 33 runs (4, 4, 6, 6, 6, 6, 1, 0) by two former RAAF crewman.

Tales From Hugh Pearce

I am grateful to Hugh Pearce of Chew Stoke Cricket Club, Bristol, England, for the stories below:

• Mark Bridges of Bristol was not much of a batsman but a good enough bowler to once capture 10 for 22 in an innings. However, he shone as a batsman when playing for Compton Dando v. Dunkerton in 1949. His team was in trouble, nine wickets down for not many runs when Mark went in to bat. His captain Billy

Thomson had instructed him to 'have a go', which is precisely what he did. He stayed only one over but what an over! He hit the first five balls for six and was caught off the sixth ball by a fielder at full stretch on long-on boundary.

His first two sixes hit two cars and the third was despatched into a river running by the ground. Surprisingly, he had never hit a six before and never did again.

- In a match between Saltford and Bishop Sutton in 1987, a bowler by name Eric (surname not remembered but known as 'Big Eric' or 'W. G.' because of his huge girth and big beard) was having a bad day. Not only were the batsmen hitting him all over the ground for fours and sixes, the team scorer kept taunting and teasing him when he fielded near the boundary.

Big Eric could take it no more and punched the scorer. As it turned out, the scorer was his wife. The fielders rushed to her aid and dragged big Eric off. Mrs Eric threw the pencil and eraser away and went home sobbing. 'The next season, however, both were back — bowling and scoring for Saltford — so they must have patched up,' Pearce concluded.

- The following year Bishop Sutton played Belmont in the North Somerset League which is a 40-overs-a-side competition. For economic reasons, only one ball was supplied for both innings, giving the side fielding first an unfair advantage.

Belmont won the toss and sent Bishop Sutton, the home team, to bat on a green top. In the second over Alan Walker hooked a short ball for a six into the garden of an adjoining house. As the fielders were searching everywhere for the ball, Norman Stuckey, a local character, winked and whispered to Sutton's captain Tim Sage: 'Not to worry, young 'un, I've hidden the ball under a flowerpot. Let them bowl with an old ball. After tea, I'll find this new ball "accidentally" and you can use it to bowl at them.'

Pearce describes this as an example of West Country cunning.

Somerset's Sixomania

If a competition were held to judge a champion six-hitting county in England, Somerset could win easily. Before World War II they had six symbols in W. H. Fowler — the only batsman to make two hits of over

150 yards (in 1882), Guy Earle, Arthur Wellard and Harold Gimblett. After WW II they included the extrovert Ian Botham and for some seasons Australia's Bill Alley and the West Indies import Vivian Richards.

The top four six-hitters in first-class cricket are all from Somerset. Wellard holds the record of hitting most sixes in first-class cricket (561 in 679 innings, an average of 0.82 sixer per innings). Botham comes next with at least 386, Gimblett 245 and Viv Richards 235 for Somerset alone in 309 innings, according to figures provided by Brodribb in a recent letter.

Somerset batsmen also rule supreme in the list of 'Most Sixes Hit in a Season'.

Sixes	Batsman	County	Season
80	I. T. Botham	Somerset	1985
66	A. W. Wellard	Somerset	1935
57	A. W. Wellard	Somerset	1936
57	A. W. Wellard	Somerset	1938
51	A. W. Wellard	Somerset	1933
49	I. V. A. Richards	Somerset	1985
48	A. W. Carr	Nottinghamshire	1925
48	J. H. Edrich	Surrey	1965
48	A. Symonds	Gloucestershire	1995

Botham and Richards thus hit 129 sixes between them in 1985. The next season they smacked 34 sixes each. Of the 90-odd instances of batmen belting 25 or more sixes in an English season, the prolific six-smacker Wellard achieved it as many as 12 times. No-one else has reached it seven times. Most sixes in a match is probably 35 at Wells in 1935 between Somerset (21 sixes) and Hampshire (14).

Even in minor grade cricket, Somerset rules supreme. West Somerset League player Rob Kelly hit 11 sixes off 11 balls in June 1993 — a unique feat at any level. Call it sixomania in excelsis.

Soaring Sixes by Kiwis

· As many as 29 sixes were hit in a Shell Trophy match between Northern Districts and Auckland at Eden Park, Auckland, in December 1991; 13 by the former and 16 by the latter. Test cricketer Dipak Patel clobbered 12 in his second-innings score of 204 in 163 minutes for

Auckland, reaching his 200 with a six. Northern Districts' Matthew Maynard, an import from Glamorgan, scored a whirlwind 195 in 181 minutes with seven sixes in the first innings and 110 in 106 minutes with three sixes in the second.

- Roger Blunt, a correct and rather dour batsman in Test matches, at times turned an aggressive batsman at lower level. For Otago v. Canterbury at Christchurch in 1931–32, he hit an unbeaten 338 in 335 minutes, then a New Zealand record. Despite this heroic knock, Otago lost the match. In a senior club championship match at Hagley Oval in Christchurch, Blunt lifted seven sixes in an eight-ball over. New Zealand author Dick Brittenden was moved to write:'Glorious, fluent strokes which put the ball high into the oaks and elms beyond the boundary'.

- Ron Talbot almost cleared Lord's Pavilion for New Zealand v. MCC in May 1931, according to Auckland journalist Nigel Smith.

- Bulky Kiwi opener Mark Greatbatch hit three towering sixes in his 68 in 60 balls against South Africa during the 1992 World Cup match at Eden Park, Auckland. One of them was lifted onto the top of the North Stand and another almost into the corporate boxes on the top of the taller South Stand.

Maynard Reaches Maiden Ton With 3 Sixes

August 27, 1985 was a memorable day for teenager Matthew Maynard. Promoted from the 2nd XI to see what a 19-year-old could do against a strong Yorkshire team at Swansea, Maynard became the youngest batsman to score a century for Glamorgan on debut. He reached his century in 87 minutes off 98 balls with five sixes and 13 fours; racing from 84 to 102 by striking three consecutive deliveries from Phil Carrick straight back into the terraces for sixes. 'There can have been few more remarkable maiden centuries in first-class cricket,' wrote *Wisden 1986*.

Frosts' Priceless Souvenir

No collection of cricket anecdotes would be complete without a Bradman classic. This pearler was brought to my attention by Fred Calcraft of Harbord, NSW, who sent me articles by George Richards ('Column 8' editor) and Philip Derriman from the *Sydney Morning Herald* of 4 and 6 July 1991.

The ball Don Bradman hit for six through Mrs Olive Frost's bedroom window in Leichhardt in 1932 was located in Seaforth in 1991, 59 years after she refused to return it until the window was repaired.

As no payment was forthcoming, the ball remained with the Frosts and is now proudly kept by Olive's son Ernie. The Frosts were living opposite the cricket ground at Calan Park Hospital where Bradman played in an exhibition match in January 1932 and scored a quickfire 143. One of his sixes off the famous Australian leg-spinner Arthur Mailey went across Balmain Road and through the Frosts' bedroom window. Ernie was 17 then and is now living in Seaforth, NSW and treasures the ball as a souvenir. 'It belongs to the family,' he told me.

When his mother insisted on payment on the day of the match, the question was: who should pay? Mailey was quoted in next day's paper as saying, tongue-in-cheek, that he had no intention of paying; the broken window was caused through 23-year-old Bradman's disrespectful treatment of his bowling.

Ernie Frost got the ball autographed by Bradman who was then working in the sporting department of F. J. Palmer's clothing store at the corner of Park and Pitt Streets in Sydney. The signature still shows on the ball, which is in remarkably good condition.

Meanwhile what about the bat which hit the ball that broke the window? Derriman is almost certain that it was the same bat with which Bradman had scored his famous century in three overs at Blackheath two months previously in November 1931.

Zoe's Six Appeal

In limited-overs internationals, 20 women have hit 26 sixes. Four batswomen have smote two sixes each, England's Sue Metcalf and Debra Maybury — both in 1990 and 1991 – Sarah Illinworth in 1994–95 and Australia's Sally Griffiths in 1993 and 1993–94. The maximum number of sixes, three, have been hit by the dynamic Aussie crowd-pleaser Zoe Goss; one against England in 1991–92 and two against New Zealand in 1993–94 and 1994–95.

Appendix

SIXES IN TEST CRICKET
(Figures accurate to 1 July 1996)

MOST SIXES IN AN INNINGS

	Batsman	Match	Venue	Season
10	W. R. Hammond (336*)	Eng. v. N.Z.	Auckland	1932–33
9	C. L. Cairns (120)	N.Z. v. Zim.	Auckland	1995–96
8	N. S. Sidhu (124)	Ind. v. S.L.	Lucknow	1993–94
7	B. Sutcliffe (80*)	N.Z. v. S.Af.	Johannesburg	1953–54
	I. V. A. Richards (110*)	W.I. v. Eng.	St John's	1985–86
	C. G. Greenidge (213)	W.I. v. N.Z.	Auckland	1986–87
6	J. H. Sinclair (104)	S.Af. v. Aus.	Cape Town	1902–03
	I. V. A. Richards (192*)	W.I. v. Ind.	Delhi	1974–75
	Haroon Rashid (108)	Pak. v. Eng.	Hyderabad	1977–78
	I. T. Botham (118)	Eng. v. Aus.	Manchester	1981
	R. J. Shastri (121*)	Ind. v. Aus.	Bombay	1986–87
5	S. J. E. Loxton (93)	Aus. v. Eng.	Leeds	1948
	E. R. Dexter (172)	Eng. v. Pak.	The Oval	1962
	J. H. Edrich (310*)	Eng. v. N.Z.	Leeds	1965
	D. T. Lindsay (182)	S.Af. v. Aus.	Johannesburg	1966–67
	G. T. Dowling (239)	N.Z. v. Ind.	Christchurch	1967–68
	B. R. Taylor (124)	N.Z. v. W.I.	Auckland	1968–69
	I. T. Botham (137)	Eng. v. Ind.	Leeds	1979
	A. R. Border (153)	Aus. v. Pak.	Lahore	1979–80
	Imran Khan (117)	Pak. v. Ind.	Faisalabad	1982–83
	Imran Khan (136*)	Pak. v. Ind.	Madras	1986–87
	Javed Miandad (271)	Pak. v. N.Z.	Auckland	1988–89
	M. J. Slater (219)	Aus. v. S.L.	Perth	1995–96

* = not out

MOST SIXES OFF CONSECUTIVE BALLS

	Batsman	Bowler	Match	Venue	Season
4	Kapil Dev (77★)	E. E. Hemmings	Ind. v. Eng.	Lord's	1990
3	W. R. Hammond (336★)	J. Newman	Eng. v. N.Z.	Auckland	1932–33
	S. T. Clarke (35★)	Md. Nazir	W.I. v. Pak.	Faisalabad	1980–81

MOST SIXES IN AN OVER

	Batsman	Bowler	Match	Venue	Season
Six Ball Over					
4 (006666)	Kapil Dev	E .E. Hemmings	Ind. v. Eng.	Lord's	1990
3 (116626)	M. W. Tate & W. Voce	A. A. Hall	Eng. v. S.Af.	Johannesburg	1930-31
(666100)	W. R. Hammond	J. Newman	Eng. v. N.Z.	Auckland	1932-33
(064066)	R. C. Motz	D. A. Allen	N.Z. v. Eng.	Dunedin	1965-66
(660612)	B. S. Bedi & B. S. Chandrasekhar	P. J. Petherick	Ind. v. N.Z.	Kanpur	1976-77
(006664)	S. T. Clarke	Md. Nazir	W.I. v. Pak.	Faisalabad	1980-81
(462660L)	A. M. E. Roberts	I. T. Botham	W.I. v. Eng.	Port-of-Spain	1980-81
Eight Ball Over					
4 (66061600)	B. Sutcliffe & R. W. Blair	H. J. Tayfield	N.Z. v. S.Af.	Johannesburg	1953-54

L = leg bye

REACHING A CENTURY WITH A SIX

Batsman	Bowler	Match	Venue	Season
J. Darling	J. Briggs	Aus. v. Eng.	Adelaide	1897–98
E. H. Bowley	W. E. Merritt	Eng. v. N.Z.	Auckland	1929–30
P. R. Umrigar	S. Ramadhin	Ind. v. W.I.	Port-of-Spain	1952–53
P. L. Winslow	G. A. R. Lock	S.Af. v. Eng.	Manchester	1955
K. F. Barrington	R. B. Simpson	Eng. v. Aus.	Adelaide	1962–63
J. H. Edrich	P. I. Philpott	Eng. v. Aus.	Sydney	1965–66
K. F. Barrington	T. R. Veivers	Eng. v. Aus.	Melbourne	1965–66
D. T. Lindsay	D. A. Renneberg	S.Af. v. Aus.	Johannesberg	1966–67
K. F. Barrington	L. R. Gibbs	Eng. v. W.I.	Port-of-Spain	1967–68
B. R. Taylor	R. M. Edwards	N.Z. v. W.I.	Auckland	1968–69
J. Benaud	Intikhab Alam	Aus. v. Pak.	Melbourne	1972–73
K. R. Stockpole	M. L. C. Foster	Aus. v. W.I.	Kingston	1972–73
K. D. Walters	R. G. D. Willis	Aus. v. Eng.	Perth	1974–75
I. C. Davis	Salim Altaf	Aus. v. Pak.	Adelaide	1976–77
R. B. McCosker	R. G. D. Willis	Aus. v. Eng.	Nottingham	1977
Haroon Rashid	G. Miller	Pak. v. Eng.	Hyderabad	1977–78
Javed Miandad	B. S. Bedi	Pak. v. Ind.	Faisalabad	1978–79
Kapil Dev	N. Phillip	Ind. v. W.I.	Delhi	1978–79

(cont.)

Batsman	Bowler	Match	Venue	Season
I. T. Botham	Kapil Dev	Eng. v. Ind.	Leeds	1979
C. L. King	G. P. Howarth	W.I. v. N.Z.	Christchurch	1979–80
J. G. Wright	R. J. Shastri	N.Z. v. Ind.	Auckland	1980–81
I. T. Botham	M. R. Whitney	Eng. v. Aus.	Manchester	1981
Imran Khan	Kapil Dev	Pak. v. Ind.	Faisalabad	1982–83
L. R. D. Mendis	D. R. Doshi	S.L. v. Ind.	Madras	1982–83
G. R. J. Matthews	V. R. Brown	Aus. v. N.Z.	Brisbane	1985–86
P. A. deSilva	Imran Khan	S.L. v. Pak.	Faisalabad	1985–86
Imran Khan	N. S. Yadav	Pak. v. Ind.	Madras	1986–87
M. D. Crowe	C. G. Butts	N.Z. v. W.I.	Auckland	1986–87
Ijaz Faqih	Maninder Singh	Pak. v. Ind.	Ahmedabad	1986–87
D. L. Haynes	N. D. Hirwani	W.I. v. Ind.	Bridgetown	1988–89
C. C. Lewis	S. L. V. Raju	Eng. v. Ind.	Madras	1992–93
D. L. Haynes	Asif Mujtaba	W.I. v. Pak.	Bridgetown	1992–93
C. L. Hooper	Nadeem Khan	W.I. v. Pak.	St John's	1992–93
P. A. deSilva	A. R. Kumble	S.L. v. Ind.	Colombo	1993–94
P. A. deSilva	Mushtaq Ahmed	S.L. v. Pak.	Colombo	1994–95
S. R. Tendulkar	C. A. Walsh	Ind. v. W.I.	Nagpur	1994–95
R. G. Samuels	D. N. Patel	W.I v. N.Z.	St John's	1995–96
S. R. Tendulkar	M. M. Patel	Ind. v. Eng.	Birmingham	1996

Note: Joe Darling brought up his century with a hit right out of the ground then necessary to be credited with a six. Stanley Jackson (Eng. v. Aus., The Oval, 1893) was the first to bring up a Test century with a hit over the boundary, then worth only four runs in England.

Ken Barrington and P.A. (Arvinda) deSilva are the only players to bring up their centuries with a 6 *three* times. The third time Barrington achieved this (v. West Indies in 1967–68), he had also reached his 50 with a six.

John Benaud's century with a six came after he had been dropped from the following Test.

Collis King brought up his 100 with a six off the last ball of the Test.

Ijaz Faqih's was his only Test century and he reached both 50 and 100 with sixes off Maninder Singh, whom he hit for four sixes. He was not in the original touring team but was called in for his off-spin bowling because of injuries.

Chris Lewis brought up his only Test century in this manner on his 25th birthday.

Desmond Haynes (W.I. v. Pak. 1992–93) reached his century off *two* successive sixes off Asif Mujtaba. Robert Samuels reached his century with a four and a six.

One source mentions that Denis Amiss (Eng. v. Ind.; Delhi, 1976–77) also reached his 100 with a six off B. S. Chandrasekhar but it is not confirmed.

In the days when a hit over the boundary was worth only five runs in Australia, Len Braund (Eng. v. Aus., Adelaide, 1901–02) went from 94 to 99 of an eventual 103 not out by driving Hugh Trumble over the fence.

WINNING A TEST WITH A SIX
(List may not be complete)

Batsman	Match	Venue	Season
E. Paynter (14★)	Eng. v. Aus.	Brisbane	1932–33
W. R. Hammond (75★)	Eng. v. Aus.	Sydney	1932–33
W. R. Hammond (29★)	Eng. v. W.I.	Bridgetown	1934–35
H. R. Lance (28★)	S.Af. v. Aus.	Port Elizabeth	1966–67
R. J. Hadlee (6★)	N.Z. v. Aus.	Auckland	1981–82
Mohsin Khan (14★)	Pak. v. Aus.	Karachi	1982–83
P. J. Dujon (17★)	W.I. v. Ind.	Kingston	1982–83
R. J. Hadlee (17★)	N.Z. v. S.L.	Wellington	1982–83
Kapil Dev (23★)	Ind. v. Eng.	Lord's	1986
A. L. Logie (6★)	W.I. v. Ind.	Kingston	1988–89
I.V.A. Richards (73★)	W.I. v. Eng.	Birmingham	1991
S. T. Jayasuriya (6★)	S.L. v. Eng.	Colombo	1992–93

Note: Suffering from acute tonsillitis, Eddie Paynter left a hospital bed to play a heroic four-hour innings of 83. In the second innings he hit a six which won the Test and regained the Ashes on the day Australia's Archie Jackson died in Brisbane aged 23.

Wally Hammond and Richard Hadlee are the only ones to win a Test for their country with a six *twice*.

SIXES IN FIRST-CLASS CRICKET

MOST SIXES IN AN INNINGS

	Batsman	Match	Venue	Season
16	A. Symonds (254★)	Gloucester v. Glamorgan	Abergavenny	1995
15	J. R. Reid (296)	Wellington v. N. Districts	Wellington	1962–63
14	Shakti Singh (128)	Himachal Pradesh v. Haryana	Dharmsala	1990–91
13	Majid Khan (147★)	Pakistanis v. Glamorgan	Swansea	1967
	C. G. Greenidge (273★)	D.H. Robins' XI v. Pakistanis	Eastbourne	1974
	C. G. Greenidge (259)	Hampshire v. Sussex	Southampton	1975
	G. W. Humpage (254)	Warwick v. Lancashire	Southport	1982
	R. J. Shastri (200★)	Bombay v. Baroda	Bombay	1984–85
	F. B. Touzel (128★)	Wst Province B v. Griqualand Wst	Kimberley	1993–94
12	Gulfraz Khan (207)	Railways v. Universities	Lahore	1976–77
	I. T. Botham (138★)	Somerset v. Warwick	Birmingham	1985
	R. A. Harper (234)	Northampton v. Gloucester	Northampton	1986
	D. M. Jones (248)	Australians v. Warwickshire	Birmingham	1989

(cont.)

Batsman	Match	Venue	Season
D. N. Patel (204)	Auckland v. N. Districts	Auckland	1991–92
W.V. Raman (206)	Tamil Nadu v. Kerala	Madras	1991–92
G. D. Lloyd (227*)	Lancashire v. Essex	Chelmsford	1996
11 C. K. Nayudu (153)	Hindus v. MCC	Bombay	1926–27
C. J. Barnett (194)	Gloucester v. Somerset	Bath	1934
R. Benaud (135)	Australians v. T.N. Pearce's XI	Scarborough	1953
R. Bora (126)	Assam v. Tripura	Gauhati	1987–88
G. A. Hick (405*)	Worcester v. Somerset	Taunton	1988

MOST SIXES IN A MATCH

	Batsman	Match	Venue	Season
20	A. Symonds	Gloucester v. Glamorgan	Abergavenny	1995
17	W. J. Stewart	Warwick v. Lancashire	Blackpool	1959

MOST SIXES IN AN OVER

	Batsman	Bowler	Match	Venue	Season
Four-Ball Over					
3 (6466)	H. J. H. Scott	S. Wade	Australians v. Yorkshire	Sheffield	1886
2 (6446)	C. I. Thornton	D. Buchanan	Cambridge Uni. v. Gentlemen	Cambridge	1871
2 (6446)	G. J. Bonnor	A. P. Lucas	Australians v. I Zingari	Scarlborough	1882
Five-Ball Over					
2 (66414)	A. E. Trott – C. M. Wells	E. J. Tyler	Middlesex v. Somerset	Taunton	1899
Six-Ball Over					
6 (666666)	G. S. Sobers	M. A. Nash	Nottingham v. Glamorgan	Swansea	1968
(666666)	R. J. Shastri	Tilak Raj	Bombay v. Baroda	Bombay	1984–85
5 (066666)	A. W. Wellard	T. R. Armstrong	Somerset v. Derbyshire	Wells	1936
(666661)	A. W. Wellard	F. E. Woolley	Somerset v. Kent	Wells	1938
(066666)	D. T. Lindsay	W.T. Greensmith	Fezelas v. Essex	Chelmsford	1961
(606666)	Majid Khan	R. C. Davis	Pakistanis v. Glamorgan	Swansea	1967
(166666)	M. H. Bowditch & M. J. Procter	A. A. Mallett	Wst Province v. Australians	Cape Town	1969–70
(646666)	F. C. Hayes	M. A. Nash	Lancashire v. Glamorgan	Swansea	1977 *(cont.)*

	Batsman	Bowler	Match	Venue	Season
(666662)	T. E. Jetsy	R.J. Boyd-Moss	Hampshire v. Northants	Southampton	1984
(646666)	F. B. Touzel	F. J. J. Viljoen	Wst Province B v. Griqueland Wst	Kimberley	1993-94

Note: Allan Border hit A. R. Dunlop (Australians v. Ireland at Dublin, 1993) for five sixes in an over (666662) but this match was not first-class. E. B. Alletson scored 34 runs (46604446) in an over which included two no-balls for Notts v. Sussex at Hove in 1911. Only Sobers and Shastri hit more runs in an over (36) and Frank Hayes same number of runs (34), as shown above.

Eight Ball Over

	Batsman	Bowler	Match	Venue	Season
4 (41366066)	D. K. Carmody & I. D. Craig	I. W. Johnson	Morris XI v. Hassett XI	Melbourne	1953-54
(60660641)	D. W. Hookes	C. G. Thwaites	S. Australia v. Victoria	Adelaide	1976-77
(06466620)	M. G. Burgess	R. W. Anderson	Auckland v. Central District	Wanganui	1977-78

Note: Most runs taken off an eight-ball over was 34 by R. M. Edwards (40446664) off M. C. Carew (Governor General XI v. West Indians, Auckland, 1968-69).

MOST SIXES OFF CONSECUTIVE BALLS

SIX: G. S. Sobers (1968), M. J. Procter (1979) (a), R. J. Shastri (1984 – 85)
FIVE: A. W. Wellard (1936, 1938), D. T. Lindsay (1961)
    M. J. Procter (1969 – 70), T. E. Jetsy (1984)

ᵃ = Procter (Gloucester v. Somerset at Taunton in 1979) hit his sixes in separate overs (66/6666).

MOST SIXES IN A SEASON (See Chapter 14).

SIXES IN LIMITED-OVERS CRICKET

MOST SIXES IN AN INNINGS

	Batsman	Match	Venue	Season
11	S. T. Jayasuriya	S.L. v. Pak.	Singapore	1995 – 96
8	C. G. Greenidge	W.I. v. Ind.	St John's	1988 - 89
7	I. V. A. Richards	W.I. v. Ind.	Rajkot	1987 - 88
6	B. L. Cairns	N.Z. v. Aus.	Melbourne	1982 - 83
	Javed Miandad	Pak. v. Ind.	Lahore	1982 - 83
	Kapil Dev	Ind. v. Zim.	Tunbridge Wells[a]	1983
	D. L. Houghton	Zim. v. N.Z.	Hyderabad [a]	1987–88
	I. V. A. Richards	W.I. v. S.L.	Karachi[a]	1987 - 88
	D. L. Haynes	W.I. v. Ind.	Georgetown	1988 - 89
	Saeed Anwar	Pak. v. S.L.	Adelaide	1989 - 90
	S. P. O'Donnell	Aus. v. S.L.	Sharjah	1989 - 90
	S. T. Jayasuriya	S.L. v. N.Z.	Bloemfontein	1994 - 95
	A. P. Gurusinha	S.L. v. Zim.	Colombo[a]	1995 - 96
	Salim Raza	U.A.E. v. Neth.	Lahore[a]	1995 - 96

[a] = World Cup   Neth. = Netherlands

MOST RUNS/SIXES IN AN OVER

Runs	Sixes		Batsman	Bowler	Match	Venue	Season
30	4	(4x66661)	S. T. Jayasuriya	Aamir Sohail	S.L. v. Pak.	Singapore	1995-96
26	4	(626066)	M. W. Gatting	R. J. Shastri	Eng. v. Ind.	Jullunder	1980-81
	3	(646460)	R. W. Marsh	B. L. Cairns	Aus. v. N.Z.	Adelaide	1980-81
	3	(464660)	B. L. Cairns	V. B. John	N.Z. v. S.L.	Colombo	1983-84
25	3	(266641)	Wasim Akram	Chetan Sharma	Pak. v. Ind.	Nagpur	1986-87
23	3	(106664)	A. L. Logie & I. V. A. Richards	J. R. Ratnayeke	W.I. v. S.L.	Karachi[a]	1987-88
22	3	(661126)	Imran Khan & Mohsin Khan	J. Garner	Pak. v. W.I.	Sharjah	1985-86
20	3	(666101)	K. Srikkanth & D. B. Vengsarkar	R. A. Harper	Ind. v. W.I.	Sharjah	1988-89

x = wide ball
[a] = World Cup

SIXES IN WOMEN'S CRICKET

TEST MATCHES (One Six Each)

Batswoman	Match	Venue	Season
R. Heyhoe-Flint	Eng. v. Aus.	The Oval	1963
E. Barker	Eng. v. N.Z.	Scarborough	1966
R. Heyhoe-Flint	Eng. v. N.Z.	Christchurch	1968 – 69
S. Tredrea	Aus. v. Eng.	Manchester	1976
S. Fitzsimmons	Aus. v. N.Z.	Adelaide	1978 – 79
S-A. Bonaparte	W.I. v. Eng.	Nottingham	1979
C. Watmough	Eng. v. W.I.	Nottingham	1979
J. Kennare	Aus. v. Ind.	Ahmedabad	1983 – 84
E. Signal	N.Z. v. Eng.	Worcester	1984
J. Dunning	N.Z. v. Eng.	Canterury (Eng.)	1984
S. Rangaswamy	Ind. v. Eng.	Worcester	1986
W. Watson	Eng. v. Aus.	Collingham, Yorkshire	1987
D. Wilson	Aus. v. Ind.	North Sydney	1990 – 91
Z. Goss	Aus. v. Ind.	Adelaide	1990 – 91
D. Edulji	Ind. v. Aus.	Melbourne	1990 – 91
S. Metcalf	Eng. v. Ind.	Hyderabad	1995

Index

Aamir Sohail, 111
Abraham, Arthur, 27
Adcock, Neil, 42
Alcock, C.W., 73
Allen, David, 54–5
Allen, 'Gubby', 82
Alletson, Edwin, 114–7, 119
Alley, Bill, 12–3, 33–4, 148
Alleyne, Mark, 109
Allom, Maurice, 81
Alston, Rex, 66
Amar Singh, 84, 86
Andrew, Tommy, 36
Angel, Jo, 137
Annetts, Denise, 141
Archer, A., 121
Arlott, John, 99, 114, 116
Armstrong, E.R., 83
Armstrong, Warwick, 20, 53
Arnold, Geoff, 34
Arthurton, Keith, 137
Asif Mujtaba, 41
Athey, Bill, 106
Azharuddin, Mohammad, 111

Baker, Horrie, 128
Bannerman, Alex, 74
Bannerman, Charles, 55
Bannister, Jack, 95
Bardsley, Warren, 58
Barnard, Dennis, 24
Barnes, Sid, 123
Barnett, Fred, 86
Barrett, Arthur, 60
Barrett, L., 130
Barrington, Ken, 24, 34–5
Basic-Six-6-Hit Awards, 46–7
Bearshaw, Brian, 88, 93, 101, 117
Bedi, Bishan, 93
Bedser, Alec, 36, 57, 66, 82, 89
Benaud, Richie, 55, 57, 88–9, 145
Best, Carlisle, 138
Bill, Owen Wendell, 128
Black, Bill, 128
Blair, Bob, 42–3
Blazey, John, 139
Blundell, Rex, 142
Blunt, Roger, 149
Bonnor, George, 13, 20, 53, 56, 58, 64, 72–3, 75, 84, 86, 94–6, 113
Booth, Brian, 57
Borde, Chandu, 132
Border, Allan, 22, 29, 99
Bose, Mihir, 63

Botham, Ian, 13, 26, 46–8, 63, 83, 88, 97, 99–101, 105, 113, 138, 148
Bowditch, M.H. 138
Bowes, Bill, 85
Bradman, Don, 36–7, 42, 59, 64, 76–7, 80, 91–2, 101, 117, 125, 127–8, 134, 136, 149–50
Brain, Brian, 102
Breakwell, Dennis, 102
Brearley, Mike, 100
Bridges, Mark, 146
Bristow, Paul, 142
Brittenden, Dick, 43, 149
Broad, F., 141
Broadbent, Alan, 24
Brock, Tom, 126
Brodribb, Gerald, 14, 18–9, 21, 29, 31, 47–8, 52, 64, 69, 76, 81, 84, 115, 120, 148
Brown, Freddie, 86
Brown, George, 143
Brown, J.H., 121
Brown, Jack, 140
Brown, Karen, 141
Brown, Vaughan, 39
Bryan, J.L. 59
Buck, Hazel, 141
Bull, Charles, 44
Bulsara, Dossu, 25
Burke, Jim, 139
Burton, Geoff, 108
Butterworth, R., 129

Cairns, Chris, 38, 40, 96, 102, 132
Cairns, Lance, 38, 102, 105
Calcraft, Fred, 149
Calvert, Julie, 141
Cameron, 'Jock', 84–6
Campbell, J.N., 136
Cantrell, Peter, 62
Cardus Neville, 36, 65, 79–81
Carr, A.W., 83, 148
Chapman, Percy, 56, 136
Chappell, Greg, 38, 41–2, 138
Chappell, Ian, 42
Chappell, Trevor, 41, 144
Chee Quee, Richard, 49
Clark, Belinda, 141
Clayton, Graham, 129, 138
Coady, Patrick, 141
Collier, John, 139–40
Collins, Herbie, 126
Compton, Denis, 76
Coney, Jeremy, 104
Constable, B., 61
Constantine, Learie, 53–4, 81–2, 91
Cooper, R., 129
Coorey, Philip, 131

Cotter, Albert, 20
Covell, Charles, 136
Cowdrey, Colin, 54
Cox, George, 115
Cranston, Ken, 58
Crawford, Frank, 76,86
Crawford, Jack, 86,126
Crompton, Alan, 139
Cronje, Hansie, 14
Cullinan, Daryll, 62

D'Oliveira, Basil, 130
Darling, D.K., 18
Darling, Joe, 13, 18–9, 74
Davidson, Alan, 13, 54–5, 61, 88–9, 135
Davis, Roger, 144
Dempster, Eric, 37
Denholm, Lynn, 141
Denning, (Lord), 30
Derriman, Philip, 54, 57, 149–50
deSilva, Arvinda, 112
Dew, John, 146
Donnelly, Martin, 53
Dossa, Anandji, 139
Douglas, Johnny, 135
Downs, Steven, 133
Duleepsinhji, K.S., 76
Dunlop, A.R., 22

Earle, Guy, 60, 78–9, 113, 148
Edmonds, Phil, 105
Edrich, Bill, 84, 89
Edrich, John, 83, 148
Edwards, Susan, 22
Ellison, Richard, 95
Emburey, John, 95

Fairbrother, Neil, 47
Farooq, Hamid, 55
Favell, Les, 98
Fellows, Walter, 52
Fender, Percy, 85, 145
Fingleton, Jack, 68, 145
Flockton, Ray, 58
Ford, N.M. 22
Ford, W.J., 72
Fowler, W.H., 53, 86, 147
Foxall, Ian, 137
Francis, F. 133
Fraser, Malcolm, 42
Fredericks, Roy, 91, 96
Freeman, Eric, 138
Freeman, 'Tich', 78, 82
Freer, Fred, 33
Frith, David, 89, 96
Frost, Ernie, 150
Frost, Olive, 150
Fry, C.B., 63, 76, 101, 120
Funnell, Jack, 97

Gascoigne, S.H. ('Yabba'), 125
Gavaskar, Sunil, 34, 93
Gee, Dan, 125
German, Gerry, 46
Gibbs, Lance, 98
Gilligan, Arthur, 65
Gimblett, Harold, 85, 148
Goddard, Trevor, 131
Goen, S.K., 129
Gooch, Graham, 103
Goodman, Tom, 53, 55
Goss, Zoe, 150
Grace, E.M., 118
Grace, G.F., 56, 72-3
Grace, W.G., 18, 23, 53, 59, 71-2, 84
Granger, Vivian, 43
Graveny, Tom, 54
Greatbatch, Mark, 149
Green, Peter, 23-4
Greenidge, Gordon, 91, 96-7, 111
Greenwood, Stanton, 146
Gregory, Arthur, 55-6
Gregory, Jack, 96, 135
Greig, Ian, 66-7
Greig, Tony, 67, 100, 106, 108, 142-3
Griffiths, Sally, 150
Grimmett, Clarrie, 79, 118
Grout, Wally, 34
Gunasekara, C.I., 145
Gunn, John, 76
Gunn, George, 115
Gurusinha, Asanka, 13-4, 112

Haigh, Schofield, 84
Hall, E.T., 56
Hammond, Wally, 36-9, 52, 59, 63, 70, 81, 96, 102, 130, 136
Handford, Peter, 97
Harper, Roger, 47, 91
Hartley, Wilson, 23-4
Havewala, Dady, 114, 117-9, 129
Hawke, Neil, 130
Hawkins, Derek, 130
Haynes, Desmond, 91, 96, 137
Haywood, Martin, 130
Hazare, Vijay, 35-6
Hazare, Vivek, 36
Headley, George, 146
Hendren, 'Patsy', 53, 136
Hendry, 'Stork', 36
Hick, Graham, 47-8
Hill, Clem, 85
Hoare, Desmond, 57
Hobbs, Jack, 58, 77, 114
Hogg, Rodney, 38
Hollies, Eric, 58, 64-5, 83
Holmes, Errol, 86, 120

Hookes, David, 13, 50, 105, 107-8
Hookey, Scott, 62
Hooper, Carl, 91, 105
Hope, D., 118, 129
Hopkins, Albert, 20, 85
Horan, Tom, 56
Hourn, David, 142
Howarth, Geoff, 41
Howat, Gerald, 121
Howell, Bill, 58, 84-5, 135
Hughes, Kim, 66
Hughes, Merv, 107
Huntington, Jack, 133
Hutchings, K.L., 21
Hutchinson, Kevin, 118, 129
Hutton, Len, 82, 88
Hyman, W., 118, 129
Hynd, Ron, 143

Ikin, Jack, 136
Illingworth, Ray, 98
Illingworth, Sarah, 150

Jackson, Archie, 136
Jackson, John, 21, 25
Jardine, Douglas, 81
Jarrett, Harold, 80
Javed Miandad, 41
Jayasuriya, Sanath, 14, 111-2, 122
Jenner, Terry, 142
Jessop, Gilbert, 20, 37, 59, 69-70, 75-7, 80, 100, 113, 144
Jones, Dean, 40, 49, 105

Kaluwitharana, Romesh, 14, 111
Kanhai, Rohan, 90-1
Kapil Dev, 13, 40, 103-5, 113
Kelly, Rob, 128, 134, 148
Kilburn, J.M., 85
Killick, Ernest, 116
King, Frank, 89
Kippax, Alan, 36, 136
Kirmani, Syed, 104
Kirsten, Gary, 14
Kline Lindsay, 145
Knee, Miriam, 141
Knight, Barry, 98
Knightly-Smith, Bill, 60

Laker, Jim, 46, 68, 89
Langer, Rob, 131
Langridge, John, 144
Lara, Brian, 52, 91
Lawry, Bill, 38
Lawson, Geoff, 38
Lee, G.M., 115
Lenehan, Jim, 57
Lever, 'Hooper', 86

Lewis, Tony, 144
Little, Bob, 24
Lloyd, Clive, 91, 93-4, 144
Lockwood, Bill, 74
Lodge, Derek, 37
Longley, Ken, 139
Lord, Robert, 31
Loxton, Sam, 105, 108
Lucas, E.V., 12, 124
Lush, Ginty, 56
Lyons, Jack, 73-5
Lyttelton, Charles, 31

Macartney, Charlie, 71, 118, 137
MacGregor, Gregor, 77-8
Mackay, Ken, 90
MacLaren, Archie, 58
Macleay, Ken, 38
Maher, Jimmy, 62
Mailey, Arthur, 58, 137, 150
Mallett, Ashley, 102, 138
Maninder Singh, 41
Mankad, Vinoo, 23, 69
Mann, Frank, 53, 85
Mark, Lyn, 139
Mark, Neil, 139
Marner, P., 31
Marsh, Rod, 42, 105-6
Marshall, N.D., 80
Martin, Andrew, 146
Martin, Colin, 24
Martin, Johnny, 13, 55, 88, 89-91
Martin-Jenkins, Christopher, 120
Matthews, Chris, 141
Matthews, Greg, 39, 137
Maybury, Debra, 150
Maynard, Matthew, 47-8, 149
McDonald, Barry, 90, 123
McKechnie, Brian, 41, 144
McKenzie, Graham, 54, 98
Meckiff, Ian, 57, 92
Mell George, 24, 26, 120
Mercantile Mutual Cup, 12, 44-6, 48-51, 62, 110
Merchant, Vijay, 36
Merry, C.A., 146
Messenger, Dally, 56
Metcalf, Sue, 150
Midwinter, Billy, 56
Milburn, Colin, 25, 97-8, 113
Milburn, Jack, 25
Miles, Thais, 143
Miller, Brenda, 29-31
Miller, John, 29-31
Miller, Keith, 13, 22, 35, 46, 57, 60, 63-70, 82, 88, 99, 102, 113
Miller, Lawrie, 42
Milton, Arthur, 60

Mold, Arthur, 76
Monckton, Walter, 28
Moody, Tom, 44, 47, 62
Morley, H., 129
Mott, Matthew, 131
Muldoon, Robert, 42
Murray, John, 97
Mushtaq Mohammad, 50

Nash, Malcolm, 25, 92, 116, 144
Nasser, Tony, 123
Nayudu, C.K., 79–81
Newman, Jack, 37
Nicklaus, Jack, 63, 65, 69
Nilsson, Tim, 129
Noble, 'Monty', 53
Nourse, 'Dudley', 128

O'Brien, Timothy, 59
O'Donnell, Simon, 105–6, 111, 137
O'Reilly, Bill, 33, 127
Oldfield, Bert, 56–7

Packer, Kerry, 27, 30, 88
Parker, Charlie, 78
Parsons, John, 21
Pataudi, Nawab of (jr.), 133
Patel, Dipak, 148
Patil, Sandeep, 132
Pavri, Faram, 25
Pawley, Mike, 139
Paynter, Eddie, 37, 120
Pearce, Hugh, 146–7
Peebles, Ian, 86–7
Philipson, W.E., 21
Phillips, John, 139
Piesse, Ken, 101
Pittioni, Paul, 130
Pollard, Jack, 52, 54, 58, 70
Pollock, Graeme, 101, 131
Ponsford, Bill, 36
Pope, Sean, 130
Prenter, Geoff, 50–1
Prittie, Terrence, 86
Procter, Mike, 101–2, 138
Pycroft, Jim, 71

Raiji, Vasant, 81
Ramsay, R.C., 73
Rankine, R.R., 140
Ransford, Vernon, 20
Reid, John, 97, 102, 109
Relf, Bob, 117
Rhodes, Wilfred, 26, 77, 84, 117
Rice, Jonathan, 123
Richards, Barry, 96, 101
Richards, George, 149
Richards, Vivian, 26, 47, 52, 91, 94–6, 111, 148
Richardson, Richie, 111
Richardson, Tom, 76

Ridings, Phil, 42
Riley, W., 116
Roberts, Andy, 100, 106
Robertson-Glasgow, R.C., 64
Robins, D.H., 97
Robinson, Gordon, 133–4
Robinson, Ray, 43–4, 53–5, 57, 68, 125, 133
Robinson, Rupert, 133
Roebuck, Peter, 95, 97
Rosa, David, 142
Rosenwater, Irving, 60, 128, 130
Ross, Keith, 140
Rush, Frank, 146
Rutherford, John, 55, 91
Ryder, Jack, 36, 118

Sage, Tim, 147
Sainsbury, Erica, 141
Salim Raza, 112
Sarbhadhikari, Berry, 80
Sardesai, Dilip, 60
Scot, Clive, 23
Scott, John, 26–7
Scott, S.W., 58
Selvey, Mike, 103
Sharma, Chetan, 41
Sharpham, Peter, 126
Shastri, Ravi, 47–8, 92, 116, 144–5
Sidhu, Navjot, 96
Simmons, Ashley, 143
Sims, Arthur, 126
Sinclair, James, 26, 84–5
Slater, Michael, 105, 107
Smith, Cammie, 89
Smith, Charles, 115
Smith, Jim, 59, 86–7, 128
Smith, Nigel, 149
Smith, Ross, 137
Sobers, Garry, 25, 57, 90–3, 116, 144
Solomon, Joe, 89
Spofforth, Fred, 56, 73
Stewart, Jim, 109
Stone, Bassie, 28
Stuckey, Norman, 147
Sullivan, K. 131
Sunderam, G.R., 139
Sutcliffe, Bert, 42–3
Sutcliffe, Herbert, 31, 35
Sutcliffe, W.H., 31
Symonds, Andrew, 13, 22, 26, 48, 83, 102, 109–11, 131, 148

Talbot, Ron, 149
Tate, Maurice, , 78–9
Tayfield, Hugh, 42, 137
Taylor, Chris, 24
Taylor, Frank, 139
Tendulkar, Sachin, 14, 52, 112
Tennyson, (3rd Lord), 84, 118

Thickeness, John, 96
Thomson, Billy, 146–7
Thornton, Charles, 20, 52, 71–2, 75, 84, 113, 116, 124
Tilak Raj, 116
Topham, Geoffrey, 28
Toshack, Ernie, 68
Tribe, George, 46
Trimble, Sam, 138
Trott, Albert, 19–20, 53, 60, 66, 73, 77–8, 84
Trueman, Fred, 57, 59, 89
Trumper, Victor, 20, 52, 59, 64, 70, 76, 125–6, 134
Tyson, Frank, 59

Ulyett, George, 73, 85
Umrigar, Polly, 132
Upham, Paul, 141

Vengsarkar, Dilip, 132
Verity, Hedley, 85
Viswanath, Gundappa, 132

Wadekar, Ajit, 132
Wakely, B.J., 17, 19–20
Walker, Alan, 147
Walker, Peter, 144
Walters, Doug, 12, 15–6, 61–2, 65, 138
Ward, John, 27
Ward, Mary, 27
Warner, Pelham, 81, 84
Wass, Tom, 115
Watkin, Steve, 109–10
Watkins, Alan, 59, 68
Watkinson, Mike, 137
Watson, A.C., 86
Watson, Garry, 131
Waugh, Mark, 14, 52, 62, 111
Waugh, Steve, 12, 41, 44–5, 50
Webber, Roy, 114, 116
Weekes, Everton, 50, 76
Weeraratna, Senaka, 145
Wellard, Arthur, 12, 46, 82–4, 113, 148
Wells, 'Bomber', 60
Whatmore, Dav, 129
Whitington, R.S., 69
Williams, Chris, 140
Williams, Reggie, 109
Willis, Bob, 12, 16, 62, 100, 132
Winslow, Paul, 136
Wood, Arthur, 85
Woodfull, Bill, 36
Wooley, Frank, 22, 52, 57–8, 70, 76, 78, 81, 83, 135
Worrell, Frank, 88, 90
Wright, Douglas, 68, 83

Yallop, Graham, 108
Yardley, Norman, 68